Dueling Discourses

OXFORD STUDIES IN LANGUAGE AND LAW

Oxford Studies in Language and Law includes scholarly analyses and descriptions of language evidence in civil and criminal law cases as well as language issues arising in the area of statutes, statutory interpretation, courtroom discourse, jury instructions, and historical changes in legal language.

The Legal Language of Scottish Burghs: Standardization and Lexical Bundles (1380–1560)
Joanna Kopaczyk

"I'm Sorry for What I've Done": The Language of Courtroom Apologies
M. Catherine Gruber

Dueling Discourses: The Construction of Reality in Closing Arguments
Laura Felton Rosulek

Dueling Discourses

THE CONSTRUCTION OF REALITY IN CLOSING ARGUMENTS

Laura Felton Rosulek

OXFORD
UNIVERSITY PRESS

OXFORD
UNIVERSITY PRESS

Oxford University Press is a department of the University of Oxford.
It furthers the University's objective of excellence in research, scholarship,
and education by publishing worldwide.

Oxford New York
Auckland Cape Town Dar es Salaam Hong Kong Karachi
Kuala Lumpur Madrid Melbourne Mexico City Nairobi
New Delhi Shanghai Taipei Toronto

With offices in
Argentina Austria Brazil Chile Czech Republic France Greece
Guatemala Hungary Italy Japan Poland Portugal Singapore
South Korea Switzerland Thailand Turkey Ukraine Vietnam

Oxford is a registered trade mark of Oxford University Press
in the UK and certain other countries.

Published in the United States of America by
Oxford University Press
198 Madison Avenue, New York, NY 10016

Library of Congress Cataloging-in-Publication Data
Felton Rosulek, Laura, author.
Dueling discourses : the construction of reality in closing arguments /
Laura Felton Rosulek.
p. cm.
ISBN 978–0–19–933761–3 (hardcover : alk. paper) — ISBN 978–0–19–933762–0 (ebook)
1. Summation (Law)—United States. 2. Forensic oratory. 3. Trial practice—United States.
I. Title.
KF8924.F45 2015
345.73'075—dc23
2014018517

9 8 7 6 5 4 3 2 1

Printed in the United States of America on acid-free paper

For my girls - Sylvia and Caroline

CONTENTS

ACKNOWLEDGMENTS

First of all, thank you to Roger Shuy for believing in this project and encouraging me to write this book. I am so grateful for your confidence in me.

Second, thank you to Rakesh Bhatt for all of your guidance over the years and all of the time and energy you put into helping me develop this research. An additional thank you goes to all of the sociolinguists at the University of Illinois for helping me think about the data in new ways, reading the early drafts of these chapters, and generally being there to support me.

Third, thank you to the linguists at the University of Montana for welcoming me while I worked on this book and for giving me an outlet to express my fascination with language.

Fourth, thank you so much to my family and friends—especially Mike, Sylvia, and Caroline. I couldn't have done this without you!

Dueling Discourses

1

Introduction

While writing this book, I was fortunate to actually serve on a jury. In that particular case, the defendant had been charged with assault after he punched another man during a fight at a party. Throughout the trial, I noticed that the defense lawyer completely ignored—or as I call it, silenced—the defendant's alcohol consumption on the night in question, despite the fact that he asked every other witness about how much they had drunk that night. By concentrating on the other people's alcohol consumption rather than the defendant's, the lawyer constructed a crime story that did not include the defendant as being intoxicated. He did not overtly deny that the young man had been drinking, but instead he did not include this information in his version of reality.

What surprised me was how my fellow jurors, who had clearly already bought into the defense's argument, interpreted this omission. Despite the fact that the prosecution had said that the defendant had been very intoxicated at the party, several of the jurors were convinced that the defendant had been sober. They then used this as evidence for why the fight must have been the victim's fault. Thus, the defense attorney's silencing of the defendant's drinking worked in his favor in this case.

This example of a lawyer ignoring a key part of the opposition's case perfectly exemplifies the claim about closing arguments[1] that I am making in this book, which is that lawyers for the prosecution and for the defense routinely silence (omit a topic in order to hide it from the jurors), de-emphasize (give a topic comparatively less attention and focus), and emphasize (give a topic comparatively more attention and focus) different topics through their linguistic and discursive[2] choices. In doing so, the lawyers present two different representations of the same reality, each framed as the only one the jurors should accept as valid. Even the smaller, often unnoticeable, and perhaps even unconscious linguistic and discursive selections that lawyers make all work together to achieve these patterns.

1 The Reasons to Study Closing Arguments

My experience as a juror and the analysis presented in this book stand in stark contrast to the depictions of closing arguments in the American media. On television and in the movies, the final summations are dramatic events. The courtrooms are usually packed full of people, and the lawyer is in full command of the audience, bringing them to laughter and to tears. Everyone is mesmerized as the lawyer's voice rises and falls, building to a dramatic climax, and the jurors' passions are swayed to find in favor of the most impressive rhetoric. Metaphors, gifted storytelling, emotional manipulations, and dramatic pleas for justice are common, if not mandatory. The closing arguments shown in many episodes of *Law & Order* or in the films *To Kill a Mockingbird* and *A Time to Kill* are classic examples of how summations are usually depicted. Such dramatic versions do occur to a limited extent in real life (e.g., in the OJ Simpson case as described in Cotterill [2003]), but the results presented in this book show that in many trials, the closing arguments are very different from those portrayed in fictional cases. The linguistic stylings of the lawyers are often much more subtle. In fact, in this book I will argue that the processes of silencing, de-emphasizing, and emphasizing are key strategies that lawyers use, rather than relying only on dramatic discursive turns and direct argumentation with the other side.

What makes the closing arguments particularly interesting both in fictional accounts and in real life is that they are a lawyer's final opportunity to plead her case, her last chance to persuade the jurors that her "version of the 'truth' is correct" (Lief et al. 1998: 11). The closing arguments are inherently important because they occur after all information in the trial has been presented, and they represent the endpoint of the lawyers' direct involvement in the case. As such, they are each lawyer's chance to bring together all of the strands of his or her argument into a single, unified discourse. During the examination and cross-examination of witnesses, lawyers are forced to present their case in a piecemeal fashion, to ask questions and to lead the witnesses into providing testimony in such a way that a certain narrative of the relevant events is created (Bennett 1979; Bruner 2002). For example, the lawyers may have had to ask one witness about the defendant's behavior before the alleged crime, another witness about his behavior afterward, and yet another—this time an expert witness—about what the defendant would have had to have done to have caused the injuries that the victim sustained. The lawyers have only been able to hope that the jurors were using the framework that the lawyers set up for them during the opening statement in order to transform all of the seemingly disparate testimony and evidence into a unified argument. However, in the closing arguments, the lawyers are finally allowed to speak directly to the jurors once again. They can weave together all of the evidence and the testimony from the trial, the relevant portions of the law, as well as the assertions, rebuttals, instructions, and pleas that they have attempted or wanted to make during earlier parts of the trial in order to present their ultimate "master narrative" (Gibbons 2003: 155) in the form of a single monologue. Because of this, the closing arguments are an ideal site to examine the linguistic forms and the discursive strategies that lawyers use as they attempt to persuade the jurors that finding in their favor is the necessary conclusion to reach in this particular case.

Although these characteristics make the closing arguments of particular interest to those who are interested in the relationship between the language and the law, they are not the limit of their appeal for discourse analysts. What makes the closing arguments unique compared to discourses that occur in other contexts is that in all sets of closing arguments, two or more speakers are constructing representations of the same general topics (the same events, people, and concepts such as the law) for the same audience. To make matters even more fascinating, the arguments are always in opposition to each other, and each is presented as the only valid representation of reality. These features make them ideal for analyzing how speakers' goals, understandings, and biases are reflected in the discourses they create.

The main question that arises from the characteristics of closing arguments I have just described is *how do lawyers utilize their linguistic and discursive choices to create opposing representations of the same defendant, victim(s), witnesses, crime, investigation, trial, and law*? To state it another way, *how do two speakers take the same reality, and solely through their linguistic skills, each try to persuade the hearers to accept their conclusions while the other side contradicts them*? As I said above, the answer to this question that I put forth in this book is that a significant way in which lawyers accomplish the creation of contrasting arguments is through the processes of silencing, de-emphasizing, and emphasizing.

This conclusion is reached through quantitative and qualitative analyses of the closing arguments presented in seventeen criminal trials in a state district court in a small city in the Midwestern United States. Trials from additional locations around the United States are also used to demonstrate the generalizability of the results. By comparing patterns such as the terms of reference used (for the defendants, victims, jurors, lawyers, judge, and witnesses), the use of pronouns (for the lawyers and the jurors), and the syntactic roles these social actors[3] play for different types of processes (Halliday 1994), both across sets of arguments and across the entire corpus, a comprehensive picture of the linguistic and discursive strategies of prosecution and defense lawyers emerges. The results demonstrate the systematicity of the processes of silencing, de-emphasizing, and emphasizing both within the individual narratives found in arguments and in the complete summations. They also show that the many lexical, syntactic, and topical choices that lawyers make all function together to serve these processes.

2 An Overview of Closing Arguments

Before delving further into the analysis presented in this book, it is necessary to expound further on the exact nature of closing arguments in the legal system in the United States. There is, of course, quite a bit of variation in the structure and form of summations, as each lawyer has his own style and his own ideas about what makes a good argument. In order to construct a comprehensive view of the general behavior of lawyers during this portion of the trial, we must turn to three sources: the ethnographic data collected for this book, the manuals and articles written for lawyers about effective trial strategies, and the published discourse analysis literature on closing arguments.

The closing arguments usually occur after the final witnesses have testified and are presented to either a jury or, in the case of a bench trial, a judge (although all of the cases discussed in this book occurred before a jury). While it differs by court system which side presents first, the prosecution lawyers generally are afforded the opportunity to have the last word with the jurors. In the corpus studied here, the prosecution lawyers gave their main arguments and were followed immediately by the defense lawyers. In fourteen of the seventeen trials analyzed, the prosecution lawyers gave a rebuttal argument, which was a relatively short response to the claims made by the defense.

The physical positioning of the lawyers during the closing arguments varies greatly. Some lawyers move about, while others stand still. Some arrange themselves behind a podium or a table, while others stand directly in front of the jurors. Trial manuals tend to instruct lawyers to not use a podium or table if possible (e.g., Mauet 2009), but as the ethnographic data gathered for this book showed, some lawyers choose to do so.

In addition to using their voices as tools for conveying their messages, lawyers often also use other materials, particularly visual aids. For example, some authors of trial manuals suggest that lawyers use presentation software such as Microsoft PowerPoint as a supplement to their oral delivery (e.g., Mauet 2009; Rogers 2006; Waicukauski, Sandler, and Epps 2009). While none of the cases in the corpus used such technological tools, some lawyers chose to draw on a whiteboard to make a visual representation of their ideas, while others came prepared with charts or drawings. For example, one lawyer drew a picture of a thermometer and marked different levels on it as a visual metaphor for understanding the standards of proof needed in different types of cases.

Lawyers sometimes utilize pieces of physical evidence in their arguments. An attorney in one of the cases analyzed here brought out the knife allegedly used during the crime to demonstrate that it actually was a dangerous weapon. Photographs and videos can also be used to give concrete visual proof of the events, people, or objects the lawyers are describing. In the assault cases in the corpus, photographs of victims were often used as a means of reminding the jurors of the actual injuries that were sustained. No one in this corpus used a video, but while collecting data, I heard a story about a defense lawyer who tends to walk in front of the prosecution's video screen when it contains damaging scenes for his client. Assuming this is a true story, this means that the lawyer silences the images on the tapes by physically hiding them from the jurors, using his body.

Some lawyers also use imaginary or metaphorical visual aids, for instance, asking the jurors to visualize the physical space they are occupying in the present as being transformed into a different place (e.g., the crime scene). In Pascual (2006), the lawyer in the case she analyzed blended the "then-and-there" of the crime narrative with the "here-and-now" by having the jurors imagine that they were at the crime scene. The lawyer then deictically pointed to places within the courtroom but referenced the location where the crime took place. By doing so, he presented the narrative in the present tense, creating a sense that the jurors were "seeing" the events as they happened. In the corpus being described here, one lawyer turned the jury box into a metaphorical continuum so that he could "point" to the different levels of proof needed in different types of trials.

The content of closing arguments is constrained by the law. Lawyers cannot introduce new evidence, nor can they make inflammatory or prejudicial claims. Additionally, lawyers are not supposed to include their own opinions on such topics as credibility, guilt/innocence, or the magnitude/importance of the evidence (Bacigal 2008). Instead, lawyers focus mainly on the testimony and evidence that was elicited at trial, the law and jury instructions, and both emotional and logical arguments for how the law should be applied in the particular case at hand (Walter 1988).

Trial manuals often instruct lawyers to construct their arguments around a theme and to make this the standout point that the jurors take with them into their deliberations (c.f., Caldwell et al. 2002; Maher 1996; Mauet 2009). In other words, they tell the jurors to emphasize a certain claim. The nature of how lawyers present this theme and the supporting material for it takes different forms, but some trial manuals suggest that the lawyer should be an educator (McElhaney 2005) and "review" (Mauet 2009: 456) the evidence and testimony while instructing the jurors about how to apply the law to it. One syntactic construction that lawyers have been shown to use in order to be more professorial is questions, which Walter (1988), Stygall (1994), and Pascual (2006) all found to be common in closing arguments. Pascual (2006), who studied the closing argument of a prosecutor in a murder trial, described the lawyer as asking and answering his own questions. She called these *fictive interactions* in which the lawyer was presenting an argumentative monologue that was, at a hidden level, a dialogue with the jurors that engaged them on a more active plane. Additionally, the lawyer used these questions to answer those that the jurors may have had, to make counterpoints to the opposing side's argument, and to preempt possible objections to his own argument. Walter (1988) also found that questions in the prosecution's argument can force the defense lawyer to answer them in her argument, thus making the arguments into an overt dialogue between the lawyers.

Although some lawyers utilize a theme while others do not, and although some lawyers try to behave like an educator while others do not, what they almost always do[4] is present a series of narratives (Bennett and Feldman 1981; Heffer 2005; Meyer 1994, 1996; Roberts 1999; Voss and Van Dyke 2001) and apply the law to them. One feature that makes the closing arguments different from other parts of the trial is that the lawyers are not just telling the "story in the trial" (Jackson 1988), which consists of the "crime story" (Heffer 2005) and the investigation story, as they did during the opening statements and the examination of witnesses. In the closing arguments, they are also telling the "trial story" (Heffer 2005) (i.e., the "story of the trial"; Jackson 1988). Thus, the lawyers combine the crime and investigation narratives with the story of what has already happened during the trial and stories about what the lawyer thinks should or will happen during the upcoming parts of the trial (e.g., the jury instructions and the deliberations). The lawyers intersperse these stories with evaluative discussions of the law and how it "should" be applied in this case based on these narratives.

In many cases in the corpus analyzed here, the lawyers also used stories or insights from sources and contexts outside the courtroom as additional means of driving home their points. Levitt (1991), in an article instructing lawyers on how to use stories from history, the Bible, and so on in their closing arguments, calls these types of rhetoric "verbal magic" (17) and "a powerful weapon" (20) for lawyers to use. The reason for this is that these stores are often mythopoetic (van Leeuwen 2007) in that they do not necessarily represent actual past events and their truth-value is unimportant. Instead, they are metaphorical, and they legitimate a certain belief or course of action. For instance, in one defense argument in the corpus, a lawyer told a story about a mother who put out poisoned breadcrumbs to kill mice. The father in the story, based on the circumstantial evidence of the crumbs being in the attic, thought his child had been eating food where he wasn't supposed to and intended to make the child eat the crumbs. The story concludes with the mother intervening before this could occur and saving the child's life. The lawyer used this story to instruct the jurors not to make a similar mistake by using circumstantial evidence against his client.

One difference between the prosecution and the defense arguments is the types of narratives they focus on, as will be discussed further later in the book. The prosecution's argument tends to emphasize the crime narrative, what the defendant did as well as where and when he did it. The defense, in some cases, offers an alternative crime narrative. However, in others, the defense focuses more on the trial (past and present) narratives (Amsterdam and Hertz 1992), other stories that might "personalize their clients" (Costanzo and Peterson 1994; Massaro 1989: 2100), mythopoetic tales, and discussions of how the law should be understood and applied.

If an argument is successful, it leads the jurors to see no other logical and/or emotional conclusion other than the lawyer's. To accomplish this, the literature on trial techniques consistently suggests that lawyers address the claims made by the opposing side, including the potentially damaging information that has been raised (e.g., Caldwell et al. 2002; Mauet 2009; Notestine 1999; Refo 2007). This is certainly done, as Walter (1988) listed refutations as an important part of the arguments that she witnessed. Even the corpus analyzed in this study includes many direct references to why the other side was wrong, as these excerpts show:

(1) *Prosecutor*—I think the defense may make this argument, that actually she was sleeping and dreamt these things and made them into reality during this emotional church night, if that were the case then why aren't they memorized?

(2) *Prosecutor*—First he said no, John didn't touch him with his mouth. A few questions later, yes, John did touch him with his mouth.

However, the argument being made in this book is that many lawyers do not do this, and a larger and more common strategy that occurs in closing arguments is to silence or de-emphasize topics used by the opposition to support its case. Even these examples can be used to support this claim. In example (1), the prosecution focused on the fact that the victim did not memorize her accusations, but in the corresponding defense argument, they silenced this issue. In (2), the prosecution did admit that the victim originally denied the abuse, but then never mentioned it again, so in the argument as a whole, the issue was de-emphasized. Thus, silencing, de-emphasizing, and emphasizing were significant processes, despite refutations such as these occurring in them.

While discussing all of these topics, the lawyers also create a multifaceted identity for themselves that combines both power over and solidarity with the jurors (Caldwell et al. 2002). This is consistent with the work in psychology that says that people are more likely to be persuaded if they find the person to be similar to them and likable but also knowledgeable and objective (c.f., Hurwitz et al. 1992; Petty et al. 1981, 1988).

To accomplish this, lawyers put on a performance (i.e., like an actor or even a magician; Corcos 2013 to try to create a certain ideal character for themselves (Hobbs 2003, 2008; Schrager 1999; Trenholm 1989). According to Hobbs (2008), just having the identity of a lawyer, at least in the United States, grants individuals a position of power and competence within the courtroom that a person who lacks the required education and training cannot achieve. However, through the image of themselves they present, lawyers still must "convey power, authority, and credibility to the opposing sides, to their clients, and where necessary, to juries as well" (Bogoch 1999: 333). As will be discussed in this book, one way that lawyers do this is by making I-statements. In other words, they refer to themselves using first-person singular pronouns as the subject of such mental processes as *know*, *think*, and *want*. They make their knowledge and opinions overt and thus relevant to the closing argument. Another way in which lawyers manage their identity, as described in Felton Rosulek (2010 a, b), is to quote the law, the judge, famous people and literature, and even the witnesses. In doing so, they rely on the authority and credibility of the original speakers as a means of making their claims more influential, and they de-emphasize their own responsibility for the messages they are presenting.

While portraying themselves as an authority figure, lawyers also try to build rapport with the jurors or the judge, to seem similar to them and more like a friend (Stygall 1994). Some instruction manuals tell lawyers to do this by showing their emotions (e.g., Roberts 1999) or telling personal stories (e.g., Levitt 1991). Another linguistic strategy that lawyers use to accomplish is code-switching between a standard form and a dialect that indexes a shared culture or identity. For example, Fuller (1993) and Hobbs (2003) both examined how an African American lawyer alternated between African American English (AAE) and a more standard variety of English, in part so that she could foreground her shared identity with the jurors, many of whom were also African American. In this book, the focus is on how lawyers emphasize their similarities with the jurors through the use of first-person plural pronouns *we*, *us*, and *our(s)*. By representing themselves and the jurors as being members of a single, unified group, despite this not necessarily being true, lawyers silence or de-emphasize the differences between themselves and the jurors and construct everyone as being in agreement about the outcome of the case.

Overall, the closing arguments are an important time for lawyers as they present their themes, narratives, arguments, and selves to the jurors for the last time. They strive to be persuasive, informative, instructional, authoritative, and likable, all at the same time. As this book will show, they are able to achieve all of these things through selectively silencing, de-emphasizing, and emphasizing information.

3 The Details of the Study Presented in This Book

3.1 THE FEATURES OF THE CORPUS

Turning now to the specific closing arguments being described in this book, the corpus used here consisted of summations from seventeen cases that all took place in the same state district court in the Midwestern United States. The size of this corpus is important because many of the previous studies that have been done on closing arguments have analyzed only a single case (e.g., Cotterill 2003; Fuller 1993; Hobbs 2003, 2005). By using such a large corpus, the findings are more robust and generalizable. Another important feature of the corpus is that the cases included in it are just average cases that took place without any special fanfare. There were no TV cameras in the courtrooms, and they did not receive any national news coverage. Unusual trials tend to receive more attention in the linguistics literature. For instance, Matoesian (2001) and Cotterill (2003) each examined a single famous trial, the William Kennedy Smith rape trial and the OJ Simpson murder trial, respectively. While studying such cases is beneficial, it leaves open many questions about what happens when there are fewer outside forces potentially affecting the case and the ways in which the lawyers try it. Therefore, by using more mundane trials, we can be more certain that these findings represent what occurs in most courtrooms.

The benefit of using arguments that all occurred in the same district court is that it permits a deeper level of analysis in that many linguistic variables (e.g., regional knowledge, dialectal variation) are controlled for, and direct comparisons can be made across and within groups of arguments. However, such a localized corpus from a single community of practice (Eckert and McConnell-Ginet 1992) leaves open the possibility that at least some of the patterns found in the book are a result of local norms, shared training and experience, and relatively dense networks of interaction (Milroy and Llamas 2013). As a result, it must be acknowledged that the specific quantitative results found in the book are not necessarily generalizable to all closing arguments. Perhaps in other court systems, lawyers tend to use other linguistic forms and strategies. However, in Chapter 7, I present an analysis of an additional trial with very different properties from those in the corpus, and I compare the results to findings presented here. They are very similar, and the larger processes of silencing, de-emphasizing, and emphasizing are again key means through which the two sides create opposing arguments. Furthermore, whenever possible, I bring in additional data from other closing arguments that took place in other locations, as well as the results of other published studies that, despite not having used the same methodology, have discovered similar patterns. For example, although Hobbs (2005) only examined a single defense argument, she, too, reported that some topics are given more emphasis by being discussed in more detail, just as is found in the larger corpus used for this book.

Additionally, the detailed analyses in the book are not being used to argue that these are the only possible linguistic and discursive forms that lawyers use. Instead, the patterns presented here are shown to be possible ways that lawyers can use language. The larger point is that lawyers' choices tend to be working together to silence, de-emphasize, or emphasize different information. In the concluding chapter, I actually put forth the argument that these processes are not specific to closing arguments, but are common to all discourses, and so the analysis presented here is simply capturing part of this larger phenomenon that is not limited to this speech community.

As for the corpus used in this book, the goal when creating it was to gather a set of cases that were controlled enough to be able to find patterns and make conclusions but also broad enough to make generalizations. The features that the cases shared were that they all involved felony charges and that they all occurred during a relatively small time frame, specifically between 1997 and 2005. The rest of the details about the cases varied to ensure that the patterns being described were not caused by the particular preferences of a single lawyer or by the nuances of a certain type of case. The arguments were given by ten defense lawyers (three female, seven male), with one lawyer having three arguments in the corpus and five having two. There were nine different prosecution lawyers (three female, six male). One had two arguments in the corpus, two had three, and one had four. Many different types of charges were represented, including criminal sexual conduct (eight cases), assault (seven cases), murder in the second degree (three), false imprisonment (one), aggravated robbery (one), kidnapping (one), manslaughter (one), and controlled substances (one). In fourteen of the cases, the defendants were adult males. However, in case #6, the defendant was female, and the defendant in case #13, although being tried as an adult, was only sixteen years old. In case #14, while the closing argument only applied to one particular defendant, his brother was also on trial as a co-defendant. With regard to the victims, there was even more variation among them. One case did not have any victims, as it involved drug-related charges. Three of the cases had more than one victim, with both cases #10 and #17 involving two victims and case #11 having six. Eleven of the victims were under the age of eighteen, and twelve were adults. Seventeen were female, and six were male.

In order to maintain the anonymity of the people involved in the cases, each of the seventeen cases in the corpus has been assigned a number, and the names of the participants have all been changed. However, the linguistically salient features of the names have been maintained. For instance, if the real name has a common nickname associated with it, then the pseudonym has one as well. Table 1.1 contains a short description of each case.

In order to obtain a large corpus of trials that were not broadcast in the media, it was necessary to analyze them through their official trial transcripts, which consisted of the "verbatim" (28 U.S.C. §753[b]) written account of the orally produced proceedings. Commas and periods were used to mark speech boundaries that the reporters felt were necessary. While the accuracy of the word-for-word transcriptions could not be verified, the literature on the subject suggests that they are an adequate source of data for this project. Not

TABLE 1.1
Summary of Each Case in the Corpus

Case #	Description
1	This case involved a criminal sexual conduct charge against a man who was accused of inappropriately touching a young girl who was a customer in his grocery store.
2	The defendant was charged with felony assault and false imprisonment after he threatened and attacked a man at a party over drugs.
3	In this case, the defendant was charged with felony assault after he attacked his girlfriend.
4	This case was another felony assault charge against a man who beat his girlfriend.
5	The defendant was charged with felony assault after he and another man were in a fight at a soccer game. The defendant was found not guilty.
6	In this case, a woman was charged with murder in the second degree after shaking a young child to death at the defendant's sister's day care.
7	The charges of criminal sexual conduct in this case were brought against the defendant based on a woman's claim that he touched her when she was sleeping at a party. The defendant was found not guilty.
8	This case also involved charges of criminal sexual conduct, this time involving a man and his girlfriend's young daughter.
9	This is also a criminal sexual conduct case with a young girl as the victim, but in this case the defendant was her adult brother-in-law.
10	The defendant was charged with criminal sexual conduct involving two victims, his girlfriend's daughters.
11	The defendant was charged with kidnapping, sexual assault, aggravated robbery, and assault after he attacked two teenaged girls and four women in a series of events that occurred over a short period of time.
12	Criminal sexual conduct charges were brought against the defendant for abusing his young stepdaughter.
13	The defendant, who was a male under the age of 18, was charged with murder in the second degree and manslaughter after the death of another young man in a fight.
14	This case involved charges for the distribution of a controlled substance. Two brothers were on trial for selling drugs, but the closing arguments that were analyzed involved only one of the defendants.
15	A charge of felony assault was brought against the defendant after he physically abused his infant daughter.
16	The defendant was charged with criminal sexual conduct, the victim being his four-year-old nephew.
17	In this case, the defendant was charged with murder in the second degree and felony assault after killing a man and wounding another during a fight.

only is it a common practice in the literature on courtroom discourse to use the transcripts (e.g., Cotterill 2001, 2003; Ehrlich 2002; Heffer 2005; Janney 2002; MacMartin 2002), but Heffer (2005) argued that there were no "perceptible differences" (58) between the syntactic and lexical items in the official trial transcripts and his own notes when he observed court proceedings. This follows Roberts and Robinson (2004), who showed that experienced transcribers, when asked to transcribe the same piece of discourse, have high levels (over 90%) of agreement for semantic content (i.e., what words were said). As court reporters are experienced transcribers, it seems likely that the transcripts are generally quite accurate with regard to the features being analyzed in this book. Also, even transcripts created by researchers often contain errors (O'Connell and Kowal 1994), so trial transcripts are not unique in that way. To further improve the accuracy of the findings, the transcripts used in this study were created by many different court reporters, so idiosyncratic transcription patterns were canceled out when the corpus was looked at as a whole. An additional benefit of using the transcripts was that this prevented the researcher's presence or the presence of cameras from affecting the behaviors of the lawyers, something Walter (1988) described as occurring when she observed the cases in her corpus.

3.2 THE ANALYSIS OF THE DATA

As could be expected, each of the closing arguments in the corpus was of a different length. Therefore, before any analysis was done, the total number of words in each was determined by the word-counting tool in the OpenOffice program *Writer*, which is a word processing program. The same program was used for all of the cases so that the method for counting words was consistent. Using this number, it was possible to calculate the frequency of the different forms and tokens being analyzed for every 1,000 words in each argument and in the corpus as a whole.

The focus of the actual analyses presented in this book was the representation of the relevant social actors—the defendants, victims, jurors, lawyers, judges, and witnesses—and their roles in the events being described. Therefore, each clause in the arguments was analyzed for either overt or covert references to one of these social actors. Covert references occurred through ellipsis, particularly in the second part of conjoined clauses or multiclause sentences, and in commands. Examples of these with the positions of the covert references underlined are:

(3) She hadn't met the judge, ____hadn't met the court reporter, ____ hadn't met the clerk.

(4) ____ Set aside that presumption of guilt.

Each overt reference was noted and categorized based on van Leeuwen's (2002) classification system for the representation of social actors, which will be described in detail in the next chapter. If the reference included more than just a single person, this was noted as well. For both covert and overt references, the person's role as an agent (responsible for the process[5]) or recipient (affected by the process) was recorded, as was the type of process involved. Halliday's (1994) categorization system, which will also be discussed in Chapter 2, was utilized to classify them. Finally, each reference was also categorized based on which narrative or voice it appeared in: the crime, the investigation, the trial, another past event, the present (the "here-and-now"), the near future (in the rest of the closing arguments), or the distant future (after the closing arguments). Descriptive statistics were used to determine frequencies and standard deviations. Since some tokens had values of zero and many others were less than five, each pair was analyzed using two-sided Z-tests for the Comparison of Proportions rather than a 2X2 Chi-Square Test (although for the comparisons with more than five tokens, the two would yield the same result; Wallis 2013). Since multiple comparisons were being made, the Bonferroni correction was used, and only results with a p-value of less than 0.01667 were accepted as significant.

4 The Findings in This Book Compared to Previous Understandings

Prior to this book, very little systematic and comprehensive work had been done to analyze how lawyers use language in the closing arguments to create opposing representations of the same people and events. The studies that have been done have tended to examine the arguments in a single case, focused on the use of a single linguistic or discursive choice, or described the distribution of linguistic and discursive features without determining their functions or how they worked together. This book has none of those issues and thus reveals many new insights about closing arguments and how lawyers construct them. Also because of the unique nature of closing arguments, this book also has much to offer people interested in critical discourse analysis more generally, as well as those interested in the linguistics of persuasion and argumentation.

What is especially interesting about the findings in the book is that lawyers are not necessarily aware of how they use silencing, de-emphasizing, and emphasizing as strategies, despite the overwhelming evidence that these are important processes. When I have talked to lawyers about my findings, they have said they would never ignore an important point made by the other side. If this were true, they would be following the advice in the trial manuals. However, over and over in the corpus, lawyers silenced topics and witnesses that supported the other side's case. So, not only are lawyers not necessarily following current expert advice, but the lawyers themselves and their sources of authority are also not necessarily aware that lawyers utilize silencing, de-emphasizing, and emphasizing for their own advantage. In fact, when I did a survey of trial manuals, the only mention of these processes was when the texts said that lawyers should emphasize a theme. In a way, it can be said that they silenced the idea of silencing. Also, when such books tell lawyers to use specific strategies, they do not seem to connect it to these larger processes. Thus, this book provides a new level of awareness of what lawyers are doing during the closing arguments that has not been described or acknowledged before.

Given this lack of awareness among lawyers, experts, and even the lay public who are interested in or affected by the legal system about how lawyers use language during the closing arguments, this book offers many new insights into their patterns. Additionally, the book builds on but greatly expands on previous analyses of closing arguments. Up until now, the literature had suggested that lawyers use specific linguistic strategies in their closing arguments, but there had not yet been an analysis of multiple cases or multiple linguistic and discursive forms functioning in the same arguments. This book does not contradict those findings, but it offers a systematic quantitative and qualitative analysis of how lawyers across cases consistently use multiple linguistic and discursive strategies, all for the purposes of silencing, de-emphasizing, and emphasizing different information.

For instance, several studies have shown that lawyers carefully control the semantic properties of their lexical choices for a specific referent in order to fit their argument. Cotterill (2003) and Luchjenbroers and Aldridge (2007) both argued that prosecution lawyers use metaphors to construct defendants as being violent. However, this book is able to show that prosecutors also use other linguistic strategies as they construct a representation of the defendants. In this corpus, they tended to silence most aspects of the defendant's identity by using functionalizations to refer to him[6] only by his role and actions in the context. They also emphasized his violent, sexual, and/or criminal behavior by frequently including him as the agent of material processes that detailed the specifics of the alleged crime. At the same time, they de-emphasized or even silenced any testimony or discourses about events in which the defendant had more positive behaviors, as well as his mental and emotional processes. Thus, multiple linguistic and discursive choices, rather than just metaphors, were all used by prosecutors to accomplish the goal of creating a criminal identity for the defendant. More important, these patterns were not just found in a single case but were shown to be statistically significant and consistent patterns in the corpus, regardless of who presented the argument and the charges against the defendant.

The results of this book are also important for sociolinguistics and discourse analysis in general. As discussed above, the closing arguments are unique in that the only differences between the two discourses are the speakers and their contrasting goals, knowledge, and beliefs. By comparing pairs of arguments, the findings presented here clearly show that speakers consistently make lexical, syntactic, and discursive choices that are informed by these types of biases. The linguistic and discursive choices they make may only be subtly influenced (rather than overtly biased or marked), but because certain forms are used consistently and other forms are never or rarely used, the resulting impact is that information not in-line with a speaker's understanding of reality is silenced, and other information is included but is either de-emphasized or emphasized, depending on its relative importance to the speaker.

The analysis of the more interpersonal functions of language presented in this book also offers important insights. It first shows the ways in which lawyers manage their identities in relation to the jurors. For example, they frequently constructed themselves as equals of the jurors by using first-person plural pronouns to refer to themselves and the jurors as a single undifferentiated unit. They also represented the jurors as already accepting the lawyer's claims with phrases such as *you know* and *you saw* rather than always overtly arguing that the jurors should believe these things. Previous work such as Stygall (1994) had noted the presence of personal pronouns in the closing arguments, but had not analyzed their functions. This book provides that necessary next step.

In addition to these more empirical results, this book also provides an important theoretical contribution in that it develops our understanding of silencing, de-emphasizing, and emphasizing; and it provides evidence for their importance in discourse production and analysis, particularly in closing arguments, when these processes explain many of the differences between the arguments presented by the prosecution and by the defense.

Silencing—the systematic omission of relevant information—is argued to be an important mechanism through which the speaker's arguably biased understanding of reality is expressed. In each pair of arguments, the speakers' contrasting points of view about the relevant events result in their silencing of different topics and information. This is shown to be true in each of the seventeen trials in the corpus and in each of the different analyses. Silencing consistently played a role in every representation included in the ideational content and in the negotiations of all the interpersonal relationships.

First, silencing occurred in the topics that the lawyers chose to include or exclude. Each side referenced different information and silenced events that contradicted their arguments. Thus, they referenced only material in their mental models of the events, and they erased information in alternative models from their discourses. In doing so, they covertly evaluated other plausible narratives and arguments as irrelevant and theirs as the only possible understanding of the events. This book not only expands the concept of silence to a new genre of discourse, but also, by examining discourses about the same topics in the same contexts, provides strong evidence for the validity of this phenomenon as being a consequence of a speaker's ideologies, biases, and understanding of the topic being discussed.

This book also extends the concept of silence from simply being about the topical choices that speakers make to also include their linguistic choices, specifically both the lexical and the syntactic forms that they use. The research then demonstrates how the linguistic mechanisms for silencing function with topical silencing to achieve silence in the discourse as a whole. For example, silencing occurred in the data in the lexical items that the lawyers chose to refer to the relevant people and those individuals' and/or groups' processes. Through the terms the lawyers selected, they highlighted only certain features of the people and processes and silenced others. While each lexical item silenced information only in the discursive moment, lawyers de-emphasized or even silenced information in their arguments as a whole by systematically avoiding certain terms. Thus, this book shows that silencing through lexical terms is another way in which speakers limit the representation of reality they create based on their own personal beliefs about reality. Lakoff and Johnson (1980) made a similar argument when they claimed that metaphors highlight certain features of the thing they represent and hide others. In this book, I show that all lexical choices function in the same way. While lexical items index certain characteristics of a person, process, or event, they ignore other aspects of them. Because these other characteristics are not activated in the mental models of the hearers, at least not by the speaker, they are silenced in the discourse.

Lawyers' syntactic choices are also shown to silence information contradictory to their arguments. For example, lawyers used passives, nominalizations, and other forms to silence the agents of processes, the recipients, and/or the dynamic nature of the process. The analysis revealed that these choices resulted from the specific goals of the speakers. While such forms have previously been described as silencing or erasing information, the important contribution here is that these syntactic choices were functioning with the lexical and discursive choices to silence information in the discourse as a whole.

The previous discussion showed how lawyers used silencing to limit the ideational (Halliday 1994) content of their discourses, but this book also shows that silencing occurs in a speaker's interpersonal (Halliday 1994) negotiations. As speakers in the data constructed the relationships between themselves and the hearers, they silenced features of the interaction that did not support the relationship they would like to be seen as having. For example, the lawyers and the jurors are in an asymmetric power relationship. However, the lawyers hid the power differential when they used first-person plural pronouns to construct themselves as having equal status to the jurors. Thus, silencing plays an important role in the interpersonal function of language as well as the ideational function.

In addition to the contributions this book makes to the theoretical understanding of silencing, this analysis also adds support to Fairclough's (2003) claim that a speaker's ideological biases and frame of understanding will affect the topics she de-emphasizes, and those she emphasizes. This book provides a methodological means of describing emphasizing and de-emphasizing, and it also shows that they operate not just at the level of the discourse as a whole. They also can occur in individual narratives and voices within a single discourse. For instance, in the closing arguments, individual social actors were de-emphasized, or even silenced, in one narrative but were emphasized in another. Many of the defense lawyers de-emphasized the defendant in the crime narrative relative to the prosecution lawyers, but they emphasized him more than prosecution did in the "here-and-now" and the future narratives. Therefore, this book shows that while an actor may be generally emphasized in a discourse, he may be de-emphasized or even silenced in certain parts (or vice versa). Knowing this can provide a more fine-grained understanding of the speaker's goals.

Additionally, this book reveals that de-emphasizing and emphasizing, like silencing, occur at the linguistic level as well as through discursive choices. As discussed above, speakers' lexical selections silence certain properties of the referent, but they also highlight (Lakoff and Johnson 1980) or smuggle in (Aldridge and Luchjenbroers 2007) other properties. By repeatedly referring to a social actor, event, process, and so on, with a single term or a set of terms that share a certain semantic property, this feature of the referent is emphasized. If the set of terms is used only infrequently, then that particular property of the referent is de-emphasized. For example, prosecution lawyers rarely referred to the defendants by name, often just once in their entire closing arguments. This de-emphasized the unique identity of the person on trial. Another example is that often in the crime narrative, the defense lawyers used general terms to refer to the criminal acts, even in denials:

(5) He did not sexually abuse this girl.

The prosecution lawyers, on the other hand, referred to the specific actions of the defendant as in this example:

(6) He put his hand on her leg.

By using generalizations, the defense lawyers silenced the details of the alleged crime, and hence they de-emphasized the crime as a whole. The prosecution included the details that the defense silenced and thus emphasized the abuse by spending more of their argument discussing it. Thus, de emphasizing and emphasizing, like silencing, must be examined lexically as well as discursively.

Previous work on silencing, de-emphasizing, and emphasizing has generally been divided into two camps, those who examine exclusion versus inclusion and those who examine de-emphasis versus emphasis. A few authors have mentioned in passing that these are related concepts. For example, Coupland and Coupland (1997) said that "near-silencing" has the same effect of silencing: "repression"; and Huckin (2002) stated that "manipulative textual silences are the ultimate form of backgrounding" (366). Despite these statements, no one has previously formulated a complete model analyzing the relationship among these processes or has shown that they form a continuum rather than being separate phenomena.

Evidence for the phenomena belonging to a continuum is found throughout the data presented in this analysis. For example, prosecution lawyers emphasize the defendants more than the defense lawyers do, particularly in the crime narratives, but they silence or de-emphasize his or her unique identity by not referring to him or her by name, not discussing his or her emotions and mental processes, and other such things. In the seventeen cases, one prosecutor never used the defendant's name, four used it once, two used it twice, and one used it three times. Thus, there is no clear separation between silencing and de-emphasizing. All of these lawyers were performing the same basic process, only at different levels. Another example shows that these processes form a continuum: in one case with multiple victims, the victim who was center of the prosecution's case was de-emphasized by only being referred to as a member of a group (six times in total) and by not being referred to at all, either individually or as part of a group, during the crime narrative.

Another issue discussed in this book that has not been addressed in the preexisting literature is that some information is included in a discourse but not overtly. Instead, some information is implied by being indexed through conversational implicature or conventional implicature (Grice 1975) or through accepted social conventions such as code-switching. However, the data analyzed here demonstrate that implicature is an important means of inclusion and that implied information can be de-emphasized or emphasized. In one of the cases in the corpus, for example, the defense lawyer insinuated that because the victim in the case was acting like a "normal" child, then she must not be a victim of sexual abuse. He emphasized this unstated claim by presenting a long list of her activities that he interpreted as "normal." It may not have had the same level of emphasis as it would have had if he repeatedly stated his claim overtly, but it was still a topic that he placed significant focus on. Therefore, an understanding of silencing, de-emphasizing, and emphasizing must address this issue, and this book does so, in the definitions of these terms and in the discussion of the data.

To conclude, this book has much to offer. Those interested specifically in language in the legal system will find a deeper understanding of how lawyers construct their closing arguments. Those interested in discourse more generally will see how silencing, de-emphasizing, and emphasizing are important multifaceted patterns at work at all levels of a discourse. Hopefully both groups can end the book with a deeper understanding of how language works, both inside and outside of the courtroom.

5 Outline of the Remainder of the Book

In the following chapters, I more clearly define the terms and issues being discussed in the book, present the analysis and a discussion of the results, and conclude by presenting an overview of how the theoretical framework used in the book can be applied more generally. Specifically, in Chapter 2, I provide a more detailed description of many of the terms and concepts used in the book, such as *discourse, text, reality, silencing, de-emphasis,* and *emphasis.* Chapters 3 through 6 contain the analysis of the data, and they are each organized around the most important people in the closing arguments: the defendants, victims, jurors, and lawyers. The book concludes with Chapter 7. This chapter begins with a summary of the findings, bringing together the multiple analyses that showed the importance of silencing, de-emphasizing, and emphasizing in lawyers' constructions of reality in their closing arguments. Following this is a discussion of the generalizability of these findings to other cases and other types of courtroom discourse. At this point, the focus will turn from closing arguments in particular to discourse more generally. The rest of the chapter will present a broader discussion of silencing, de-emphasizing, and emphasizing as theoretical constructs and how they may be seen in other genres.

2

The Theoretical Framework

In the chapters that follow, I describe specific linguistic and discursive patterns found across the corpus of closing arguments from seventeen criminal trials to argue that silencing, de-emphasizing, and emphasizing are processes through which lawyers create opposing representations of the same realities. Before turning to the actual analysis of the data, in this chapter I will describe the theoretical framework and assumptions on which this book relies.

1 Critical Discourse Analysis

At its heart, this book falls within the general scope of critical discourse analysis (CDA) in that the overarching goal is to unmask and de-naturalize the patterns of linguistic and discursive behavior that let the powerful[1] (the lawyers) maintain their control over the less powerful (the jurors) (van Dijk 1995). The focus of the book, then, is not to simply describe how lawyers use language but to uncover the essential patterns they use to restrain how the jurors understand certain aspects of reality.

It must be noted that while the power balance between the lawyers and the jurors is highly asymmetric, it is also quite complex. At the end of the trial, it is the jurors who have the power to decide the outcome of the case, to choose the verdict they deem fit. However, during the closing arguments, they have almost no overt power. They cannot ask questions, nor can they contribute their own opinions about the topics at hand. They cannot decide that some topics should be given more or less attention or that certain terms or constructions should be introduced into the proceedings. In fact, they cannot even ask for clarification if something is unclear. Instead, the lawyers are the ones who make the lexical and syntactic choices, who select the topics to be included or excluded, and who determine the manner and order in which they all are presented. To make the situation still more complicated, even the lawyers do not have complete control over their own arguments. They are constrained by the law, the rulings of the judge, and the objections of the opposing counsel. In fact, in some ways, the closing arguments can become a dialogue, with each side questioning and responding to the other (Pascual 2006). Despite all of these factors, though, it is the lawyers whose power is relevant for this book in that it is their choices and strategies that ultimately select what information the jurors receive and the form in which they obtain it.[2]

This book, by revealing the common patterns used by the lawyers in the corpus, will not alter this power distribution, nor will it necessarily make the strategies ineffectual. Instead, it will simply provide all of the parties who are involved in the American judicial system with more knowledge about how language is functioning within it, and it will provide clues into what is occurring in other similar contexts (e.g., political speeches, advertising).

2 Systemic Functional Linguistics

While CDA provides the general framework of understanding used in this book, as well as the research questions and the definitions of key terms (e.g., *power*, *ideology*, and *bias*), the methodologies used in the analysis of the corpus mainly originated in the related field of systemic functional linguistics (SFL) (Halliday 1973, 1978, 1994). One issue for all work within CDA is that it does not offer a single consistent methodology but instead simply provides a theory of how discourse functions within societies. SFL has helped fill this gap and is a framework that has been frequently utilized by many researchers in CDA (e.g., Fowler et al. 1979; Martin 2000; Wodak and Meyer 2009; Young and Harrison 2004).

Both SFL and CDA acknowledge the fact that language, context, culture, and meaning are interrelated or dialectical in that they simultaneously constrain and create each other (Dunmire 2011; Young and Harrison 2004). The benefit of SFL as a supplement to CDA is that it is more focused on descriptions of patterns of language use so it provides systematic tools for discourse analysis. More specifically, SFL views linguistic forms as having developed to serve distinct functions and to create meaning within a context (Halliday 1994). The goal of the researcher, then, is to determine the patterns of linguistic choices that speakers make from among the many different options they possess. To this end, SFL has created a series of categorization systems so that speakers' selections can be consistently captured and described (Halliday 1994). Martin (2000) describes these categories as a "technical language for talking about language" (275), and that is how SFL is being used in this book: as a system for describing the linguistic patterns observed in the corpus that lawyers use to control the representations of reality that they create for the jurors.

By utilizing SFL's pre-existing categorization systems, undertaking both qualitative and quantitative analyses, and describing patterns across a large corpus, this book demonstrates how the goals of CDA can be accomplished using a large corpus of data and systematic methodologies, just as authors such as O'Halloran (2011) have called for. The goal is to remove as much influence from outside forces (including the researcher) as possible and to present a nuanced but neutral description of the discourses being analyzed.

3 Discourses and Texts

Within CDA and SFL, as in the discourse analysis literature more generally, the term *discourse* often goes undefined. When its meaning is specified, the characterization is highly variable and dependent on the source and the theoretical tradition in which it is being discussed (Wodak and Busch 2004; Young and Harrison 2004). A very general definition that circulates throughout the literature and that is being is adopted in this book is that discourse is language use in any form (written, spoken, signed, etc.) in social contexts (Brown and Yule 1983; Fairclough and Wodak 1997). Importantly, this differs from the traditional definition of *discourse* as "language above the sentence or above the clause" (Stubbs 1983: 1) in that the focus is on how language actually operates in social contexts rather than on its length or complexity. A single word can be a discourse (e.g., "No!"), or a series of texts can be. Based on this definition, the closing arguments are each discourses in that language is being used in them to communicate a message from one person to others within a given social setting.

The term *discourse* also carries a more abstract meaning as well, following the work of Foucault (e.g., 1972). According to van Leeuwen (2005), discourses are "socially constructed knowledges of some aspect of reality" (94). In other words, a discourse is a representation of some aspect of the world that is created and circulated within a community. The term *knowledge* is being used here to mean an understanding or interpretation of an aspect of reality rather than access to "facts" or the reality itself.

This definition greatly informs the understanding of *discourse* in this book. First, it captures the idea that an individual instance of language use does not exist in isolation. It is part of a larger pattern of communication about a particular topic or related topics. For instance, when lawyers discuss particular points of law, they are not creating their own definitions or ideas from nothing. They are drawing on previous discussions of that law that they are familiar with, and these all form a discourse that is part of the repertoire of this segment of society. Additionally, each discourse contains parts of other previously created discourses. Lawyers, like all speakers, include references to these other discourses and even re-create other texts. When a lawyer quotes someone, for instance, he or she links the current discourse to any prior ones in which the quote appeared.

Relatedly, while each closing argument represents a single discourse, it is also part of larger discourses. For example, each lawyer's argument is simply one segment of the discourse that includes everything their side in the case communicated to the jurors during the trial. The closing arguments are simply a new genre and structure in which the lawyers can present the same information. Therefore, when the term *discourse* is used in the book, it may refer only to a single closing argument, or it may refer to a larger discourse of texts all containing the same understanding of reality that the closing argument is part of.

Finally, this definition acknowledges the fact that an understanding of reality is a social product in that it is dependent on the information and means of interpretation that are part of a person's social system. This is exemplified in the closing arguments. For instance, in a murder trial, the lawyers' arguments about whether the defendant's actions can be considered murder or not is determined by how the lawyers define the concept, the related events, and the participants in them. At its most basic level, *murder* means that one person died because of the actions of another. However, it is never this simple. If it were, a person who is shot in a war and a person who is shot during a fight in his home would both be murdered; for many people, only the person in the second scenario was. Many different factors go into characterizing something as murder. For instance, the degree of causation must be defined. While in some cases it is clear-cut, in many it is not. Often, lawyers are simply drawing a line in the sand. In one case in the corpus, two boys attacked another young man, and the victim died. Only one of the attackers was charged, despite the other one being the leader. The prosecution's charge of murder against the defendant was based on him having dealt the fatal blow, but the defense argued that the other boy was more responsible because he had started and participated in the fight. In the end, the jurors had to decide which interpretation of *murder* they accepted. Other issues in determining if something is murder or not include the type of action involved (e.g., one person strangling another compared to a judge sentencing something to the death penalty); the status of the victim (e.g., an unborn baby, someone involved in a criminal act, or an enemy combatant); the degree of planning on the agent's part; all of the participants' intentions; and the possibility that a person was acting in defense of their self, their property, or another's life. For example, in a case described in Danet (1980a), a doctor who performed a late abortion was on trial for murder. One side called the victim a *fetus* while the other referred to him as a *baby*. The outcome of the case was determined in part by how the jurors defined the victim and, by extension, the defendant's actions involving him. The basic facts did not change, but as in any case, the definition of reality depended on the discourses being created.

The word *text* is also used frequently in this book. A text is a particular instantiation of a discourse. More specifically, a text is the linguistic and communicative output produced in a speech event by a speaker or set of speakers. There are several important distinctions between a text and a discourse. First, a text is bound: it has a start and a finish, a limited number of participants, and a specific context in which it was created and usually interpreted (this is not necessarily true of written texts, however). It can be re-created later in other contexts, but this also produces a new text while pointing back to the original creation of the text. A discourse may be unbound. It is re-articulated and redefined indefinitely by any members of a community in any context, and its meaning, shape, and form do not remain static. Also, a single text can contain many different discourses within it, as texts are often not limited to a single topic. In this book, each closing argument, in addition to being a discourse, is also a text. These terms will often be used interchangeably when referring to individual closing arguments, although a *text* will only ever refer to the linguistic data from a specific closing argument and a *discourse* will also include the meaning and representations of reality being created.

4 Functions of Discourses

Having defined *discourses* and *texts*, we now turn to the purposes they serve, the reasons they exist. However, looking at discourses as singular, undifferentiated objects ignores the diversity within them as well as the micro-functions of the individual parts that all work to serve the larger goals. Therefore, it is necessary to examine the functions of each level of a discourse both individually and as part of a larger system. We will start at the broadest level and work our way downward until we arrive at individual word choice.

One understanding of the functions of discourses comes from Halliday (e.g., 1978, 1994). He pointed out that whenever people (particularly adults) use language, there are two levels of meaning being simultaneous created (Mathiessen 1995). They communicate the speaker's knowledge about reality[3] (this is a discourse's *ideational* meta-function) and construct a social world (this is a discourse's *interpersonal* meta-function) (Halliday and Hassan 1985). Both of these can be seen at the level of the clause, the utterance, and the discourse.

To be more specific, the ideational meta-function of language represents the fact that discourses are how people distribute their understanding of the world, their experiences with it, and their understanding of it. This is true whatever the topic. As in examples (1)–(3), whether a person is telling a story about what she did the night before, is discussing philosophy, or is declining an invitation, she is always conveying an interpretation of the world.

(1) I went to a movie.
(2) A statement can be both true and false.
(3) I cannot come to your party.

At the same time, because discourses are interactions and because they are a means for people to build, negotiate, and maintain social relationships (Halliday 2002), they always have an interpersonal meta-function. Speakers must define the speech event while negotiating their own roles in the exchange; the hearers' roles; and the relationships they have with each other, with the immediate context, with the larger world, and with the discourse content. Through discourses, people define themselves, they express their evaluations and emotions, and they facilitate interaction with each other (Halliday 1994; Halliday and Matthiessen 1999). These activities construct a new social world. To put this in the context of the closing arguments, the lawyers are managing several identities for themselves and constantly redefining their relationship with the jurors.

While Halliday's description provides important insights into discourses' meta-functions, it does not capture the more practical side of discourses. Another way to discuss their functions is to examine what specific acts or outcomes are being accomplished for the participants. There are two common[4] discourse acts that are relevant here: *informatives* and *directives* (Sinclair and Coulthard 1992). *Informatives* are the distribution of knowledge while *directives* are the dispersal of instructions for how the speaker wants the world to be changed. This is completely compatible with Halliday's ideas of interpersonal and ideational functions of discourse. It is only through the communication of understandings of reality (the ideational function) and constructions of the social world (the interpersonal function) that speakers are able to inform and to direct. The processes of spreading knowledge, creating and negotiating identities and relationships, and trying to affect the world are all interconnected and occurring simultaneously.

The closing arguments are *informatives* in which lawyers report their understanding of the crime, the investigation, the trial, the law, themselves, and the jurors. Among other things, lawyers provide the jurors with descriptions of the relevant events and social actors, educate the jurors on aspects the law, offer their analysis of the relationship between the law and the particulars of the case at hand, indicate which identities they want to be considered as having and those that they think the jurors have, and provide a meta-discourse (i.e., a commentary on the linguistic acts they have done, are doing, and will do). Much of this information is communicated directly in the referential nature of the linguistic forms that the lawyers produce. However, there are also ways in which lawyers, or all speakers for that matter, also communicate implicitly, especially when managing the interpersonal topics in a discourse. For instance, when lawyers use esoteric vocabulary and syntactic structures representative of legalese, they are not only informing the jurors about the details of the law, but they are also indexing their education and status as attorneys. In other words, they indirectly remind the jurors of their identity as lawyers—and that they are the ones who have direct access to the requisite knowledge in this case.

While lawyers provide the jurors with a lot of information, it is not done simply to increase the jurors' knowledge base. The lawyers are providing these representations of reality and their evaluations and understandings of the case in order to guide the jurors into accepting their argument so that they can successfully direct the jurors to decide in their favor. In other words, all of the information is meant to persuade[5] the jurors, and that is why the closing arguments are also *directives*. Lawyers direct through commands and requests, but much of the time, it is accomplished more subtly, through the distribution of information in a manner that will potentially manipulate the jurors' future behaviors. Lawyers provide the jurors with their own description of how the world is and, based on that, how it should be in the future. Then the lawyers covertly or overtly direct the jurors to make the world fit the lawyer's vision of it (i.e., decide in their favor).

At this point, it should be clear that discourses both distribute an understanding of reality, but they also help define the social world. For closing arguments, both the ideational and interpersonal functions are managed with the same goal: to increase the lawyer's success at informing and directing.

The functions of discourses can only be accomplished if the individual clauses or sets of clauses within them are all ultimately working together to accomplish the larger goals of the text. Unlike the functions of discourses, the functions of individual clauses, which are often referred to as speech acts (Austin 1962; Searle 1969), are much more diverse. For example, speakers such as lawyers represent the world as it was, is, or will/could be (i.e., inform) through such acts as assertions, predictions, proposals; they change the world (i.e., direct) by producing such forms as namings, oaths, promises, predictions, requests, and commands; and they manage their relationships through apologies, greetings, and other similar personal acts. Lawyers have been shown to use many of these speech acts in their closing arguments (Walter 1988) and to use certain types for strategic purposes, for example, questions can create a fictive dialogue among all of the lawyers involved and the jurors (Pascual 2006). In this book, it is important to understand that when lawyers choose one type of speech act over another, they are managing the larger functions of the discourses. Thus, when lawyers request rather than command, they are still directing the jurors, but they are also controlling their interpersonal relationship with the jurors as well. When lawyers apologize, they are not only negotiating their relationship with the jurors, but they are also informing the jurors of the lawyer's own knowledge and mental state.

The larger functions of discourses are not only managed at the clause level but also in the lexical and syntactic forms used within clauses. It is here that meaning is negotiated and nuance is created (Halliday 1978). When speakers construct a clause, they select from a wide range of options for the structures and the components to fill them. Each of the choices they make represents their understanding of reality as well as the social world they are constructing.[6] Additionally, each choice allows them to distribute a specific piece of information or to try to change the world. Therefore, the linguistic level is ultimately very important, as the greater functions of a discourse could not occur without certain patterns of choices being made here.

Specifically, the ideational function of a discourse is conveyed linguistically through the categories of lexical items speakers select when representing the people, concepts, entities, and events (i.e., noun phrases), the structures they embed them in, and the syntactic and thematic roles they assign them (Halliday 1994). If speakers have different knowledge of reality or different interpretations of the same events, then they are going to make unique sets of choices and thus their ideational output will differ. For example, in a case where the defense claims self-defense, it is only logical that the prosecution is likely to include the defendant as the agent of processes while the defense includes him as the recipient of them. Thus, the different interpretations of the defendant's agency will be seen in the syntactic structure.

The interpersonal function of discourse has traditionally been examined through grammatical mood (e.g., imperatives, subjectives, declaratives) and modals, as well as the indicators of the speaker's affect and stance (Young 1990). However, these factors really focus more on the relationships that speakers construct between themselves and the text or the message. In this book, the interpersonal function is further expanded to also include any linguistic form with a relationship-negotiating discourse role such as personal pronouns, vocatives, and so on, because these are also ways in which a speaker positions himself or herself with relation to the hearer, the discourse, and the context.

To conclude, discourses consist of words organized into phrases, which are grouped into clauses, which then pattern together to create texts and discourses. While individual lexical items, syntactic forms, clauses, speech acts, and so on, have their own micro-purposes, it is important to remember that they all ultimately serve the greater functions of the discourses. In this book, since we already know the goals of the closing arguments, we can easily examine how speakers' linguistic and discursive choices all work together to serve their greater objectives. We can determine how seemingly unimportant selections (such as the use of a first-person plural pronoun rather than a singular one) result in a certain understanding of reality being distributed, directions being given, and relationships being negotiated as lawyers try to persuade the jurors that their version of reality is correct.

5 Discourse as a Reconstruction of Reality

The idea that all discourses have an ideational meta-functions means that discourses are representations of reality, or, to put it another way, that they are descriptions of events, objects, or concepts that are part of the real world or are in some imagined world (Halliday 1978). These worlds can be either/both external (physical) and internal (cognitive, emotional) to the speaker, and an understanding of them is gained either through personal observation, logic, and experience,[7] or through the speaker being the recipient of others' discourses. When a speaker transforms his or her knowledge into linguistic output, he or she re-create part of reality in a new form, that is, a discourse. The original event, object, or concept is transformed into something different as it is recast or recontextualized (Bauman and Briggs 1990) into this new medium. For example, when a lawyer describes a robbery during his or her closing argument, the robbery itself has already occurred in a different time and place. It does not re-occur before the jurors' eyes. Instead, a discursive depiction of that robbery that is separate and inherently different from the original robbery is created. While this is obvious for narratives of past events, it is also true for any topic in the present or future. Even a meta-discourse, or a discourse about a discourse, is still a separate and different entity from the discourse it reflects upon.

This distinction between reality and the discursive representation of it is a crucial concept for this book. In any trial, the jurors did not observe most of the events being discussed in the closing arguments,[8] and they are unlikely to be familiar with many of the legal concepts being examined. The discourses presented in the trial are the only sources of information that the jurors possess in order to understand the crime, the investigation, the law, and even their own future actions. Because of this, the "true" reality of what occurred cannot be captured and no longer really matters in the legal context. The physical manifestations (e.g., recordings, physical evidence) as well as the discursive representations of those products and the events themselves are all that will move forward and are the only things that the jurors will base their verdicts on. This book, then, is not concerned with reality or what really happened. Only the linguistic reconstructions of it are relevant.

Not only does the construction of a discourse create a new object that is separate from the reality it represents, but it also forces the speaker and any hearers to label and thus assign meaning to their world (Wodak and Meyer 2009). To construct a discourse, a speaker must separate objects and processes into distinct entities or events so that they can provide them with linguistic markers. As part of this, they create order and analyze the relationships among objects and concepts, giving them additional layers of meaning as a result. This can be seen at all levels of a discourse, including the lexical items, syntactic forms, and discourse structures that a speaker selects.

More specifically, by choosing a word or phrase to refer to something, a speaker carves out the features the referent has, selecting some and rejecting others. For instance, by labeling something a *robbery*, a lawyer—or any speaker, for that matter—forces it to be understood as a criminal or illegal act, an act of taking of someone else's property through force or manipulation. This rejects any other possible understanding of the event and any other characteristics it might have. By labeling someone a *robber*, a speaker silences the other aspects of his or her identity. The point of view of and biases[9] of the speaker will be reflected in the lexical items they choose (Kress 1989; Trew 1979b; van Dijk 1983, 2009). A prosecutor, as someone who abhors those who break the law, may describe the robber with such terms as *the thug* or *the thief* and the victim as *the poor man* and *the innocent owner*. On the other hand, a defense lawyer who empathizes with his client may label him *a desperate man* and *a victim of society* while calling the victim *the rich property-owner* or *an unfortunate casualty of war*. The same is true of a speaker's syntactic choices. If a person says, "Joe robbed the store," then Joe had agency and has responsibility for this robbery. When the speaker instead says, "The store was robbed," then the identity of the agent is silenced. Speakers always have choices among the lexical, syntactic, and discursive possibilities, and their biases and points of view will influence their output and make language *loaded* (Bolinger 1980).

Labeling an event, object, or concept with a linguistic term brings the different elements of that referent together and erases their individual existence and weight. Distinct and disparate elements become inherently linked and equal. For instance, when someone is referred to by name, this evokes all aspects of their physical, emotional, and mental self and all properties of their possible identities. No element is given any more importance than any other (alternatively, if a term other than a name is used, then one aspect is given importance while the others are grouped together and ignored). When a series of processes are given a single overarching label, this makes them all just components of the larger event rather than independent events themselves. Returning to the robbery example, when a lawyer refers to a series of processes (e.g., opening a door, walking to a counter, holding up a gun, demanding money, being given money, leaving the store, and running down the street) as *robbing*, this forces those processes to all be understood as components of a single process and as elements of a bounded event. This linguistic choice emphasizes the interrelatedness of the processes but de-emphasizes the fact that in reality they were separate and distinct actions.

Additionally, because of the nature of narratives, a speaker has to create artificial boundaries for any event she describes by picking a starting point and an endpoint for it, despite the reality being that there was a continuous flow of interrelated processes. When a robbery actually takes place, time does not start and stop for the participants. However, a narrative version of a robbery has to take an almost infinite series of interrelated processes and determine that some were part of the robbery and some were not. As a result of the storyteller's choices,[10] actions that could be seen as unrelated (e.g., a person opening a door and a person pulling out a gun) are now linked under the heading of a single larger event, the robbery. Processes that could logically have been considered part of the same event (e.g., the robber walking to the store or the victim crying at home afterward) are now excluded and are part of separate events. Once the narrative has been presented, it may seem natural that an entire set of processes are all a single event, but a speaker with a different point of view may have chosen different starting or ending points or may have included different processes (e.g., the defendant losing his job and needing money to feed his family could have been included, or the opening of the door could be excluded if the speaker knew the robber had not yet decided to demand money when he did that). When different processes are included/excluded, this not only creates a very different version of reality but constructs unique links, relationships, and meanings among the different processes.

When an object or entity is referenced instead of an event, the same types of issues apply. Solid objects have easily defined boundaries based on human sensory knowledge, but for many referents, this is not the case. If we just take the simple example of a *store*, the elements included by this term are often discursively constructed. Is the store the internal space of a building, or is it the physical walls and roof as well? Does it include the property and people within it? Is the ground the store sits on part of it? If so, are the sidewalk and the street surrounding it also part of the store? Does its online presence count? All of these answers depend on the speaker's point of view and are reflected in how they discursively define the store.

A final point is that a speaker who is creating representations of the world can only include some aspects of reality, and other information must ultimately be excluded (Walter and Helmig 2008). This is partly due to the limitations of human perception and cognition, as we simply cannot have access to, notice, process, or remember all input. It is also a result of the discourse medium. There is usually necessarily enough time or resources in any speech event to represent every detail of the speaker's knowledge. Instead, speakers can often only include a limited amount of information, and this has a profound effect on the resulting depiction of reality. In the discursive representation, the excluded elements do not exist. They play no overt role in the re-created version of reality, and their role and impact are silenced. Returning to the robbery example, one can imagine a situation in which everyone ignores a certain witness to a crime. Perhaps no one notices him at the time of the event, no one believes him during the investigation, or no one thinks that he helps their case. Regardless, if no one ever mentions this person or even if he just does not appear in the final discursive representation of the event that circulates in the society, then the person's existence is a non-issue. His effects on the events are hidden. It does not mean that the witness was not real or never existed, but it does mean that information about his presence is lost for all people whose knowledge of the event is dependent on the circulating discourse. For a jury, people's stories about the crime are frequently the only sources they have for making their decision. So, if a jury never hears about a witness, then in effect, that witness was not there because he will have no impact on the verdict.

To summarize, there is no neutral discourse (Bolinger 1980), no unbiased understanding of reality (Fowler, Hodge, Kress, and Trew 1979), no "raw," uninterpreted, "theory-free facts" (Trew 1979a: 95). The very process of representing a topic through linguistic means recontextualizes it, and in this process, certain information is retained, and other information is lost. Some relationships are strengthened, and others are dismissed. The end result is a new product that is separate from reality and is defined by the discursive processes that created it.

6 Discourse as Constructions of a Social World

As discussed earlier, discourses are more than just the communication of information. They are also social interactions, and through them social worlds are created, delineated, enacted. Some have even gone as far as to argue that there is no social reality unless it is constructed in a discourse (see Phillips and Hardy 2002; Wodak and Meyer 2009). Whether or not we accept such an extreme claim, the truth is that discourses are a site in which various identities and relationships with the text and the hearers are negotiated.

A speaker's identity in a discourse is a complicated matter and is constructed in the moment-to-moment details of the interaction. During a trial, whenever lawyers communicate, they are putting on a performance (Hobbs 2008) and trying to create a certain ideal image or character for themselves (Hobbs 2003; Schrager 1999; Trenholm 1989). They have to convey both power and credibility (Bogoch 1999). In order to do this, like all speakers, they take on different "partial selves" (Ochs and Capps 1996: 22) or "roles and relations" (Matthiessen, Teruya, and Lam 2010: 126). These roles have also been called *footings*[11] (Goffman 1981) and *voices*[12] (Bakhtin 1981; Hill 1995; Koven 2002, 2007; Wortham 2001), and there are three overarching sets of them that any speaker can inhabit: a *narrator*, an *interlocutor*, or a *character voice* (Koven 2002, 2007). Additionally, within these general roles, speakers, by using vocabulary, syntax, and stylistic patterns that are indexical of different socially defined characters, present clues about the nature of the identities they are constructing for themselves and the hearers and more clearly define their relationships (Hill 1995; Koven 2002, 2007; Schiffrin 1996; Wortham 1999, 2001).

When using the narrator voice, speakers present descriptions of events with no mention of the "here-and-now" of the speech event or their own responsibility for the discourse. References to the discourse participants (e.g., the lawyers and the jurors) as they are in the present context are absent, as are any overt forms of evaluation. In the corpus analyzed for this book, this voice is often (although not exclusively) used when the lawyers present narratives[13] (about the crime, investigation, trial, future, outside events, etc.), and when they educate the jury about the judicial system, their role in it, the law, the ways they think it applies in this case, and other related topics. The importance of this information being at least partially delivered in a narrator voice is that when lawyers inhabit it, their role as creator of the discourse is not overtly highlighted. This can make the information seem less personal, and lawyers, like speakers in any discourse, can use this role to send the message that they are just neutrally representing the world as it is, rather than how they want it to be (Hill 1995; Koven 2002, 2007).

Speakers also present parts of discourses as their present self in an interlocutor voice, and, by doing so, show themselves as having an active and responsible role in the discourse creation. This is when the text is in the "here-and-now." The speaker includes a meta-discourse or meta-narration (Babcock 1977; Bauman 1986) and gives their own evaluative and affective response to the representation of the world being presented (Koven 2002, 2007). For instance, in the interlocutor voice the lawyers tell the jurors what they should currently be thinking or how the lawyers themselves are feeling. They also ask the jurors questions and command them to undertake certain actions. The message that this voice sends is that the speaker is personally involved in the discourse and is responsible for it and the information being distributed in it.

Additionally, speakers use character voices, which is when they quote someone or something, either directly or indirectly. When this occurs, speakers stop representing themselves as responsible for the message they are conveying and instead overtly assign someone else, who presumably has more authority on the matter (Felton Rosulek 2010a, b), as the source or *author* (Goffman 1981).[14] The current speaker is then interpreted as only the *animator* (Goffman 1981) of the discourse. Lawyers use character voices to put on an air of objectivity and to position themselves as having "reduced personal responsibility" for the content (Besnier 1992; Goffman 1974: 512). They also use quotations to increase their status as orators/storytellers by making the arguments potentially more vivid and engaging if it seems as if the events are unfolding in front of the jurors (Hymes 1973; Labov 1972; Rosen 1988; Tannen 2007 [1989]).

As was stated before, within these general footings, lawyers also adopt more specific voices that allow them to reconfigure their local identity, adopt new rules for the "rights and obligations" (Myers-Scotton 1993) of themselves as speakers and the jurors as hearers, and distribute a framework for how the discourse content should be interpreted. Bakhtin (1981) argued that language is "saturated with intentions and accents" (293) so that each word or phrase "tastes" (293) of the previous contexts in which it was used. To put it another way, each time linguistic forms are used in society, they pick up new meanings and associations that then continue to circulate in each additional discourse in which they are used. To put it another way, linguistic choices and patterns index certain social groups or contexts and, by extension, the characteristics usually assigned to them. A speaker can simply insert words, phrases, or syntactic forms or shift among genres,[15] styles, or dialects/languages that have socially recognized associations (Agha 2005; Bakhtin 1981; Johnstone 1996; Koven 2002, 2007; van Dijk 1997; Wortham and Locher 1996) and bring the attached meaning into the current discourse.[16] Lawyers, like all speakers, use this to create certain identities for themselves. For instance, Fuller (1993) and Hobbs (2003) both described a lawyer using African American English to establish a more relatable persona. Similarly, Cotterill (2003) described Johnnie Cochran using an African American preacher style to emphasize his message in the OJ Simpson case. These code-switches were not just rhetorical devices; rather, the speakers were adopting voices that sent a message about who they were, what relationships and characteristics they had, and how their discourse should be understood.

Describing speakers as adopting different voices or footings helps us understand how lawyers construct and manage their identities throughout the closing arguments. However, this is only one aspect of the creation of a social world. Another is the development of the relationship between the speaker and the message he or she is sending. This is referred to as stance-taking or evaluation, which is:

> The expression of a speaker or writer's attitude or stance towards, viewpoint on, or feelings about the entities or propositions that he or she is talking about. (Thompson and Hunston 2000: 5)

Given this definition, most aspects of a text, particularly when a speaker is in the interlocutor voice, are forms of evaluation. For instance, lexical and syntactic choices (referring to a piece of testimony as a *claim* rather than a *statement*, using adverbs such as *supposedly*) (Hoey 2001; Thompson and Zhou 2000) or even rhetorical devices such as metaphors (Lakoff 1991) all reflect a speaker's point of view, his or her particular theory of reality (Fowler et al. 1979). Modals (e.g., *will, could, might*), hedges, and lexical items that function similarly reflect a speaker's position about the truth-value and the certainty of the proposition (Halliday 1994).[17]

Evaluation is also seen in the personal responsibility that speakers take for their messages and the amount of their self or personal face that they risk. It is seen in how much stake and personal interest in the discourse they acknowledge or hide, how much certainty and consensus they suggest, and how much they try to appear neutral (Potter 1996). Many of these activities are managed through the adoption of different footings and the use of character voices, but they are also accomplished through references to the lawyers themselves, the labels they overtly give themselves (e.g., *lawyer, father, citizen, average Joe)* and their claims about their own mental states (e.g., *I think . . . , we all know . . . , I suppose . . .*). All of these types of strategies permit the speakers to construct a claim as if it were a fact or as if it were a personal opinion (Potter 1996), and they allow the speaker to insert his or her own beliefs and attitudes toward it.

Yet another important part of the construction of social reality is the definition of the roles of the speakers and the hearers and the negotiation of their relationship(s). For instance, by using vocatives, speakers remind the hearers that they are the intended recipients of the discourse. Including overt references to them in the meta-discourse also does the same thing. When lawyers say, "Let's now discuss . . ." or something similar, they are portraying the hearers as active participants in the creation of the discourse.

One way that the speaker's and hearers' relationships are negotiated is through the speaker providing labels for groups of individuals. The act of assigning people to pre-existing or new social categories delineates the group's boundaries and the referents' identities. A common example in a courtroom setting is when the twelve people sitting in judgment of the defendant are transformed into a group by being referred to as *the jury*. While they were all doing the same job before the application of this term, the label makes them a single entity, erases their unique status as individuals, and excludes others who are not members. As this example demonstrates, when a speaker selects a certain set of people as all forming a bound unit, this defines them as having a shared identity and represents them as distinct from non-group members. The differences among the group members are erased, and their shared features and identities are highlighted (Bloome et al. 2005; van Leeuwen 2002).

Plural pronouns are a particularly useful way for speakers to create social groups. In the closing arguments, lawyers often use first- or second-person plural pronouns (e.g., a lawyer using *we* to create a group that refers to herself and the jurors; Stygall 1994) for this purpose. Because pronouns are deictic and thus do not have a set meaning prior to their use, they are much more flexible than noun phrases in their ability to "both refer to and establish an interactional group" (Wortham 1996: 332) that was not necessarily a recognized unit before the use of the pronoun (c.f., Morford 1997; Silverstein 1981). Pronouns involving the speaker and hearers are unique in that the two parties are serving very different roles in the current context so their being equal group members is only forced on them and naturalized by the pronoun's use.

Whether a speaker uses a noun phrase or a pronoun, the discursive construction of social groups divides the world into categories, making some people more alike and some people more different, based on a limited set of characteristics. It creates a shared identity for some people, and this is often exploited to index properties that are associated with group membership or to extend the features of one member of the group to all members. For example, defense lawyers in the corpus studied here often referred to themselves, the jurors, and the defendants as all being citizens of the United States, and argued that this status meant that they all shared certain rights and responsibilities. If the jurors would expect to receive a fair trial and a presumption of innocence when charged with a crime, then the defendants deserved this as well since they were members of the same category of people. Another example is that the lawyers frequently said *we know* . . . with the pronoun referring to the lawyers, the jurors, and maybe but not necessarily the other people present. Such phrases often occurred when the proposition supposedly accepted by the group was in fact controversial. The lawyer making the claim might have "known" it, but the jurors did not necessarily agree. However, by assigning a feature of one person (the lawyer) to the rest of the group (the jurors), the lawyers portrayed everyone as being in agreement.

Speakers, when defining their relationship with the hearers, also manage the level of social distance between them. There are several ways that this occurs that are relevant for this book. The first is through group membership, as discussed earlier. By definition, a common classification decreases social distance, while distinct groupings increase it. Another strategy is formality. Although this term has been used to refer to many distinct concepts (see Irvine 1979), it is understood here as the opposite of intimacy or the creation of greater social distance. Formality is generally measured by the number of rules defining the behavior of the participants, the use of specific styles and genres associated with relationships or social settings of a certain status or social distance, the positioning and labeling of the different participants and referents, and the centrality of the focus (whether there is high degree of shared focus or not). More formal discourse tends to have more rules, a higher status register, less assumed shared knowledge, less or no acknowledgment of a deep or previous relationship, and a high level of shared focus. In the courtroom, this means the use of titles and last names rather than first names (O'Barr 1982), the use of legalese or complicated syntax and vocabulary, and infrequent references to the lawyers or the jurors. This indexes a large power differential, a lack of a shared identity, and little to no personal relationship. More colloquial and interactive speech, the use of first names, and other forms of casual behavior lessen this social distance and create a shared identity or at least a personal relationship. Also, because the context of the closing arguments is a legal trial, which is inherently formal, more formal discourse reflects a respect for the context, while informal discourse de-emphasizes the local context and its impact on the lawyer's speech.

Politeness strategies are another way that speakers decrease social distance, build a positive relationship with the hearer, and manage social relationships (i.e., the interpersonal function of the discourse). Every culture has different rules assigned for politeness, but in the courtroom it often occurs through the recognition of other's social status, speech acts such as apologies and thank yous, respect for local rules and traditions, and the use of more formal speech styles. Politeness, while it does not necessarily redefine social roles, is a way in which speakers discursively manage their relationships with the hearers and maintain their face needs (Brown and Levinson 1987).

To conclude, a discourse such as the closing arguments is a microcosm in which a certain social reality is created. The speaker is able to put on and take off different personas to create a multifaceted identity. By playing these different roles, speakers are able to project themselves as having different characteristics that better serve their goals, and by shifting among an assortment of personas, speakers are able to highlight various identities at different times. Speakers, while managing their relationship with the ideational message they are distributing, can also represent themselves as having more or less personal responsibility for it, depending on the evaluative measures they use. Additionally, speakers are able to determine the type of relationship they have with the hearers. While they manage the level of social distance between them, they also create or redefine social groups so that they can portray themselves as either more or less similar to the jurors. Thus, discourse allows speakers to construct social roles and group memberships for themselves and others as suits their goals, biases, and ideologies.

7 The Factors Shaping Discourses

Representations of both the social and the non-social worlds are not just influenced by the process of the being transformed into a discourse. They are also shaped by cultural patterns, the features of the participants creating the discourse, and the context in which it is constructed.

To start with, many of the rules for deciding what aspects of reality to include and how to linguistically represent them are predefined by the culture in which the discourse is created. At the most basic level, the patterns and limits of the language and dialect can have a direct effect on what is possible to say or what is most like to be said.[18]

Additionally, people's knowledge of the world is mediated through the culture in which they have been socialized. Every culture has its prevailing ideologies and systems of belief about reality and how it should be interpreted, classified, and organized (Bruner 1991; Hodge and Kress 1993; Shore 1996; Trew 1979a; van Dijk 1993, 1995). More specifically, cultures provide people with frames or schemata for understanding and interpreting reality and for giving it meaning (Coulson 2001; Goffman 1974; Snow et al. 1986; Spiro 2003). Frames allow people to "locate, perceive, identify, and label" (Goffman 1974: 21) elements in the world so that they can be organized into a coherent picture of the world that is then reflected in discourse. One example is that some cultures believe in supernatural forces that can affect the world, while others do not. Individuals from cultures with opposing views on this issue will interpret the same event, such as a natural disaster, very differently and will focus on different aspects of it. Another example is that cultures differ on what they define as food. A person from a culture in which people eat meat who sees animal flesh may recognize it in terms of its edibleness. A person from a vegetarian culture might consider its other properties.

Another cultural issue is the genre (the socially recognizable discourse structure; Richards and Schmidt 2010) within which the discourse is created. In any culture, including that of the American legal system, there are identifiable discursive forms whose properties are widely known within the society. There are rules for who can say what to whom, where, and in what way (van Dijk 1993). Some of the features that are often defined for genres include the key structures and the order in which they appear, the subject matter to be included/excluded, and the contexts in which the genre is likely occur[19] (Duranti 1983; Locke 2004). For example, a newspaper article is a common genre. In American culture, it occurs either online or in paper form, and there are many articles about different topics appearing in the same place at the same time. An individual article starts with a headline in a bigger font than the rest of the text, which is sometimes followed by a subtitle and then a byline. The actual article provides a chronological narrative about what occurred, and this is interrupted with quotations from knowledgeable authorities such as eyewitnesses. Authors make no overt references to themselves or to the audience, and they generally do not mention the methodology they used to gather their information.

Because of the power of genres on how people produce discourses, speakers start with a small set of possibilities for how to interpret reality and how to transform it into a text. They are relatively limited by the genre as to what is appropriate to include/exclude and how they can linguistically refer to it. As a result, speakers are not creating representations of reality on their own but are working within predetermined rules and patterns. For instance, if we return to the newspaper example, the genre and the social structure in which it functions have already determined what information is relevant in a newspaper article and what is not. Apparently, the personal identity and role of the reporter have been deemed unimportant and therefore must be excluded. Uncertainly or doubt should ignored, and the point of view of those without power or status is usually excluded or at least minimized (Huckin 2002). Depending on the newspaper, information that goes against the powerful discourses circulating about a topic is often omitted as well (Fowler 1991).

Because of issues of power and authority, the individual reporter has little to no opportunity to include these additional issues, and because the public has become naturalized to this genre's rules, they do not necessarily realize or question the fact that many possible topics are missing.[20]

The closing arguments in criminal trials are a unique genre (Walter 1988), as they exhibit "generic homogeneity" (van Leeuwen 2008: 4) in terms of form, structure, and linguistic patterns.[21] The importance of the genre's rules and patterns are actually magnified for closing arguments, in comparison with discourses that occur in non-legal contexts, because the social rules for what is relevant and possible are formally policed and externally controlled. Non-compliance can have significant real-world consequences. The lawyers' personal feelings about the case, for instance, cannot be included in the closing arguments, and the opposing side or judge will usually interrupt the production of the summation if they are referenced. However, for many topics, there are no relevant legal rules, but instead, social pressures are so strong that it has been naturalized that they will appear either in both arguments or in one argument but not the other. For example, it may seem obvious that the prosecution would not discuss the defendant's positive qualities or that the defense would not mention the heinousness of the crime. However, there is no logical reason that they could not acknowledge and address these issues. The lawyers have simply been socialized not to.

While genre-based patterns provide a common structure to follow, speakers also use the linguistic rules and patterns common to their speech communities (Labov 1972) or communities of practice (Eckert and McConnell-Ginet 1992). The communities that speakers participate in provide them with sets of possible linguistic choices and styles, as well as the rules for how to use them in different contexts and the meanings that can be evoked through their use (Hymes 1974).[22] The importance of these social registers is that they provide the common lexical and syntactic forms to use to describe reality, thus shaping how individual speakers transform that reality into a discourse. As an example, prosecution lawyers often refer to the person on trial as *the defendant* rather than by his name or another more personal term. They did not each come to the conclusion that this is a good term to use independently. Instead, because they are all members of the same community, they have been socialized into using it.

Another way to think about the issues of genre and style conventions is that every speaker in any discourse is recycling and recasting past discourses (Bakhtin 1981, 1986). They are not saying or doing anything truly new. When a lawyer creates her closing argument, she consciously or subconsciously turns to all of the past closing arguments she has heard, the books she has read and classes she has taken on effective litigation, the persuasive speeches she has heard, and so on. Using these previous forms as models and inspiration, she creates a new discourse from them.

In addition to the genres and speech communities in which speakers are working, the particular properties of the discourse participants' personal understanding of reality also alter the ways in which it is transformed into discourse. For instance, the identity of the speaker will have a large impact. Each individual speaker will produce a somewhat unique discourse, as each has her own experiences, patterns of behavior, and conceptual understandings of the topics at hand.[23] It is unlikely that two speakers would ever independently produce the exact same discourse or representation of reality, because a speaker cannot help but produce a representation of reality from his or her own point of view (Duranti 1994). The biases, beliefs and attitudes, and ideologies that the speakers have adopted are all discursively expressed through how they represent reality and construct the resulting text(s) (Berger and Luckmann 1966; Hodge and Kress 1993).

Speakers almost always possess only a fraction of the possible information about a topic, and this is mainly due to the means through which humans gain knowledge: either through personal experience or through access to circulating discourses about a topic. If someone observes an event, she only collects information from her vantage point and only has access to sensory data and evaluative procedures within the limits of human cognition. She cannot see what happened before or after she was present, what is occurring in locations that are blocked from the range of her senses (e.g., on the other side of a wall or large obstruction, beyond earshot), or what the mental and emotional processes and states of the other participants are. Additionally, the human brain can process only a limited amount of the sensory input it has access to and receives (Starr and McMillan 2012). The data that the person does process will be influenced by his past experiences, his cultural patterns, and his brain's functions. As everyone's cognitive system functions slightly differently (Rathus 2012), even people who observe the same event or entity from the same vantage point will have a unique perception and understanding of it.

If, instead of a speaker's knowledge coming entirely from personal experience, she has some or all of her knowledge from discourses, she will still only have a partial understanding of the topic. First of all, she likely has only had access to a portion of the discourses that are circulating about the topic. Second, even the discourses in which she has participated have been biased because humans created them. Those discourses have been shaped by the cultural frames and the individual limitations of the people who constructed and shared them.

While the effects of a speaker's biases are an important component of the representation of reality being created, the role of the hearer is an essential part as well. Especially in more dialogic genres,[24] the discourse and reality are co-constructed (Duranti 1994). Together, the participants create meaning. The situation is slightly different in more monologic discourses such as those being studied here. In these contexts, the jurors, as the main audience, have a much less active role. As they cannot speak, their role is mostly limited to eye contact, body language, and other forms of non-verbal communication. However, their very presence is an important factor since the lawyers are trying to manage their relationship and the amount of social distance between them. The jurors' potential knowledge, backgrounds, and understandings all affect the discourse the lawyers create.[25]

To summarize, through the process of transforming reality into a linguistic medium, that event is recontextualized and necessarily transformed. Its boundaries are set, while its parts are located and labeled. Some of it will be included, but some will be excluded from the discourse and thus lost. In the end, the output will be a representation but not a perfect re-creation of the original. These processes are all dependent on the genre of the discourse being created, the point of view and biases of the speaker, and the effects of the hearers.

8 Silencing, De-Emphasizing, and Emphasizing as Discursive Means for Representing Reality and Constructing Social Worlds

Thus far, the argument has been made that discourses, while representing, organizing, labeling, and creating realities, are reliant upon the biases of the speaker, which are both personally and culturally determined. While this discussion has been aided by examples, the full nature of how this occurs in discourse has not been explained. In Chapter 1, I argued that it occurs through silencing, de-emphasizing, and emphasizing. In this section, I expand on those claims and provide more detailed definitions of the relevant issues. For those interested in discourse analysis beyond just the courtroom, this will be the most important insight of the book.

According to the model being put forth here, there are four important issues facing any potential piece of information. The first is whether it is included or excluded from the discourse. Inclusion is when the topic is communicated to the hearers through symbolic content. Exclusion, then, is when it is not communicated. There are two general categories for excluded information: it is either silenced or presupposed. A topic is silenced (Huckin 2002) when the speaker excludes it, it is not recoverable from common-sense knowledge, and it is not a logical implication of claims about reality that were made. The fact that the hearers could already be aware of the excluded information or that they could possibly discover the existence of the topic from another discourse or through personal experience does not matter. All that matters is that this particular discourse does not include it in its representation of reality. Presupposed information is also excluded, but the difference is that it is assumed to be part of the interlocutors' "common ground" (Stalnaker 2002), information that the speaker assumes is shared knowledge.

There are two separate issues for all information that is included in a discourse. The first is whether it is explicitly stated or just implied. Implicit inclusion means that instead of being overtly referenced through linguistic content, the information was indexed through entailment, conversational implicature, conventional implicature (Grice 1975), or other socially determined conventions such as code-switching. The other distinction relevant for included topics, whether they are referred to implicitly or explicitly, is whether they are de-emphasized (given less focus, prominence, or attention), included neutrally (given no more or less focus, prominence, or attention) or emphasized (given more focus, prominence, or attention). These three concepts fall along a continuum with completely excluded topics at one end and the most emphasized topics at the other. A visual representation of the issues can be seen in Figure 2.1.

The importance of inclusion/exclusion has been discussed by a wide variety of authors including Trew (1979a, b), Hall (1985), van Dijk (1986), Jalbert (1994), Dressen (2002), Johnstone (2002), van Leeuwen (2002), Fairclough (2003) and Kurzon (2007), and has long been considered important, both within the field of CDA and outside of it. It has been consistently shown to be affected by a speaker's biases, particularly those of an ideological nature, and to affect the representation of reality created. In fact, Johnstone (2002) said, "in addition to being shaped by what is said, the worlds evoked and created in discourse are also shaped by silence." As discussed above, a discursive representation of any type of reality cannot contain all possible information, not even all sensory input or knowledge about an event or entity that a speaker has. There has to be some "discursive simplification" (Jessop 2002). Therefore, the limits of a speaker's knowledge and his or her biases, the patterns of ideology and behavior dictated by the society, and the features of the speech event and discourse context will all act as selective "filters" (Fairclough 2003: 139), allowing some information to make it into the construction of reality and some to not.

A few examples of how inclusion and exclusion have been shown to function in discourses will demonstrate the importance of these concepts. Van Leeuwen (2008) examined discourses about schools and found that different

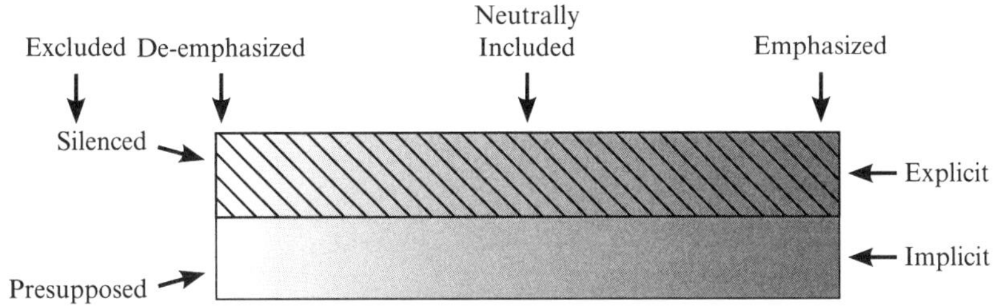

FIGURE 2.1 The possible level of inclusion for any piece of information.

social actors were excluded based on the target audience of the texts. Texts for teachers omitted fathers while texts for upper-class members of society ignored people whose social class was below the level of the teacher (e.g., custodians, cafeteria workers, etc.). By following these patterns, the discourses revealed who these groups considered to be unimportant or unnecessary participants in the schooling process. Peled-Elhanan (2010) examined Israeli textbooks, and showed that one textbook's coverage of a massacre by Israeli police silenced the killers' motives/reasons, the suffering of the victims, and many details that could have caused people to negatively evaluate the Israeli government. By ignoring this information, the actions of the state of Israel were legitimated. A final example comes from Huckin (2002) and his analysis of the coverage of homelessness in newspapers. He found that in a conservative newspaper editorial, the author ignored how such issues as racism, domestic abuse, government spending cuts, job training, and treatment programs are all related to the issue of homelessness. This occurred despite these topics being part of more liberal public discourses. As all three examples showed, biased representations of reality were created because relevant information was excluded and information that fit the speaker's cultural ideologies and personal biases was included.

In this book, when excluded topics are being discussed, the focus is on those that are unrecoverable to the hearers because, by not being included, they are lost from the particular model of reality the speaker has constructed. Following Huckin (2002, 2010), this type of the omitted information is referred to as *silenced*.[26] Its role and impact are metaphorically mute because it plays no overt role in this version of reality from the point at which the discourse is created and onward.[27] Irvine and Gal (2000) describe a similar process and use the term *erasure*. Although they are referring to discourses more broadly and are focused more on ideologies, the idea is basically the same. Information is excluded from discourses because it does not fit the speaker's beliefs, goals, understanding of the world, and so on. For example, it was mentioned earlier that van Leeuwen (2008) found that in first-day-of-school narratives directed at teachers, the fathers were often excluded. This is an example of silencing. The teachers have no other information about the children in the stories so they cannot assume that they actually have fathers who are actively involved. This text is the extent of the teacher's knowledge, and so in their understanding of these children's worlds, there are no fathers. The potential importance of this is that if the teachers start to relate these stories to the lives of their actual students, then the role of those children's fathers is likely to also be ignored because it simply is not part of the pervasive discourse.

Not all silences are equivalent in that not all happen for the same reasons. Some occur because the speaker wants to send a message by not saying anything when they are expected to say something, and this is called a "speech act silence" (Huckin 2002), or a "meaningful silence" (Dressen 2002). An example is when someone asks a question, and the other person refuses to answer or else provides a "dispreferred response" (Sidnell 2010) such as a non-relevant statement or another question.

Other silences occur simply because a speaker was not thinking about the topic for some reason (e.g., distraction, forgetting, chance; Dressen 2002; Huckin 2002). Most people have experienced a time when they meant to say something and they forgot to do so, or an instance when they said the first thing that popped into their head, despite thinking of better things to have said when given more time to review the situation.

Some silences reflect the biases of the culture in which they occur or those of the speaker who produces them. Cultures tend to declare certain topics, linguistic forms, and so on, to be taboo either in all situations or in some, depending on characteristics of the speaker, the hearers, and the context. By respecting these rules, a speaker is "discreet" (Huckin 2002) by remaining silent about topic. For instance, in American culture, it is generally not acceptable to talk about bodily functions in formal settings and so these topics, even if they are on someone's mind, are generally silenced. In other instances, the cultural ideologies affect the form of genres in such ways that it becomes naturalized that a certain topic will not be included in them (Dressen 2002; Huckin 2002). How this works in newspaper articles was discussed earlier. Finally, there are "manipulative" silences (Huckin 2002), which occur when a speaker excludes relevant information in order to hide it from the hearer. For instance, when a politician only discusses the positive benefits of a military strike and ignores all of the civilian casualties, this is a manipulative silence. Whether it is the effect of the individual speaker or the group in which they belong, the fact is that because of biases, certain relevant information gets erased.

In the closing arguments, the most important silences are genre-based silences and manipulative silences, but the distinction between these two can be difficult to tease apart. Since the prosecution and the defense closing arguments are both individual sub-genres, we expect to find similar patterns used by lawyers of the same type, and the analysis in this book shows that they do behave quite consistently. However, the patterns found are often done to hide specific information from the jurors—to exclude it from the version of reality the lawyers are creating so that the jurors do not include it in their own models of the people, events, and concepts. Thus, they are manipulative silences as well. Also, while the general patterns may be characteristic of the genres, the details of how they actually occur are specific to the individual cases. Therefore, for the purposes of the book, items that are defined as silences should be considered to be both unless otherwise stated.

Several additional points need to be made about silences. The first is that while silences occur in the output of a discourse, this is not necessarily where they originate. They may be in the speaker's knowledge base from which she is creating the discourse, or they may be purely discursive. For instance, a speaker's biases may be so strong that she has not even considered other opinions, or a genre's effects may be so pervasive that the speaker did not even notice aspects of reality that she was unlikely to include. Second, when a discourse silences a topic, this does not mean that it is impossible for the speaker to get the information elsewhere. It simply means that he must turn to another discourse to obtain it, and when he does, it will already have been inserted in a different and perhaps incompatible representation of reality. For instance, in the closing arguments, the jurors are receiving the information that was silenced in one argument from the other argument. However, it is not necessarily possible for them to reconcile the different narratives being presented or to understand how claims made by one side, if true, would fit into the other's version of reality. Chilton (2004) stated that coercion was partly accomplished by "making assumptions about realities that hearers are obliged to at least temporarily accept" (45). Jurors have to accept certain silences while listening to each side because it is the only way to interpret this particular version of reality.

Third, despite being "out in the open," silencing is in fact often hidden. When lawyers stand in front of the jurors and present an alternative model of the world that omits certain information, the silenced information is simply lost. The representation created without it still seems complete, and that is how the silence is the most effective (Thiesmeyer 2003). For instance, when lawyers present a narrative of what happened during the crime, they usually try to present a believable story, despite not including events or people the other side included. The speakers themselves may not even be aware that they are silencing information; they are just presenting information as they know and understand it.

The other type of excluded information, recoverable knowledge, is being referred to as *presupposed* information in this book.[28] To put it simply, speakers and hearers all enter into discourses with a large amount of shared knowledge or "common ground" (Clark 1992; Karttunen and Peters 1975; Stalnaker 1978, 2002) that they rely on for interpreting the exchange. A speaker can omit from the discourse "propositions whose truth he takes for granted as part of the background of the conversation" (Stalknaker 1978: 321). In other words, speakers can exclude topics that they already know and accept and that they assume the hearers already know and accept, either from prior knowledge or from the context of the discourse (Chapman and Routledge 1999; Chilton 2004; Huckin 2002; van Dijk 2005; Yule 1996). For example, in the courtroom context, the lawyers do not have to introduce everyone (e.g., the different lawyers, the defendants, the judge, the jurors) during the closing arguments because they can assume that the jurors already learned this information earlier in the trial. Therefore, people's names and roles are presupposed. Other types of common knowledge might be "interpersonal knowledge" (from previous shared interactions), "group knowledge" (information widely distributed within a social group; e.g., legends and myths among those who belong to the same religious faith, technical know-how among practitioners in a field), "institutional or organizational knowledge" (information about how an institution functions, its rules and regulations, and its terminology), "national knowledge" (information that circulates within a certain political boundary), and "cultural knowledge" (van Dijk 2005).

For presupposition to work in a cooperative interaction, the speakers must truly believe that the hearers accept the presupposed knowledge to be true, and in order to understand what is going on, the hearers have to agree (Chilton 2004). However, for various reasons including ideological viewpoints and manipulative intentions, speakers omit information that the hearers do not necessarily accept in order to represent the hearers as already being in agreement with a proposition (Bekalu 2006; Chilton 2004; Flowerdew and Leong 2010; van Dijk 2005;). This has been called *presumption* (Chilton 2004; Flowerdew and Leong 2010; van Dijk 2005), but in this book, this is understood as a form of silencing, as the speaker is excluding the hearers' doubts and dissension as well as other possible interpretations of the world. For example, prosecution and defense lawyers in the corpus analyzed here often presumed that a victim of a crime would act in a certain way, and they indicated this by judging the victim in the case as either acting like a true victim or not doing so, depending on the lawyer's point of view. On the surface, this seems like the lawyers were simply making a presupposition about the jurors being in agreement about the ways victims behave, when in reality, they are silencing the large amount of variation in victims' reactions and behavior. Basically, whenever a blanket statement about a group is made and not supported, this is a presumption that silences data that does not fit.

The difficulty in studying exclusion is that the data are undefined and unlimited in that they are simply everything that is not included. The first step for completing such an analysis is deciding on relevance. For the purposes of this book, a topic is relevant to all arguments in a case if it is included implicitly or explicitly in a proposition made in any of the related texts. Basically, if one speaker makes it relevant, then it is a potential topic in any text in the set. Additionally, this definition means that the pragmatic implications and presumptions that follow from a speaker's stated propositions are relevant in that text and in the others. If those implications are not stated or addressed, then they are excluded. For instance, when a lawyer says to the jurors, "you know . . . ," this implies that the lawyer is aware of the jurors' mental processes and that they are actually in agreement with the following claim. However, this is not necessarily true since the lack of communication between them means that the lawyers likely do not know what the jurors are thinking. Thus, the lawyer is excluding either the source of his knowledge about the jurors or his own lack of certainty about the truth-value of this statement.

So, the lawyer made these additional issues relevant by implying them, but excluded them when he did not address them.

The other issue for analyzing exclusion is determining if something is presupposed or silenced. Information not included in any of the arguments in a case but that could be relevant is considered to be presupposed. This includes information the jurors received in other parts of the trial (e.g., the identities of the different participants), common-sense knowledge that an average member of the community in question would likely know (e.g., what county the trial is occurring in, the names of the major institutions located in the area, etc.), and information that is not contentious or more beneficial to one case over the other (e.g., the specific distance between the different sites in which the crime took place, the number of children the defendant had). Contentious information (i.e., propositions whose truth values were not necessarily accepted by all participants) that is beneficial to one side but that is excluded from the other's argument is labeled as *silenced*.[29]

In addition to understanding exclusion, it is also important to understand degrees of inclusion. It has long been noted that information in discourses receives different levels of "importance" (Fox 1983: 250), that some topics are more relevant to the "global theme" or what the discourse is about (Tomlin et al. 1997: 95). However, the terminology used for this phenomenon has been inconsistent or has tended to not be well-defined. Sets of terms that have been adopted include *mainline* topics and *supportive* topics (Longacre 1989, 1996), *main structure/part* versus *side structure/part* (van Kuppevelt 1995), *prominent* and *backgrounded* (Fairclough 2003), and *high, average, and low occurring frequencies* (Faber 2006). Others have simply commented that topics can be *backgrounded* (Huckin 2002) or *near-silenced* (Coupland and Coupland 1997) but have not defined the other end of the spectrum.

One pair of terms that has been used quite frequently, although with slight variations in meaning, is *foregrounding/backgrounding* (e.g., Chvany 1990; Givón 1987; Grimes 1975; Hopper 1979; Hopper and Thompson 1980; Jones and Jones 1979; Labov and Waletzky 1967; Mukařovský 1964 [1932]; Tomlin 1985). The key idea that these words capture is that certain information is more central to a discourse and therefore is given more attention and made more "conscious" (Mukařovský 1964 [1932]: 226). Specifically, a topic is in the *foreground* if it is more important (Tomlin 1985) and contributes to the main goal of the discourse (Hopper and Thompson 1980). Background topics are less important or less crucial (Tomlin 1985), and support the foregrounded material by elaborating on it or providing the context for it (Hopper and Thompson 1980). While it is easy to see these two categories as a rigid dichotomy, in reality they are steps on a continuum, a matter of degree (c.f., Jones and Jones 1979; Tomlin 1985;[30] Wårvik 2004).

There are problems with these terms for the present study, however, mainly because of their association with narratives. Following Labov and

Waletzky (1967), the *foreground* has often been limited to clauses that describe actions and events that move the plot forward, while the *background* provides descriptions about states and properties of characters, places, and events (Labov and Waletzky 1967; Longacre 1996; Polanyi 1982). However, this denigrates the importance of evaluation, discussion, explanation, and description, particularly in non-narrative or multi-narrative discourses; it fails to recognize that some elements are given more prominence than others, regardless of their foreground or background status (Khalil 2005); and it does not help us describe the focus given to particular referents, concepts, or even larger themes since the *foreground/background* distinction is mostly used to describe processes and clauses. Therefore, while these terms will be used as synonyms for *emphasis* and *de-emphasis* in the book, their potentially clouded meaning will limit their use overall.

This idea that certain topics are more important or activated in a discourse has also been referred to with the terms *prominence* and *salience* (Halliday 2002; Khalil 2000; Swales 2004). Halliday (2002) discussed *motivated prominence* as another term for *foregrounding* or "linguistic highlighting" (99) and defined it a state where "some feature of the language of a text stands out in some way" (99). Khalil (2000) makes a distinction between the two terms. He defines *salience* as "the relative conspicuousness of schema categories" (66). *Prominence* describes the ways in which "sentences and their components stand out" (67) because of their syntactic and semantic properties. Thus, salience has to do with concepts and ideas and prominence with linguistic forms, but both are describing the idea that certain discourse structures receive more focus than others. The problem with these terms is that they are often used for the interpretation of discourse references and so, like *foreground/background*, are laden with additional, irrelevant meanings for this particular book.

As was mentioned before, the terms *de-emphasis, neutral inclusion*, and *emphasis* will be mainly used in this book. Coe et al. (2004) and Gerbner (1985) used the term *emphasis* to refer to topics that were referred to more frequently. Van Dijk (2000, 2008) used the term *emphasizing* for the more prominent topics although his term for the lower end of the spectrum varied (*de-emphasis* in van Dijk [2000], *marginalization* in van Dijk [2008]). Gerbner (1985) defines *emphasis* as "a measure of the relative importance of a unit of attention in the sample. Emphasis directs attention to some units at the expense of attending to other units" (22). He also states that measures of *emphasis* capture "degrees of intensity, centrality, and importance" (21). In this book, emphasis, as in all of these others studies, is understood only in comparison with other topics and structures. Something is emphasized if it is given a higher degree of importance than something else. Neutral inclusion means they have the same degree of importance, while de-emphasis means the one topic has been given less importance than another one.

Now that *de-emphasizing* and *emphasizing* have been defined, the difficulty is in operationalizing them for analysis. There are many different linguistic and discursive ways in which topics and information are made more prominent and given more focus. For instance, in Halliday (2002), the choice of one syntactic structure more frequently than others made it locally prominent. Huckin (2002) labeled topics as *foregrounded* if they occurred very early in a discourse. Labov (1984) discussed strengthening adverbs and other linguistic devices as means of adding intensity to increase the force of an illocutionary act. Another way to analyze textual prominence is through the given/new or theme/rheme structure with the theme being given the most emphasis (Caffarel, Martin, and Matthiessen 2004). In oral discourses like the closing arguments, emphasis can be provided through extra-linguistic means such as stress, volume, and pausing, while in texts it is done through font, text size, physical separation, and other visual means of setting something apart. All of these methods of analyzing emphasis are potentially valid, but the analysis in this book is mainly focused on the frequency of inclusion as a means of emphasis (although other means will be discussed from time to time). When examined with nuance and caution, the frequency of certain lexical items within a corpus can help reveal what topics the texts are focused or centered on (Baker 2006). In this book, we extend this type of analysis to other linguistic forms and discourse structures, as all aspects of meaning-making are influenced by ideology (Fairclough 2010). The reason that *frequency* was selected is that it can mean one of two basic things: either that more information and details are being provided about a topic, or that the same information is being repeated. Both keep the topic at the forefront of the speaker's attention and focus. When a topic is referred to less frequently and less information is provided about it, then it is de-emphasized. The assumption is that speakers with different conceptualizations of a topic and with different goals give different amounts of focus to topics. The lawyers in the corpus analyzed here support this assumption.

The other issue for inclusion, which matters regardless of the level of emphasis, is whether or not the information is explicit or implicit (van Dijk 1977). Explicit information is directly encoded in the lexical and syntactic choices of the speaker. In contrast, implicit information is indexed through entailment (van Dijk 1977), conventional implicature (Grice 1975), and socially defined forms of conversational implicature (Levinson 2000).

Entailment is the property of a stated proposition that other propositions can follow from it as a logical consequence. To put it another way, a proposition A entails a proposition B if every time A is true, B must also be true and if every time B is false, A must also be false. For example, the sentence *my client is an honest man* entails *my client is a man*. If the sentence *my client is an honest man* is true, then this person has to be a man. If he is not a man, then the sentence *my client is an honest man* cannot be true. Another example is that *my client is an honest man* entails *I have a client.*

Conventional implicature is closely related to entailment. It is the additional meaning that accompanies the main assertion that is encoded by the choice of linguistic forms, even the function words—for example, *but, therefore, even, still, manage to* (Potts 2005). For example, if a person says, "Emily managed to get through the book," this entails that she read the book and conventionally implies that it took effort. If someone says, "Even Jim read the book," this entails that Jim read the book and conventionally implies that Jim was less likely than others to have read the book. While some such as Bach (1999) deny that conventional implicatures even exist and insists that they are higher level speech acts or simply additional entailments, the important message for this book is that speakers can avoid stating certain propositions by implying or suggesting them through the nuanced meanings attached to the lexical forms and syntactic structures they include.

Finally, there is conversational implicature (Bach 1994; Grice 1975; Levinson 1983, 2000), which captures the idea that more information is communicated than just the literal meaning of the linguistic forms (Levinson 1983). While this, too, is a much debated and much theorized topic in pragmatics, the relevant insight for this book is that as Levinson (2000) stated, speakers add additional levels of meaning "by utilizing the form, the structure, and the pattern of choices within the utterance" (6). Speech situations have unmarked or predictable conventions for how they are constructed. Following these patterns implies that a hearer can interpret the event and the linguistic output as having the usual sets of meaning that are attached them. Making a marked or atypical choice indicates that the speaker is deviating from the typical meaning and indexes other possible interpretations of the utterance. There are generally rules for what is relevant in a discourse, and when a speaker says something that appears to be irrelevant, the message generally is that either the information is relevant or that the speaker does not have something relevant to say for some particular reason (Grice 1975). Shifting among different styles, codes, or voices is another means of creating additional layers of meaning through implicature. We return once again to Fuller's (1993) and Hobb's (2003) description of lawyers using African American English to connect with African American jurors. In such instances, the lawyers did not have to directly state that they were someone the jurors could trust, but they implied it by displaying a marker associated with being a member of a common social group.

To summarize, the content included in a discourse cannot only include what is explicitly or literately stated but must also include what is implied through logical inference and standard and accepted forms of implicature. Speakers and hearers communicate multiple levels of information, particularly about themselves and their relationship to the context, the hearers, and the information being communicated. This cannot be omitted from a theory of inclusion. It must be noted that there may be differences between explicitly and implicitly referenced information with regards to the degree to which it is made salient to the hearer. A psychological measure of this is beyond the scope of the book although implicit and explicit references are kept separate for quantitative purposes throughout the book.

In the remainder of the book, the analysis of the data will demonstrate the importance of silencing, de-emphasizing, and emphasizing in both the explicit and implicit communication strategies that lawyers use. The patterns described here will demonstrate the significance of these phenomena in all aspects of discourse. They occur in lexical and syntactic forms and in individual clauses, narratives, texts, and discourses. They aid in both the interpersonal and the ideational functions of language, and they help speakers both inform and direct. While individual instantiations of them may occur randomly, the general patterns of silencing, de-emphasizing, and emphasizing occur because of speakers' individual and cultural biases.

3

The Defendants

With the theoretical framework discussed in the previous chapter in mind, we now turn our attention to the data from the corpus. The current chapter and the three immediately following it each focus on a specific set of social actors: the defendants, the victims, the jurors, and the lawyers. The decision to focus on the people involved in the trials rather than any other topic is based on two main factors. First, the events surrounding and the actions of these social actors are what the crime, investigation, and trial narratives are likely to be about in any closing argument, regardless of the charges or the specifics of the crime. Therefore, these people are the natural place to start when trying to compare across a large number of trials. Second, Heffer (2005) and Felton Rosulek (2008, 2009) found that the prosecution and the defense differed in the focus they placed on the defendant and the victim. Thus, there is pre-existing evidence that the representations of these social actors are key to understanding how lawyers create opposing arguments.

In this chapter, we start with the defendants, as they are the ones who are most directly affected by the outcome of the case. They will be punished if found guilty and will be redeemed if found not guilty. Regardless of the specifics of the case, the prosecution and the defense have distinctly different goals with regard to how the jurors view the defendant. In a criminal trial, ultimately the prosecution wants him or her to be found guilty,[1] while the defense wants him or her to be found not guilty.

Given these differing viewpoints and the more theatrical qualities of the closing arguments (Cotterill 2003; Hobbs 2003; Meyer 1994), it might be expected that each side would use a full range of linguistic constructions to dramatically create images of the defendant as either a sinner or a saint. This does happen. Prosecutors have been known to use metaphors and name-calling to demonize the defendants. Cotterill (2003) describes OJ Simpson as being compared to a *ticking time bomb* and Bishop (1977) reports names such as *ape*, *snake*, *assassin*, *as low as the most lecherous animal that ever crawled the earth*, *thug*, and *filthy pervert*.[2] However, Felton Rosulek (2008, 2009) did not find such terms to be common. Instead, the prosecution used the term *defendant* most of the time. At the same time, trial manuals consistently urge defense lawyers to humanize the defendant (e.g., Berg 2006; Mauet 1998, 2009; Perrin et al. 2011). To this end, lawyers have been shown to use the defendant's name (Felton Rosulek 2008; Walter 1988) and to provide personal and sympathetic details about his or her life (Costanzo and Peterson 1994; Meyer 1994). While these patterns are interesting, they provide us with a very narrow and stereotypical view of the representation of defendants in closing arguments. They are what we would expect to see if we watched a dramatized case on a television show or a movie. In this chapter, I present a much more nuanced version of how lawyers linguistically construct opposing representations of the same defendants.

The analysis is broken up into several sections. The first describes how frequently the defendants are referred to, the second examines the terms that are used to reference them, and the third examines their roles in the different narratives and voices that make up the arguments. Each section starts with a description of the corpus as a whole and then turns to the specifics of a selection of the individual cases. Because this is the first chapter of data analysis, each section also includes a description of the methodology used for analyzing the data.

1 Frequency of Reference

There are two important differences between the prosecution and the defense with regard to the frequency at which they referred to the defendants: (1) the prosecution emphasized the defendants more than the defense did, and (2) the defense emphasized the victims and the jurors more than they emphasized the defendants. Both of these results can be seen in Table 3.1, which presents

TABLE 3.1
Frequency of Reference

	Prosecution	Defense	Rebuttal
Defendants	38.6 (3,490)[1, 2]	27.5 (2,239)[1, 3]	34.5 (634)[2, 3]
Victims (excluding cases with more than one victim)	35.0 (2,179)	30.1 (1,993)	27.3 (397)
Jurors	23.8 (2,146)[4, 5]	28.3 (2,307)[4]	27.4 (516)[5]
Opposing side	2.3 (207)[6, 7]	7.2 (590)[6, 8]	8.2 (155)[7, 8]
Lawyer who was speaking	15.1 (1,366)[9, 20]	18.0 (1,469)[9]	20.3 (382)[10]

Note: The first number in each square is the number per 1,000 words; the actual number of tokens follows in parentheses. The difference between values with matching superscript numerals are statistically significant for $p<0.01667$.

the number of explicit references to the defendants both as a frequency and as a total number and includes data for other social actors[3] for the purposes of comparison.

The prosecution referred to the defendants much more frequently than the defense did, both in terms of the total number of references (3,490 for the prosecution compared to 2,239 for the defense) and the frequency of those references per 1,000 words (38.6/1,000 for the prosecution in the main arguments and 34.5/1,000 in their rebuttals, compared to 27.5/1,000 for the defense arguments). As will be shown repeatedly in this chapter, this means that the prosecution emphasized the defendant more than the defense did. In the prosecution arguments, the defendant played a more central role in the events, was involved in more processes and events, and was kept in the foreground even more. In contrast, the defense included less information about the defendants, and thus, their arguments focused on them less. This is not to say that the defense completely de-emphasized or silenced the defendants. They still referred to them quite often. It just means that compared to the prosecution, the defense provided less information about the defendants and that other topics were discussed more.

The two sides also differed significantly with regard to which actors received the most emphasis. The prosecution referred to the defendants the most frequently, then the victims, and then the jurors (followed by all other people). During the rebuttals, the order was similar in that the defendants were still mentioned the most often, although the jurors and the victims were referred to at roughly the same rate. However, in the defense arguments, the victims were discussed the most often, the jurors were next, and then finally, the defendants were referred to less frequently than either of them. This is important in that it clearly demonstrates that the prosecution and the defense arguments were focused on different social actors and different topics. For the prosecution, the defendant was the most important social actor in the case, while for the defense attorneys, other people and topics were more vital to their argument.

When each closing arguments is analyzed individually, rather than analyzing the corpus as a whole, the same patterns emerge. As Table 3.2 shows, in almost every case (fifteen of the seventeen), the prosecution lawyers referred to the defendants more frequently than the defense lawyers did.[4]

In the fifteen cases in which the prosecution referred to the defendant more frequently than the defense did, they mentioned the defendants an average of 12.9 more times per 1,000 words than the defense did, and in one case, #13, the difference was as high as 24.7 references per 1,000 words. In several of these cases, the prosecution referred to the defendant twice or even thrice as often than the defense did.

For example, in case #5, the defense only referred to the defendant thirty-five total times, or 9.7 times per 1,000 words. The prosecution referred to him

TABLE 3.2

References to the Defendants

Case	Prosecution	Defense	Rebuttal
1	24.2 (38)	18.8 (52)	27.3 (25)
2	45.7 (330)[1, 2]	22.1 (194)[1, 3]	31.2 (66)[2, 3]
3	45.3 (265)[4, 5]	32.3 (156)[4, 6]	10.0 (9)[5, 6]
4	24.9 (58)	20.6 (69)	0.0 (0)
5	30.8 (82)[7]	9.3 (35)[7]	17.9 (13)
6	28.4 (271)	27.1 (217)	33.0 (37)
7	*34.2 (159)*[8]	*62.5 (228)*[8]	*46.9 (28)*
8	35.7 (51)	23.9 (87)	28.5 (19)
9	31.0 (158)[9]	14.7 (53)[9]	—
10	25.6 (193)	20.4 (33)	16.6 (25)
11	38.2 (192)[10]	14.1 (28)[10]	—
12	39.6 (116)[11]	19.0 (88)[11]	25.2 (30)
13	46.1 (396)[12, 13]	21.4 (103)[12]	28.5 (28)[13]
14	42.6 (294)[14]	19.5 (138)[14]	—
15	*34.6 (279)*[15]	*38.0 (474)*[16]	*51.0 (181)*[15, 16]
16	34.7 (79)	29.5 (79)	24.4 (50)
17	61.5 (529)[16]	45.5 (205)[16]	53.9 (123)

Note: The first numbers are the number/1,000 words; totals are in parentheses. Differences that are statistically significant are given matching superscripts.

82 times, or 30.8 times per 1,000 words. In this particular case, these disparities were the result of the prosecution emphasizing the defendant and his role in an assault during a fight at a soccer game, and the defense focusing on the problems with the witnesses' testimony. Since the defense mostly ignored the events that allegedly occurred at the crime scene, the defendant had comparatively little importance in their argument.

Another example comes from case #13. This one is particularly interesting because the prosecution mentioned the defendant at an especially high frequency of 46.1 times per 1,000 words (396 times), but the defense referred to him less than half as often (21.4 times per 1,000 words/103 times). This was another case involving people in a fight, but in this particular instance, there were multiple perpetrators. The prosecution emphasized the defendant and what he had done, while the defense gave him a comparatively smaller role in their version of the fight. They admitted that he was involved but only depicted him as being relatively inconsequential. Because of the contrasting levels of importance given to the defendant in the key events, he was assigned different levels of emphasis in their arguments.

Several arguments did not fit the general pattern of the corpus and thus deserve further discussion. The first such set consists of the arguments presented in cases #1, #4, #8, and #16. In terms of the frequency of reference per 1,000 words, these arguments fit the general pattern in the corpus. However, in cases #1, #4, and #8, the defense actually referred to the defendant more times than the prosecution did, and in case #16, the two sides referred to him the same number of times. The explanation for this is simple—the prosecution had relatively short closing arguments in these cases in terms of total number of words,[5] while the defense arguments were average. The prosecution still emphasized the defendants in their arguments, making them a focus in the depiction of the reality they created, while the defense did the opposite. The defense just discussed so many more topics that the prosecution ignored that this diluted the additional references to the defendants in their arguments.

In only two cases (the italicized entries), #7 and #15, did the defense refer to the defendant more frequently than the prosecution did. Case #7 will be discussed more later, but the reason for the unusual pattern in this particular case is that the defense was claiming that instead of this case being about rape, as the prosecution argued, it was about consensual sexual acts. To prove this, they went into great detail about the sexual events (something most defenses do not do) but portrayed the defendant as the recipient instead of the agent of the acts more frequently. In case #15, the difference between the frequencies for the two sides was not significant, and the prosecution, in their rebuttal, referred to the defendant at an especially high rate, 51.0 times per 1,000 words, which resulted in them still emphasizing the defendant more overall than the defense did.

An additional key point that should be noted about these two cases is that the unusual results were not the result of the prosecution lawyers de-emphasizing the defendants; rather, they occurred because defense lawyers mentioned the defendants exceptionally frequently. In fact, these two cases represent the defenses' highest and third highest frequencies of reference for the defendants in any of the cases. As a result, these cases show that unless the defense discussed the defendants more than they typically did, the prosecution emphasized them more than the defense did. Another thing these two cases had in common is that they both were instances when the defense admitted the events in question occurred but gave them a different, noncriminal explanation. To do so, they emphasized the defendant more than the defense did in a typical case.

A final point is that the prosecution lawyers were much more consistent in how frequently they referred to the defendants than the defense lawyers were. The standard deviation for the prosecution was 7.4 times per 1,000 words, while the defense had a standard deviation of 13.2 times per 1,000 words. One explanation for the increased variation among the defense arguments when compared to the prosecution arguments is that while all of the prosecution lawyers were arguing that the defendant did certain things and was therefore guilty, the defense strategies differed. For example, in case #5, in which the defendant was significantly de-emphasized, even when compared to other defense arguments, the lawyer argued that the alleged victim of the assault invented the accusations. Because of this argument, they did not present an alternative crime narrative. In case #7, when the defendant was mentioned the most often by his lawyer, the defense was admitting that sexual activity took place, but said that the alleged victim had consented to it. They thus presented a crime and investigation narrative that highlighted the defendant's innocent acts and lack of agency. The disparate strategies of the defense led to differences in how frequently they referred to the defendant.

While very little comparable work has been done on arguments that occurred in other communities, the findings presented here do follow from the differences seen in individual cases in Heffer (2005). Specifically, Heffer (2005) found that in a set of closing arguments, the prosecution highlighted the behavior of the defendant, while the defense centered their argument on the anger of the complainants/victims. This fits exactly with the frequencies of reference here. Since Heffer's case occurred in England, and the cases in this corpus occurred in the United States, this is positive evidence that this is a generally widespread phenomenon. More support for this finding, although indirect, is that Hobbs (2005), who studied a single defense argument, showed that the lawyer emphasized relatively inconsequential details, which presumably would have taken the focus off the defendant.

2 Terms of Reference

We turn now to a more detailed analysis of the actual lexical items being used in these references. Terms of reference, like all lexical items, categorize and evaluate referents, indexing aspects of their identity and the social groups to which the speaker thinks they belong (Wortham and Locher 1996: 562). They indicate the speaker's stance toward the person being referenced and how the speaker perceives them as fitting into the context and events being constructed.

2.1 METHODOLOGY

The analyses of terms of reference in this chapter and in those that follow were conducted by classifying each reference based on (1) if it referred to only the relevant social actor, in this chapter the defendant, or to others as well (individualization versus assimilation; van Leeuwen 2002), and (2) which category it represents in van Leeuwen's (2002) framework for "the representation of social actors." In order to make the findings comparable across cases, the frequencies were normalized by calculating the number of times references appeared on average per 1,000 words, and descriptive and comparative statistics were calculated as described in Chapter 1.

In van Leeuwen's system, references to social actors are broken down into different categories, several of which are relevant here. An important distinction is whether or not the term personalizes the referent, highlighting his or her "humanness." One type of personalization is *nomination*, or the use of someone's name. This points to his or her "unique identity" (van Leeuwen 2002: 322). Nominations are further divided into three sub-categories. The most formal type are a person's surname, often but not always preceded by a title or another honorific (e.g., *Anderson* or *Mrs. Anderson*).[6] Even a witness's role in the case can serve as a title, and O'Barr (1982) found that trial practice manuals instructed lawyers to "distance [themselves] from an opposition witness" (34) by referring to them by their role, first name, and then their surname (e.g., *defendant Emily Anderson*). This follows the findings of Brown and Ford (1961), who argued that in the American system of address a title plus a last name is the equivalent to a V pronoun and indexes social distance, formality, and often respect. The next sub-category is semi-formal nominations, which are the use of both the given name and the surname (e.g., *Emily Anderson*). Finally, there are the informal nominations or the given name only (e.g., *Emily*). In the same study by O'Barr (1982), trial manuals were found to suggest that lawyers should personalize their own witnesses by using only their first names.

An additional category that includes nicknames needs to be added to this classification system. These forms usually represent a personal and often informal relationship, what Foley (1997) calls "extremely high solidarity" (318). The need for this category was clearly demonstrated in Felton Rosulek (2008). In the case described in that article, the prosecution referred to the victim with a nickname, *Lizzy*, while the defense used her full name, *Eliza* (and often included her last name as well). While both sides used a nomination for her, the difference between the two sides is not captured in van Leeuwen's categories as they are. Of additional interest in that particular case was that the nickname was a diminutive. Also, the prosecution often referenced her young age, focusing on how someone her age could only know as much as she did about sexual intercourse through abuse. The result was that the prosecution emphasized her youth, and the use of the nickname was part of this strategy.

Another type of personalizing term of reference is a *categorization*, which are personalizations that reference an aspect of the referent's identity that they share with others. Within categorizations, there are two sub-types: *functionalizations* and *identifications*. Functionalizations are references to what someone does (e.g., *the police officer*, *the driver*), that is, their role in the context. For example, in Danet (1980b), the prosecution lawyer frequently referred to the victim with functionalizations that pointed to her role as a soldier in order to counteract the negative depiction of her that the defense created. In the discussion below, we will see that referring to the person on trial with the functionalization, *the defendant* is a means for the prosecution to silence many of the person's more positive or at least unique characteristics.

Identifications are references to "what [people], more or less permanently, or unavoidably are" (van Leeuwen 2002: 324). Identifications are further divided into *classifications*, which point to the person's "age, gender, provenance, class, wealth, race, ethnicity, religion, sexual orientation, and so on" (van Leeuwen, 2002: 324) (e.g., *the woman* or *the black man*), *references to relation* (e.g., *Suzanne's son*), or *references to physical characteristics* (e.g., *the brunette*). For instance, in Bennett (1978), a lawyer, when cross-examining the defendant's mother, repeatedly referred to the defendant as *your son*. They emphasized this relationship because the lawyer was arguing that as the defendant's mother, the woman was likely to be lying to protect him.

Overall, categorizations allow a speaker to classify a referent as part of a group and thus to assign the characteristics and responsibilities of members of that group to the individual while ignoring his or her other features.

Nominations and categorizations personalize social actors because they are terms that have the semantic property of humanness associated with them. However, it is also possible to use *impersonalizations* (van Leeuwen 2002: 239), and there are once again several sub-categories of these. The first type is *spatializations*, which are references to a person or group as the place they are associated with (e.g., *the United States* to refer to all people living here). The second type is *utterance autonomization*, in which "social actors are represented by means of reference to their utterances" (329). For example, this occurs when, in the closing arguments, the lawyers say, "The report stated . . ." instead of saying, "The medical examiner wrote . . ." or "The lab technician found . . ." The next category is *instrumentalizations*, or references to individuals by an object they use (e.g., *the getaway car* in the sentence "The getaway car sped off . . ."). Finally, in *somatizations*, a social actor is referred to by a body part (e.g., *his hand* and *her neck* in "She felt his hand tighten around her neck.") All impersonalizations, including those that don't fit into these sub-categories, like calling lower class people *problems*, "background the identity and/or role of social actors" (330). For example, when a lawyer is discussing what happened during an instance of alleged sexual abuse, he or she often refers to the victim's body parts as the object that was touched, instead of the individual being the recipient. This puts distance between the action and the recipient of it. Also, as is the case with categorizations, impersonalizations can also bring the associations that hearers have with the literal meaning of the term to their conception of the social actor (330).

Overall, if an actor is included in a discourse, he or she can be personalized or impersonalized. If he is personalized, his unique identity is more strongly focused on if a nomination rather than a categorization is used to refer to him. If a functionalization or an identification is used, aspects of the referent's role or a specific aspect of her identity is emphasized, and she is constructed as belonging to a certain social category. All of the hearer's evaluations of and associations with that category are activated, and the speaker's stance toward and conceptualizations of the referent are indexed.

2.2 RESULTS FOR THE ENTIRE CORPUS

The analysis of the data shows a set of very definitive patterns, as can be seen in Table 3.3. When not using a pronoun, the prosecution lawyers consistently used functionalizations to refer to the defendant, while rarely using a nomination or an identification. In comparison, the defense almost always used a nomination and almost never used one of the other two types. In terms of the numbers, the prosecution used a functionalization, almost always *the defendant*, 32.1% of the times they referred to him or her in their main argument, but the defense used a functionalization (and nearly never *the defendant*) only 4.7% of the time. The defense used a nomination for their client 27.8% of the time compared to the prosecution, who used one 6.1% of the time in their main argument and 7.6% of the time in their rebuttals. Neither side used an identification very often, but as will be discussed later, they still used them very strategically to include certain aspects of the defendants.

The effects of these differences is that the prosecution de-emphasized each defendant's unique identity as well any personal relationship the jury may have felt toward him, instead limiting the person's identity mostly to the fact that he had been accused of a crime and was now on trial for it. At the same time, the defense de-emphasized this very aspect of the person's identity and emphasized his name and everything that went with it. They focused on him being an individual, with all of the feelings, inspirations, fears, and rights that anyone has in our society. Thus, the two sides constructed two very different people, simply through their patterns of use for terms of reference.

TABLE 3.3

Non-Pronominal Terms of Reference for the Defendant

		Prosecution	Defense	Rebuttal
Nominations	Percent of references	*6.1%*[1]	*27.8%*[1,2]	*7.6%*[2]
	Number per 1,000 words	2.4[3]	7.6[3,4]	2.6[4]
	Total number	214	622	48
Functionalizations	Percent of references	*29.8%*[5]	*4.7%*[5, 6]	*30.3%*[6]
	Number per 1,000 words	11.5[7]	1.3[7,7]	10.3[8]
	Total number	1,039	106	192
Identifications	Percent of references	*3.6%*	*3.2%*	*3.3%*
	Number per 1,000 words	1.4[9]	0.9[9]	1.1
	Total number	126	71	21

Note: Differences that are statistically significant are given matching superscripts.

2.2.1 Nominations

The two sides both varied greatly in the actual nominations they used. Table 3.4 shows the distribution of the different types. Case #15, the shaken-baby assault case, is an outlier in that the defense lawyer referred to the defendant with an informal nomination eighty-five times, compared to there otherwise being sixty-five tokens total of only the given name in the other sixteen cases combined. Therefore, the results are also included for when that case is excluded from the defense corpus, and the statistics were run both with and without that case.

As Table 3.4 shows, the prosecution and the defense both used the semi-formal given name and surname construction the most frequently. Interestingly, they used it even when it was not linguistically necessary to use the surname, as it was not being used to distinguish one person from another with the same given name, as in the following example:

(1) So we can tell that the blunt force trauma which killed Chris Britt was the punch by Don Selke and, therefore, Don Selke caused the death of Christopher Britt.

In this example, as in most throughout the corpus, both the first and the last names of both people referred to are used. One explanation for the use of the

TABLE 3.4

Types of Nominations for Defendant

		Prosecution (n = 214)	Defense (with case #15) (n = 622)	Defense (without case #15) (n = 525)	Rebuttal (n = 48)
Informal (given name)	Percentage of nominations	*21.0%*[1]	*24.8%*	*13.0%*[1]	*20.8%*
	Number per 1,000 words	0.5[2,3]	1.9[2,4]	1.0[3]	0.5[4]
	Total	45	153	68	10
Semi-formal (given name and surname)	Percentage of nominations	*33.6%*[5]	*37.5%*	*43.4%*[5]	*27.1%*
	Number per 1,000 words	0.8[6, 7]	2.9[6, 8]	3.3[7, 9]	0.7[8, 9]
	Total	72	233	228	13
Formal (surname)	Percentage of nominations	*22.0%*[10, 11, 12]	*6.8%*[10]	*8.0%*[11]	*6.3%*[12]
	Number per 1,000 words	0.5	0.5	0.6	0.2
	Total	47	42	42	3
Formal (title and surname)	Percentage of nominations	*23.4%*[13, 14]	*30.7%*	*34.9%*[13]	*45.8%*[14]
	Number per 1,000 words	0.6[15, 16, 17]	2.3[15, 18]	2.7[16, 19]	1.2[17, 18, 19]
	Total	50	190	183	22

Note: Differences that are statistically significant are given matching superscripts.

full name in examples likes this is that this is the norm in the social context of the courtroom. Not only is it stated in the rules for this district court system that first names only are not to be used for adults (which was not the case in example (1) anyway), but it is a more formal context in general. What is more surprising is that formal nominations (a title and the last name) were used less often than semi-formal terms, given the formal context and given the fact that formal terms were used by the lawyers for each other. One explanation is that the defense wants to lessen the social distance between the defendant and the jurors, and the prosecution wants to lessen the respect afforded to the defendant. Despite the contrasting goals, the same terms of reference satisfy both.

An interesting finding shown in Table 3.4 is that when case #15 is excluded as an outlier, the defense rarely chose to use an informal nomination when they used the defendant's name, at least compared to the prosecution. Informal nominations can represent three things—informality, a personal relationship, or a lack of respect (at least when compared to when a formal nomination is expected). The context for these discourses was always formal, so the use of these forms was unlikely to index informality. Additionally, it was the defense lawyers who had personal relationships with the defendants and who may have wanted the jurors to feel like they had one with them, so it is unlikely that the prosecution lawyers would have been using the first names only to signal this. This leaves us with the third option, that the prosecution lawyers used the first names of the defendants to signal a lack of respect as the most likely explanation for why they used them and why the defense lawyers tended not to.

This raises the question of why the defense lawyer in case #15 took the opposite approach and almost exclusively used the defendant's first name only. In doing so, he foregrounded the level of familiarity in their relationship and perhaps tried to make the jurors feel less distanced from him. It was obviously an uncommon strategy, but one that has a reasonable explanation.

These findings, although they occurred in an unpublicized trial far away from California, echo the patterns seen and remarked on in the OJ Simpson case. In fact, Johnnie Cochran, the main defense lawyer, said early in his closing arguments:

(2) Now, in this case, you are aware that we represent Mr. Orenthal James Simpson. The prosecution never calls him Mr. Orenthal James Simpson. They call him "defendant." (quoted in Tiersma 1999: 188).

Not only did Mr. Cochran refer to the defendant by his full name (not his nickname) and a title, but he directly remarked on the fact that the prosecution did not do this. Thus, he noted the pattern being described in this book.

Although he obviously did not directly state that the functionalization was being used as a means of silencing or de-emphasizing the unique identity of the victim, Mr. Cochran used the defendant's name repeatedly to counteract this and to emphasize his individuality.

Overall, though, the defense lawyers tended to use nominations that reflected the formal context and to construct a more respected, distanced, and formal identity for the defendant. The prosecution lawyers sometimes respected the context and did the same thing, but at other times they did not. However, regardless of what sub-category of nominations the two sides used, it must be remembered that the prosecution was generally de-emphasizing, often to the point of silencing, the defendant's unique complex identity as an individual person by usually not using any form of his or her name, while the defense was comparatively emphasizing it.

2.2.2 Functionalizations

As discussed earlier, instead of using the defendant's name, the prosecution lawyers tended to use functionalizations. In fact, they referred to them as *the defendant* with particular frequency (10.4 times per 1,000 words, or 29.1% of the prosecutions' references to them), just as Johnnie Cochran had described as occurring in the OJ Simpson case in the quote noted earlier. The defense rarely used a functionalization (1.3 times per 1,000 words, 4.7% of references to them), and especially did not use *the defendant* (0.6 times per 1,000 words, 2.3% of references to them). Eight of the seventeen defense lawyers never referred to their client as *the defendant*, four only did it once, two did it three times, and one did it four times. Only the defense lawyers in case #1 (twelve times) and in case #14 (twenty-four times) used it with any notable frequency.[7] On the other hand, all of the prosecution lawyers used the term. The maximum number of times it was used was 139 times in case #14. The minimum was six times in case #4, but he only referred to the defendant fifty-eight times in his entire argument.

The scope of the emphasis being placed on the term *defendant* by the prosecution is seen not just in how frequently it was repeated but also when it was used unnecessarily. As the example in (3) shows, it was often the term of choice when a pronoun would have sufficed:

> (3) The *defendant* would come in once or twice a week for a period of a year, year and a half. And the *defendant* at various times would engage in different sorts of sexual abuse, but part of it, once or twice a week, was the *defendant* would . . .

Another particularly interesting finding about the term *defendant* was that it was used in all parts of the closing arguments, not just the trial narratives when it was a relevant identity for the person. Other functionalizations were more limited to certain narratives. For instance, terms like *caretaker*, *driver*, and *aggressor* were used in the crime narratives when they were relevant functionalizations and *witness* was used in some trial narratives. In contrast, *defendant* was used to refer to the person in narratives that described times when they did not yet have that particular identity, when they had not yet been charged with a crime and were not on trial. This can be seen in an excerpt in example (4), which is from the prosecution's crime narrative in case #6:

(4) The defendant just shook Serena Hu and shook her to death.

In this example, the victim was referenced by name but Carolyn Jakobson, the defendant, was referred to by her role in the "here-and-now" of the discourse event. Her identity at the time of the crime was completely silenced. The prosecution lawyers in some cases even went as far as to use *the defendant* in direct quotations from the time of the crime, as in example (5) from case #12:

(5) Lizzy would say, "I wish you would divorce the defendant."

Since the person being referenced in the quotation did not have this identity at the time the original speaker produced the utterance and because the close relationship between the speaker and the defendant makes it unlikely she would have used this term, we can be sure the lawyer altered the quotation. In doing so, they further silenced the person's identity and emphasized his limited identity as a person on trial for an alleged crime. This was something the defense lawyers did not do but the prosecution lawyers did very frequently. Thus, the contrasting linguistic choices the two sides made allowed them to create opposing representations of the same people by silencing, de-emphasizing, and emphasizing different aspects of their identities.

If the defense lawyers used a functionalization at all, they generally used *my client*. The defense lawyer in case #3 used this 2.7 times per 1,000 words, which was 8.2% (thirteen) of his references to his client; the lawyer in case #11 used it 1.5 times per 1,000 words, or 10.7% (three) of the times she referenced him; and the lawyer in case #12 used it 1.9 times per 1,000 words, or 13.2% (nine) of the times he referenced the defendant. The use of *my client* pointed to the fact that the lawyer and the defendant had a very specific relationship and that the lawyer was speaking on behalf of the defendant. In other words, the repeated use of this term emphasized the relationship between these two people.

2.2.3 Identifications

The final type of term of reference used with any frequency for the defendants in the closing arguments were identifications. Both sides used fewer identifications for the defendants than any other type (3.7% of all references by the prosecution in their main argument, 3.2% of the defense references, and 3.3% of references in the rebuttal).

TABLE 3.5

Distribution of Identifications for the Defendant

		Prosecution	Defense	Rebuttal
Classifications	Percentage of references	*2.6%*	*2.7%*	*1.6%*
	Number per 1,000 words	1.0	0.7	0.5
	Total	89	60	10
Relational identifications	Percentage of references	*1.1%*[1]	*0.5%*[1, 2]	*1.7%*[2]
	Number per 1,000 words	0.4[3]	0.1[3, 4]	0.6[4]
	Total	40	11	11

Note: Differences that are statistically significant are given matching superscripts.

Identifications were broken down into type types: classifications (by age, by gender, by personhood, etc.) or relationships. Classifications were the more common of the two types, as can be seen in Table 3.5, and no lawyer used a purely physical identification.

An example of a classification, a gendered classification in this sentence from case #2, can be seen in (6), where the prosecution was discussing how the victim must have been assuming the defendant was one of the people kidnapping him or he would have taken a different action:

(6) If he doesn't think *this man* had anything to do with it, why doesn't he just ask him to stop the car and let him out?

This limited the defendant's identity in this discursive moment to his being a male adult.

The importance of identifications, although relatively rare, was that in certain cases, they were used to emphasize a particular feature of the defendant. For instance, case #10, the trial of the stepfather who was accused of sexually abusing his two stepdaughters, was where twenty-three of the forty relational identifications in the corpus of prosecution arguments occurred. The reason for this was that this prosecutor was using terms to emphasize the fact the defendant and the victims formed a family. As the lawyer argued, it is a rule in our society that father figures are not supposed to see their daughters as girlfriends, but this defendant did. References to the group as a family highlighted the rules these people were supposed to have followed that were egregiously broken. The defense silenced the fact that this was a family and that the defendant was the victims' stepfather. This is similar to Bennett (1978), mentioned earlier, who described a lawyer referring to the defendant as *your son* when talking to his mother to bring attention to the social rules usually placed on this relationship.

Identifications also allowed the lawyers to include a characteristic of the defendant. In case #17, the defense referred to the defendant as *a 49-year-old man* in the following construction:

(7) You also heard that Tracey Beardsley, *a 49-year-old man*, was clearly playing a young man's game.

The message here was that the defendant was out of his element, and he thus thought he had to use a knife to put himself on even footing with the other people. The defense lawyer in case #11 used a reference to ethnicity for strategic purposes:

(8) Mr. Meyer is *a black man* accused of serious crimes against six women.

While the lawyers did not emphasize these aspects of the defendants by using the terms repeatedly, they did discretely bring these characteristics to the jurors' attention through these terms of reference.

One type of identification that we would have expected to find is metaphors. The idea is that by representing the defendant as a member of a group to which he or she does not logically belong, lawyers can associate the features of this classification with him or her. In previous studies, prosecutors have been shown to use this linguistic device to associate the defendants with violence (Cotterill 2003; Luchjenbroers and Aldridge 2007). Specifically, as Cotterill (2003) described, the prosecution repeatedly referred to Simpson as a ticking time bomb as they tried to force the jury to see him as powerful, explosive, and volatile. The defense then played on this metaphor, claiming there was no fuse and the bomb never exploded. In a similar vein, Luchjenbroers and Aldridge (2007), through an analysis of several trials, showed that prosecutors portrayed defendants as being inherently violent by using animal metaphors and the use of terms such as *predator* to accomplish this. However, metaphors were rarely used in the particular corpus of closing arguments studied here, particularly for the defendants, and they were never used to imply that the defendant had a violent nature. This could be a feature of this particular speech community studied here or just an indication that metaphors, while used by some lawyers, are relatively rare overall.

In only one case, #14, did the prosecution lawyer repeatedly refer to the defendant with a metaphor. Specifically, they called him a *big fish*. In fact, the prosecutor used this phrase sixteen times (2.3 times per 1,000 words), or 5.4% of the times he referred to the defendant. The reason, as can be seen in examples (9) and (10), was the lawyer was developing the idea that the defendant, who was accused of being the head of a drug-dealing ring, was the target of the entire investigation, which he compared to a fishing trip.

(9) The defendant here is a big fish. He's such a big fish that he sells once ounce quantities of cocaine for thousands of dollars. He's such a big fish that he sits around in a living room with almost $10,000 laid out on a coffee table and the floor in front of him.

> (10) [The police] didn't bring the little net to catch the little fish. They brought the big net. . . . And the net they brought with them was a strong net.

Strikingly, the metaphor only appeared in the lawyer's speech at the beginning and end, not in the middle, despite being in the crime, investigation, trial, and future narratives. This gave it a different type of prominence, as it framed the rest of the argument.

The previous discussion focused mainly on the individualization (van Leeuwen 2002) of the defendants, the references to them as individuals, but it is also noteworthy that in one of the cases, there was actually more than one defendant. In case #14, while the particular set of arguments analyzed here were only focused on one man, Mike Tercero, in fact his brother, Carolos, was also a co-defendant. The prosecution lawyers grouped these two men into a single unit and thus de-emphasized their unique identities. By combining this with the coordination of references and relational identifications, the prosecution was able to background Carlos's individual personhood.

To be specific, of the times that the prosecution referred to Carlos, 72.9% (thirty-five) of them included a reference to Mike. Examples of this included *the defendant's brother*, *his brother Carlos*, or *they*. Eighteen of these references were of them as a single unit or group—*they*, *Carlos and Mike*, *the two men*, and so on. Of the times that the defense referred to Carlos, only 5.7% (two) included references to Mike. Instead, they referred to him simply as *Carlos* or *he*. The differences between the prosecution and defense can be explained by the arguments each side made. For the prosecution, both of the men were on trial, even if this was only the argument against Mike Tercero. Their argument centered on the idea that the two brothers were working together, and Mike was the leader. For instance, they said:

> (11) The evidence in this case from the beginning showed that the defendant and his brother Carlos are in this together. It's a joint operation, and they're both participating.

Since the prosecution did not talk about Carlos having a role of power but only doing activities that Mike did, the lawyer discursively depicted the two men as functioning as a single unit (a topic he emphasized) or else Mike acting on his own. On the other hand, the defense argued that Carlos was the boss of the drug ring and the one selling the drugs to the informants and the police. They focused on him doing the criminal actions on his own. For example, the lawyer said:

> (12) Carlos is not only in possession of some additional drugs but also has some of the buy money in his wallet. This defendant has no drugs on him and has no buy money on him whatsoever.

Since the lawyer wasn't talking about Carlos and Mike doing activities together, he did not refer to the two men as a single unit. He created an opposing representation in which they were two social actors functioning separately, and their relationship was de-emphasized.

In the following section, I analyze three individual cases in even more detail, but to first summarize the findings in this section, the defense and the prosecution systematically used very different terms to refer to the defendants. Their contrasting patterns of linguistic choices resulted in their creating opposing representations of the same person. While others have found that lawyers were using the very salient choices of metaphorical terms to create certain identities for the defendants, this analysis found that the patterns can be much more subtle. Instead, simply using or not using the defendant's name or a functionalization allowed the lawyers to silence, de-emphasize, and emphasize different aspects of their identities.

2.3 THREE CASES IN DETAIL

These three cases were chosen so that three different charges and defense strategies, as well as six different lawyers, were represented. Also, case #6 was chosen to examine if there were any differences for female defendants. Otherwise, there was nothing special about these three cases that would set them apart from the rest of the corpus.

2.3.1 Case #3

The first case to be examined in detail is case #3. In this case, the defendant was charged with assault after attacking his girlfriend. The prosecution's case was based on the testimony of the witnesses who saw the event. The defense claimed that another person was responsible, as both the defendant and the victim had stated during the trial. What is different about closing arguments in this case from many of the others is that the prosecution actually used nominations for the defendant and the defense used functionalizations. However, the prosecution still favored functionalizations, and the defense preferred nominations. Also, the actual terms they used were different.

Specifically, the defense used a nomination for the defendant 31.4% of the times they referred to him and significantly more than the prosecutor did, as he only used one 7.9% of the times he referred to Mr. Hills. The defense used formal constructions, either *Mr. Hills* or *Hills*, with only two exceptions, when they instead referred to him with a semi-formal reference. The prosecution, on the other hand, tended to use a semi-formal nomination, usually his full legal name *Steven Jay Hills*, or an informal nomination, including the most informal shortened form, *Steve*, as can be seen in Table 3.6.

In the prosecution's argument, ten of the eleven references to the defendant with an informal nomination were in the voices of the witnesses, those

TABLE 3.6
Nominations for Case #3 Defendant

	Prosecution (*n* = 265)	Defense (*n* = 156)	Rebuttal (*n* = 9)
Personal name	7.9% (21)[1, 2]	31.4% (49)[1]	44.4% (4)[2]
Steve	3.0% (8)	—	—
Steven	1.1% (3)	—	—
Steve Hills	1.1% (3)	0.6% (1)	—
Steven Hills	—[3, 4]	0.6% (1)[3]	11.1% (1)[4]
Steven Jay Hills	2.3% (6)[5]	—[6]	22.2% (2)[5, 6]
Hills	—[7]	6.4% (10)[7]	—
Mr. Hills	0.4% (1)[8, 9]	23.7% (37)[8]	11.1% (1)[9]

Note: Differences that are statistically significant are given matching superscripts.

people who had an informal and personal relationship with the defendant. The lawyer was just recreating what the people who knew the defendant well said, as in the following example:

(13) Steven came back and came in and grabbed me out of bed.

The other time the prosecution used an informal nomination was directly following the re-animation of what a witness had said during the commission of the crime, and that witness had used an informal nomination.

(14) He went to the door and said, "Steve, let the woman out." *Steve* opened the door

So, for the prosecution, the use of informal nominations was not tied to their trying to represent him more personally but in trying to accurately represent the terms that witnesses used. In contrast, the references to the defendant with a formal title were in the "here-and-now" when the attorney was speaking as an interlocutor rather than a character or narrator. This reflected the distant relationship between the two men in the context of the courtroom.

In the defense's argument, the two semi-formal nominations were the first two references the defense lawyer made to the defendant and were in parallel constructions:

(15) No one saw David Brooks strike Suzanne Benneton. . . . No one saw Dave Brooks hit Suzanne Benneton.

After that, they used the formal nominations. This emphasized the level of respect being given to him by the lawyer. However, as will be discussed below, the lawyer also used formal nominations for the victim, so this could just be a personal preference for referring to the most important social actors in this context. Since this was the only case for this particular lawyer in the corpus, there is no way to confirm or deny this assumption. Why he started using semi-formal terms for both and then switched to formal constructions is unclear.

While the prosecution did use nominations for the person on trial, they more frequently used functionalizations. Specifically, they referred to him with a functionalization thirty-seven times (6.3/1,000 words), or 14.0% of the times they referred to him. The defense lawyer, who only used one eighteen times (3.7/1,000 words), actually had a similar percentage at 11.5%, but contrastively, this was much less often than he used nominations. What truly separated the two sides, however, was the actual terms they used. The prosecution almost always used *the defendant* (thirty times) but also referred to him with such terms as *fiancé* and phrases like *the one man that had promised to marry [the victim]* to highlight the fact that his alleged behavior did not fit with the social role he was supposed to be filling. On the other hand, the defense never used such a term. The terms they used were *my client* (fourteen times) and *witness* (four times). The repetition of *my client* served to emphasize the fact the lawyer was representing this person and the use of *witness* occurred because their side claimed that another man had committed the crime. Thus, the functionalizations the two sides used emphasized different characteristics of the same person, and thus were used to create very distinct representations of him.

Only one identification was used repeatedly by either side, and that was when the prosecution lawyer referred to the defendant by his gender. Specifically, he used *man* or *guy* six times when reminding the jurors that the defendant and the victim had been in a relationship. As they used this term, they contrasted her behavior toward him with how she acted toward other men. In doing so, the term served a unique purpose, and the repetition provided it with a minor amount of emphasis.

Overall, while the general quantitative results for this case make it appear that it did not follow the common patterns, it in fact did. The two sides used very different terms and mainly silenced or at least de-emphasized those used by the opposing side. Through their linguistic choices, they were able to create different representations of the same individual.

2.3.2 Case #6

In case #6, a woman was tried and convicted of shaking to death a toddler who had been in her care while she assisted at a day care. As in the corpus as a whole, the prosecution relied mainly on functionalizations, while the defense used nominations to refer to her. In other words, the prosecution de-emphasized her individuality, while the defense emphasized it.

As can be seen in Table 3.7, the prosecution de-emphasized the unique identity of the defendant, almost to the point of silencing it, by rarely referring to her by name (only three times, which was 1.1% of their references to her). The defense used her name more often but actually less than the average case as only 11.1% of the references to her were nominations. However, unless the defense used a pronoun, they almost always used a nomination.

TABLE 3.7
Nominations for Case #6 Defendant

	Prosecution (n = 271)	Defense (n = 217)	Rebuttal (n = 37)
Personal name	1.1% (3)[1, 2]	11.1% (24)[1]	13.5% (5)[2]
Carey	0.4% (1)	—	—
Carolyn	0.4% (1)	2.3% (5)	2.7% (1)
Carolyn Jakobson	0.4% (1)[3, 4]	8.3% (18)[3]	8.1% (3)[4]
Carolyn Joan Jakobson	—[5]	0.5% (1)	2.7% (1)[5]

Note: Differences that are statistically significant are given matching superscripts.

As in the other cases, most of the prosecution's nominations for the defendant, particularly the information nominations, appeared in quotations from witnesses, and therefore, the responsibility for them was given to someone else. Both informal nominations that the prosecution used were attributed to someone else. The other use of her name came when the prosecutor was explaining exactly what he needed to prove:

(16) Now the State has the burden of proving to you beyond reasonable doubt that Carolyn Jakobson caused those injuries.

The defense's use of informal nominations also mainly occurred in their recreation of the voices of others, with only one occurring when the lawyer was taking responsibility for the words:

(17) The fact that she might have said two different things to Serena Hu's mother does not mean that that came from Carolyn.

The really interesting finding from this particular case is that neither side ever used a formal nomination for the defendant. The fact she is a woman perhaps explains why her surname was not used by itself, as this has traditionally been a more masculine term of reference (Romaine 1999). However, there is not a good explanation for why neither lawyer used a title for her, as both used one when referring to several of the witnesses and for each other. Her status as a female defendant makes this particularly interesting and suggests an avenue of further study. While this diminished the level of respect being shown to her, something the prosecution would want to exploit, it also made her appear more familiar and less distanced from the lawyers and jury, which the defense would have wanted. Regardless, the most important finding here is that the prosecution de-emphasized the unique identity of the defendant by very rarely referring to her by name.

While the prosecution only referred to the defendant by name three times, he used a functionalization for her 127 times (13.3/1,000 words), or 46.9% of the times he mentioned her. One hundred and eighteen of these functionalizations were *the defendant*. Thus, he emphasized her role in the case, de-emphasizing and silencing all other aspects of her identity. In fact, example (4) is from this case and demonstrates how the prosecutor, by referring to this woman as *the defendant* even in the crime and investigation narratives, ultimately de-emphasized her other identities and roles.[8] One of the other functionalizations was particularly interesting, *child killer*, which was used in the following way:

(18) He's rushing to help a child killer avoid justice, which apparently is his major occupation these days.

This is perhaps the worst identity anyone could have in our society, and the prosecutor gave this woman this label. Thus, he did not need to use metaphors or any other rhetorical device. He just made this her identity.

The defense attorney, as could be expected, never referred to her client as *the defendant*. In fact, she only used a functionalization for her three times (0.4 times per 1,000 words), which was 1.3% of her references to her client. She did, however, use functionalizations to bring attention to the fact the police had zeroed in on her from the beginning (e.g., *the prime suspect*).

Identifications were also used by both sides, not necessarily to emphasize any aspect of the defendant's identity but to bring attention to a characteristic at certain moments. For instance, the defense referred to her as *an individual person* three times to suggest that the defendant was in a difficult position because, according to them, the power of the entire state was being focused on her:

(19) Now when you think about reasonable doubt, this case has a title and the title is "State of ______ vs. Carolyn Joan Jakobson." And if you think about it, that's kind of a heavy thing. The State of ______ versus this woman sitting over here. Okay. The State versus an individual person. And you think, well, gee, that's pretty unfair, the State versus an individual person.

What was particularly interesting is that the prosecution actually addressed this first thing in their rebuttal, but replaced *individual person* with *the defendant*:

(20) This case is captioned the State of _____ vs. Carolyn Joan Jakobson. That's the caption that applies in every criminal case, whether a minor criminal case or a major criminal case. It is the State versus the defendant. Defendant has been accorded her constitutional rights and you are expected to apply them just as in any other case. There's nothing unusual about this case.

The prosecution did not deny that the defendant was an individual person; instead, they just replaced this term with another word when addressing the more general issue being discussed. In doing so, they effectively ignored the point the defense was making by suggesting that since she had been given her rights and this case was not unusual, the jurors should not worry about it. As a result, the two sides discussed very different things, and silenced the argument made by the other side.

Overall, as in the other cases, the prosecution de-emphasized this person's unique identity while instead emphasizing her role as the person on trial. The defense did the opposite and thus, through their patterns of linguistic choices, they created opposing representations of the same woman.

2.3.3 Case #7

In case #7, the charges of criminal sexual conduct were based on a woman claiming she was sexually touched while she was sleeping at a party. The defense argued that the acts were consensual, and the defendant was eventually found not guilty.

With regard to nominations, the prosecution de-emphasized the defendant's unique identity by only referred to him by name once, or 0.2 times per 1,000 words, and this appeared in the lawyer's first set of clauses after his greeting:

> (21) My job here over the last few days has been to present to you the case of State versus Ernest Ayres.

On the other hand, the defense referred to him with a nomination forty-two times, or 11.5 times per 1,000 words. Additionally, the defense lawyer never used the man's given first name, *Ernest*, but instead she always used his less formal nickname by which he was more commonly known, *Ernie*. While this could have been a purposeful decision, perhaps to lessen the social distance between the defendant and the jurors in this context, it just as easily could have been because this is what she was accustomed to calling him. The distribution of the terms used can be seen in Table 3.8.

The distribution of the defense lawyer's choices of nominations within their actual argument was also important. Specifically, she used the formal construction of title plus last name only four times, but all four are in the first forty-five clauses (out of 732 total) or the first 239 words (out 3,648 total),

TABLE 3.8
Nominations of Case #7 Defendant

	Prosecution (n = 159)	Defense (n = 228)	Rebuttal (n = 28)
Nomination	0.6% (1)[1]	18.4% (42)[1]	3.6% (1)
Ernie	—	2.2% (5)	—
Ernie Ayres	—[2]	14.5% (33)[2]	—
Ernest Ayres	0.6% (1)	—	—
Mr. Ayres	—	1.8% (4)	3.6% (1)

Note: Differences that are statistically significant are given matching superscripts.

which was when the lawyer was greeting the jurors in an interlocutory voice and outlining her argument in both the narrative and interlocutory voices. This was the only form of nomination she used for him in this passage, but during this section, she referred to the victim with a semi-formal construction (in fact she only used a formal nomination for the victim once, which will be discussed later), as can be seen in the following example:

(22) Mr. Ayres and I are very, very grateful for that. . . . Of course Mr. Ayres has an interest in the outcome of the case. He entered a not-guilty plea because he believed he was not guilty. Bridget O'Day has an interest in the outcome of this case.

As the underlined nominations for the defendant and the victim were in parallel constructions, it is noteworthy that she used the formal construction for the defendant, as it showed the respect she was giving him in this portion of her argument, and its repetition at the beginning of the argument gave it added saliency.

After this initial section of the defense lawyer's argument, she almost exclusively used the semi-formal combination of his nickname and surname. However, there were five instances when she referred to him with an informal nomination, *Ernie*. Two of them were in the voice of the victim. The other three tokens of this type were during the re-creation of the voice of the police officer who investigated the charges or when the lawyer was describing what he said in her own narrator voice:

(23) Ernie's very disbelieving. He even asks Officer Kelton, "Are you joking?"

As these incidents occurred during the crime and investigation narratives and mostly through the voices of people who testified, it is possible that they simply represented the witnesses' original terms of reference and their familiarity with the defendant. Regardless, what is clear in this case is that the prosecution silenced the defendant's unique identity while the defense emphasized it, originally with a term highlighting the formality of the situation but mostly with semi-formal nominations.

As in the other cases, instead of using nominations, the prosecution used functionalizations (forty-two times, or 9.0/1,000 words, or 26.4% of references to him), specifically *the defendant* (forty times). He often used it in juxtaposition with a nomination for the victim as in the following:

(24) Who are you going to believe, Bridget O'Day or the defendant?

This even occurred in the crime narrative when his status as a person on trial was not yet part of his identity:

(25) That the defendant touched Bridget O'Day's intimate parts?

Through the lawyer's repeated use of this term and the contrast between how he referred to the victim and the defendant, the prosecution emphasized the defendant's role in the case. At the same time, the defense lawyer de-emphasized this aspect of his identity, although they did not completely silence it (there were four references using this term in the defense argument).

The prosecution further de-emphasized the defendant as an individual by referring to him as *a man* or *a person* nine times, or 5.7% of the times they referred to him. This was especially pronounced in the crime story, as can be seen in the following excerpt:

> (26) She got to tell about waking up with a man rubbing his penis on her vagina, a man.

The repetition in just this sentence highlights that this is not an acceptable behavior by a person of this gender, but also, by repeatedly not using his name and replacing it with terms such as this, it further de-emphasizes all other aspects of this person's identity. He is a male person who sexually touched her, and that is it.

In conclusion, this is yet another case in which opposing representations of the defendant were created by the prosecution and the defense referring to him with very different sets of terms. The prosecution de-emphasized who he was outside of this crime, while the defense gave him a name and a unique identity. They helped the jurors create a relationship with him.

2.4 CONCLUSIONS

Despite the importance of the defendants in criminal cases, very few studies prior to this one have actually examined how lawyers refer to them in the closing arguments, or even in trials more broadly (although exceptions to this include Cotterill 2003; Danet 1980a; Luchjenbroers and Aldridge 2007). This study not only provides a detailed analysis of this topic, but the results presented here mostly support the few earlier findings that do exist. In fact, Danet (1980a) analyzed the trial of a doctor charged with manslaughter after performing a late term abortion. She found that the defense referred to the defendant by his title, doctor, and his surname, thus marking his elevated status in society. The prosecution referred to him as *the defendant*, ignoring his position and unique identity. Although the trial in her case occurred over twenty years before the arguments analyzed here and took place in a different part of the United States, she found the exact same pattern seen in this corpus.

The results presented here are also not unexpected given the results of studies (e.g., Cotterill 2001, 2004; Drew 1992; Eades 2006, 2008; Goodwin 1994; and Kozin 2008) that, while not looking specifically at terms for defendants, have demonstrated that lawyers systematically select noun phrases with semantic properties that fit their point of view and covertly or overtly reject those used by the opposing side. For example, a witness in Eades (2008) used the phrase *a group of friends* to describe himself and the people he had been with, while the lawyer referred to them as *a gang* and *a group of louts*. Reinterpreted in the framework being presented here, these studies show that lawyers select terms to silence or de-emphasize certain properties of the referents and to include or even emphasize other properties. While the details of the specific terms they select may vary from lawyer to lawyer, case to case, and location to location, the basic patterns are the same.

The only surprising finding, as discussed earlier, was the lack of metaphors in this particular corpus. This could be the result of the culture in which the cases took place or the fact that they were very ordinary trials, unlike the OJ Simpson case being described in Cotterill (2003). However, metaphors serve the same general purpose as other terms of reference: they point to a characteristic or set of characteristics of the referent. Some lawyers may emphasize this through metaphors or use metaphors to appear more poetic, but the end result is the same. Lawyers silence, de-emphasize, and emphasize different characteristics of the defendants, based on which side of the case they are on, all through the terms of reference they use.

3 The Roles of the Defendants in Clauses

While terms of reference are one linguistic means through which lawyers create biased representations of the defendants, another form they manipulate is the processes involving the defendants. Based on the analysis of this corpus and on results published in the literature, this section of the book argues that prosecution and the defense portray the defendants as having different effects on and experiences with the world, and silence or at least de-emphasize those included by the other side. Even when they use negation to argue that the other side's claims about the defendant were wrong, the main force of their arguments is constructed around different sets of events and processes involving the defendant.

3.1 METHODOLOGY

Before turning to the actual analysis, we must first discuss the methodology used for analyzing how any of the social actors were included/excluded from processes and the roles they played. The basic assumption is that reality is "made up of processes" (Halliday 1994: 106) (i.e., actions, activities, states), and these are represented in language through clauses, which describe a "state of affairs" or "something that can be said to occur, take place, or obtain in some world" (Dik 1997: 51). Discourses, then, are strings of clauses describing series of processes that together compose an event or topic. To create a clause, speakers must decide, according to their own understanding, which process best represents the state of affairs they are describing (Fairclough 2003) and what role, if any, each relevant social actor plays in that process.

For this book, there are three specific choices that speakers make that are examined in detail. First, we are concerned with determining which processes were included in each argument and which were excluded for each social actor being studied (in this chapter it is of course the defendants). For any process included in one argument, they opposing side could have (1) included the same or a similar process but recontextualized it, (2) included the same process with the same social actors but negated it, (3) included the same process but had different actors as the agents and recipients (or not have included people in these roles), (4) excluded the process and replaced it with a very different process involving one or all of the social actors, or (5) not included any process from the context or time period in question. As an example, if a prosecutor argued that the defendant pushed the victim, the defense argument was analyzed for whether they claimed (1) that the defendant did push the victim but there was a non-criminal explanation for it, (2) that he simply did not do it, (3) that someone else pushed the victim, or (4) that the defendant was doing something else at the time in question (which implies that he did not push the victim) or if they ignored the issue of the push altogether and focus on other topics (e.g., the victim's clumsiness or reasonable doubt).

Another issue analyzed was the role given to the social actor for each process they were included in because this determines the level of agency and involvement given to the individual. The same event is interpreted very differently depending on whether the person is portrayed as the cause of the process, the recipient of it, or simply a bystander present during its occurrence. The degree of agency given to the person helps determine his or her responsibility for the events. For example, a hearer will presumably perceive an event very differently if he is told that the defendant pushed the victim, that the victim pushed the defendant, or that a third party pushed the victim into the defendant.

The final issue addressed in this section was the lexical choices the lawyers made to encode the processes they choose to include, even if they negated it, as this determined which properties of the process were indexed and which were ignored or denied. If one side said that the defendant *shoved* the victim, while the other side said that he *nudged* him, then this included different information about the level of violence and silenced the details given by the opposition.

In order to systematically analyze the patterns in the prosecution and the defense arguments for each social actor's roles in processes, five steps were undertaken: (1) each clause containing a reference to the actor (in this chapter, the defendant) was classified by its narrative or voice: crime, investigation, trial, present, future, or other; (2) the thematic role the actor played in that clause was determined; (3) the type of verb used to represent the process was classified using Halliday's (1994) system, which is described later in this chapter; (4) the lexical properties of the verb were noted using van Leeuwen (1995); and finally, (5) statistical analyses on the quantitative results were performed.

According to Halliday (1994), processes can be broken down into six different types: *material*, *mental*, *relational*, *behavioral*, *verbal*, and *existential*. Material processes are "processes of doing" (109) that have an actor, someone doing an action to or creating or "bringing about" (111) another entity. Importantly, these are processes that the actor has control over rather than processes that happen to them (Dik 1997). An example of clause with a material process is:

(27) He punched him in the head.

In this sentence, *punch* is the verb depicting the material process. An actor, the defendant, did the action of physically injuring another person.

Mental processes represent what a human agent "feels, thinks, or perceives" (114). To again borrow from Dik (1997), these processes are [+ experience] in that there is a sensory or cognitive aspect to the verb. To put it another way, these are describing the cognitive processes of animate objects. Halliday includes senses such as *see* and *hear* as mental processes, but I do not, as they also include physiological processes and are not purely cognitive. Example clauses with mental processes are:

(28) I want . . .
(29) They both know him.
(30) He was angry.

Relational processes are "processes of being" (119). Traditionally, these have been called *states* (Chafe 1970), as no change in the world is occurring dynamically (Dik 1997). In Halliday's system, these are further broken down into three sub-categories. With an intensive relational process, a person either has an attribute as in (31), or an identity as in (32):

(31) The defendant is guilty.
(32) The defendant is an honest man.

The next type of relational processes is circumstantial relational processes, which describe a physical or temporal location.

(33) He's within a foot or two away from her.

Finally, possessive relational processes show possession in either form that English allows (i.e., with a verb such as *have* or a possessive's marker).

(34) You have the defendant's own statements.

The next category of processes are behavioral processes, which represent "physiological and psychological behavior" (Halliday 1994: 139). Even according to Halliday, the boundaries of this category are not distinct, but processes in this category are both mental and physical at the same time. Examples are verbs such as *cry*, *smile*, *breathe*, *faint*, or *perspire*, as in:

(35) Why would the defendant be perspiring?

In order to give this category more definition, I limit it to all physiological and psychological processes that tend not to be consciously controlled. Thus, while *fall* is included, *dance* and *sit* are not, even though they are included in Halliday's opinion. Halliday categorized verbs of the senses, such as *see* and *hear*, as mental processes but *look* as a behavioral process. I instead deem *see and hear* to be behavioral because they are physiological actions that are not purely conscious choices, and they are not purely mental in nature. I categorize *look* and *listen* as material because they are typically actions you consciously choose to do. You use your eyes and ears as tools, just like you use your other body parts for other material actions. I consider behavioral processes to be more reactions and physiological processes, while material processes are actions.

The next category is verbal processes, when the agent or subject is the *sayer*. These are any verbs that involve the production of language and discourse such as say, tell, and so on. For example:

(36) The defendant, himself, said
(37) As the defendant testified

Verbal processes can also be represented by more evaluative terms such as *claim* and *imply*, and some verbs are only verbal in context, such as *demonstrate* and *go*.

Finally, there are the existential processes. These "represent that something exists or happens" (Halliday 1994: 142). An examples is:

(38) There were two of them.

Often, a dummy *there* and a *be* verb are used in existential processes.

To summarize, there are six different types of processes and many subtypes that can represent events. As discussed earlier, speakers with different models of reality may choose different process types to represent it. A pair of hypothetical examples can be seen in (39) and (40). In (39), a person's material behaviors are described without evaluation, while in (40), the person is described as having had a negative quality based on the behaviors, but his actual material and verbal processes are ignored.

(39) Oskar pushed the other children and did not share his toys with them.
(40) Oskar was rude.

Two speakers will have different points of view, frames of reference, or goals, so they choose different processes to represent and evaluate the same event.

Halliday's framework accounts for the types of processes that can be represented in English. However, his system says nothing about the specific terms within process types that speakers may select. For example, if a defendant is said to have patted a victim rather than hit or smacked her, this is a significant difference. Thus, speakers can categorize an event differently, even if they both see it as the same type of process. When they select a term to refer to the process, the semantic properties of the term will evaluate it and will place it within a specific category of processes. It will create a representation that will raise any associations the hearers have with the term used.

Terms to refer to processes do not just categorize and evaluate. They can also limit or increase the information provided about the process (van Leeuwen 1995). This work is complementary to Halliday (1994), but it focuses on how linguistic manipulations can affect representations. First, there is deactivation, in which processes are referenced as "entities or qualities rather than dynamic processes" (Halliday 1994: 93). In other words, instead of being referenced as verbs, processes are referred to with nouns. This not only hides how the process takes over time, but it can also result in what van Leeuwen calls "de-agentalization." This is when the human agency for a process is erased through it being turned into a noun and the actor being ignored. For example, one could say "the abuse happened" rather than "he abused her." This hides the responsibility of the social actor who did the material action. This is similar to the use of passives in English; in these constructions, the actor who did the process can be omitted.

Another set of strategies is generalization and abstraction. In these related forms, several specific processes are collapsed into a single general or even abstract process. Compare the following:

(41) Her boyfriend grabbed her by the hair and hit her across the face. Then, he pushed her down the stairs.
(42) Her boyfriend abused her.

Both (41) and (42) describe the same events. However, in (41), several distinct abusive processes are referenced, while in (42) they are all generalized into a single process.

Van Leeuwen (1995) also highlights the importance of metaphors and how they can foreground a specific quality or evaluation of the process being referenced. This limits or changes the representation of the process. However, metaphors are not alone in doing this. As described above, any term selected to represent a process will activate some semantic properties and not others. Metaphors simply relate a process to one that it might not normally be associated with or that it differs from in some significant ways.

Overall, the semantic properties of the specific term used to refer to a process are as important as the type of process being referenced. They allow the speaker to categorize and evaluate the process based on how it fits into their mental model.

Finally, as mentioned above, the representation of events is not just about the type of process and the specific term used to refer to it. It is also about how the social actors are portrayed or not portrayed as participating in it. Participants can fill four main roles (Halliday 1994: 144), only three of which are relevant here. The first is the logical subject, the one who does the process. Depending on the type of verb, this role can receive many titles—*actor*, *behaver*, *senser*, and so on. In this book, the actor in this role, regardless of the type of verb, will be called the *agent*. A participant in the role of actor is given agency or an active role in the process. Especially for material and verbal actions, he or she is portrayed as having responsibility for the process having occurred.

Another relevant syntactic position is that of the goal of the process. This is the direct object of traditional descriptive grammars. In example (42) (*Her boyfriend abused her*), *her* is the recipient. A participant in this role lacks agency and therefore is represented as more passive.

The next role is that of the *beneficiary*—the traditional indirect object. This is the participant the process is done for. In the following example, it is *us:*

(43) The law gives us some help to this predicament.

Like the goal, the beneficiary does not have agency. He or she thus also does not have responsibility. Therefore, for the purposes of this book, the roles of goal and beneficiary are conflated into a single category of *recipient* that refers to a social actor being represented as having a lack of agency over the process. The process happens to them, rather than their doing the process.

3.2 RESULTS FOR THE ENTIRE CORPUS

Returning now to the analysis of the defendant's process, as can be seen in Tables 3.9 and 3.10, the defendant played the most roles in both of the prosecution and the defense's crime narratives. This was followed by the investigation story and then the trial story. This is true for when the defendant was an agent of processes and when he was a recipient. The present, future, and other narratives contained the least references to the defendant as either an agent or a recipient of a process. Also shown in Table 3.9, in the crime, investigation, and trial narratives, the prosecution emphasized the defendant's agency more than the defense did.

3.2.1 The Crime Narrative

With regard to the crime story, the defendant was the agent of a process 25.2 times per 1,000 words in the prosecution main arguments and 15.0 times per 1,000 words in the defense arguments.[9] Additionally, as can be seen in

TABLE 3.9

Distribution of Processes with the Defendant as the Agent

		Prosecution	Defense	Rebuttal
Crime	Material	14.6[1,2]	7.9[1]	8.0[2]
	Verbal	1.5[3,4]	0.8[3]	0.8[4]
	Behavioral	0.6	0.6	0.9
	Mental	1.9[5]	1.1[5]	1.6
	Quality	2.0[6]	1.3[6]	1.4
	Location	0.7	1.0	1.0
	Possessive	3.8[7,8]	2.3[7]	1.7[8]
	Existential	0.0	0.0	0.1
	Total	25.2[9,10]	15.0[9]	15.7[10]
Other	Material	0.6[11,12]	0.3[11,13]	—[12,13]
	Verbal	0.2[14]	—[14]	—
	Behavioral	0.0	0.0	—
	Mental	0.0	0.1	—
	Quality	0.0	0.0	—
	Possessive	0.1	0.0	—
	Total	0.9[15,16]	0.5[15,17]	—[16,17]
Investigation	Material	1.1	1.0	1.2
	Verbal	3.1[18]	2.5[18]	3.0
	Behavioral	0.1	0.1	—
	Mental	1.0	0.8	0.9
	Quality	0.3	0.6	0.7
	Location	0.0	0.1	0.1
	Possessive	1.3[19]	0.5[19,20]	1.6[20]
	Total	6.8[21]	5.3[21,22]	7.5[22]
Trial	Material	0.9	0.6[23]	1.2[23]
	Verbal	2.3[24]	1.4[24,25]	2.8[25]
	Behavioral	0.0	0.0	0.1
	Mental	0.4	0.4	0.7
	Quality	0.5	0.4[26]	0.9[26]
	Location	0.1	0.0	—
	Possessive	0.5	0.3[27]	0.8[27]
	Total	4.6[28,29]	3.2[28,30]	6.5[29,30]
Present	Material	0.0[31]	0.1[31]	0.1
	Verbal	—[32]	0.1[32]	—
	Mental	0.0	0.1	—
	Quality	0.0	0.0	—
	Possessive	0.5	0.5	0.6
	Total	0.6[33]	1.0[33]	0.6

continued

TABLE 3.9
(continued)

		Prosecution	Defense	Rebuttal
Future	Material	0.0[34]	0.3[34]	0.1
	Verbal	—	0.0	—
	Behavioral	—	0.0	—
	Mental	0.0	—	—
	Quality	0.1	0.1	—
	Location	0.0	0.0	—
	Possessive	0.3	0.2[35]	0.6[35]
	Total	0.6	0.7	0.7

Note: Differences that are statistically significant are given matching superscripts.

Table 3.10, the defendant was the recipient of processes in the crime narrative significantly more frequently in the prosecution arguments (2.9 and 2.7 times per 1,000 words in the prosecution arguments and rebuttals, 2.0 times per 1,000 words in the defense arguments). More specifically, the prosecution included the defendants as the agents of significantly more material, verbal, mental, quality, and possessive processes and the recipient of more material processes during the crime story in the prosecution arguments.

The prosecutions' stronger emphasis on the defendant's role in the crime narrative when compared to the defense occurred across almost all of the cases. In fact, in only three of the seventeen cases in the corpus did the defense include the defendant as the agent of a process during the crime more frequently per 1,000 words than prosecution did. One of those cases, #7, will be discussed in more detail later. In some of the cases, the differences between the two sides were especially exaggerated. For instance, in case #10 (the sexual abuse case involving a man and the two daughters of his girlfriend), the prosecution included the defendant as the agent of a process during the crime story 22.8 times per 1,000 words, while the defense only had him as an agent 1.2 times per 1,000 words in this narrative. This result is striking because the numbers clearly show that the prosecution emphasized his role in the alleged criminal events while the defense de-emphasized him and in fact almost silenced him.

The prosecution's increased emphasis on the defendant's roles in the crime is exemplified in the following two excerpts from case #14, both of which describe the exact same event that took place during the alleged crime. The prosecution in (44) repeatedly refers to the defendant, emphasizing his role in the crime, while the defense silences it in (45):

(44) And then again, they see the defendant's Malibu come driving up with the defendant in the driver's seat and his brother Carlos in the passenger seat. They honk the horn. Crowley comes out, gets in the car, and then they kind of slowly drive around a couple of blocks where the defendant sells that ounce of cocaine to Crowley. . . .

TABLE 3.10

Distribution of Processes with the Defendant as the Recipient

		Prosecution	Defense	Rebuttal
Crime	Material	1.5[1]	1.0[1, 2]	1.6[2]
	Verbal	0.2	0.1	0.2
	Behavioral	0.1	0.0	—
	Mental	0.1	0.2	—
	Relational	1.1[3]	0.7[3]	0.9
	Possessive	—	0.0	—
	Total	2.9[4]	2.0[4]	2.7
Other	Material	0.1	0.1	—
	Verbal	0.0	—	—
	Mental	0.0	—	—
	Total	0.1	0.1	—
Investigation	Material	0.6	0.5	0.6
	Verbal	0.4	0.5	0.3
	Behavioral	0.0	—	—
	Mental	0.0	0.0	—
	Relational	0.5	0.5	0.7
	Possessive	—	—	—
	Total	1.5	1.5	1.7
Trial	Material	0.4	0.3	0.3
	Verbal	0.1	0.0	0.1
	Behavioral	0.1	0.1	—
	Mental	—	0.0	—
	Relational	0.3	0.2	0.4
	Possessive	—	—	—
	Total	0.8	0.5	0.9
Present	Material	0.0	0.1	—
	Relational	0.1	—	—
	Possessive	0.0	0.0	—
	Total	0.1	0.1	—
Future	Material	0.3[5]	0.3	0.7[5]
	Verbal	0.0	—	—
	Behavioral	—	—	0.1
	Mental	0.1	0.0	0.2
	Relational	0.0	0.1	0.1
	Total	0.5[6]	0.4[7]	1.0[6, 7]

Note: Differences that are statistically significant are given matching superscripts.

(45) All we know is that this car comes, and it drives around the block slowly with Crowley in the back. And there's some activity going on. But all you have really is Crowley's word about what goes on in there. For all we know, he could have been selling drugs that he just got in that building. Could have been selling drugs. Could

have been paying off a loan. Could have been doing anything. Demonstrating a card trick, for all we know. All you have is his word.

The defendant in (44) is the owner of the car, is in the driver's seat, honks, drives, and sells cocaine. In (45), he is completely silenced. It is as if the car drove itself, and he was not even there. By constructing their story in this way, the defense did not need to deny that the defendant had done the actions the prosecution discussed. They simply did not include him as the agent of them in their argument.

The functional result of these quantitative differences is that the defendants' role, particularly their active role and agency, in the crime was emphasized in the prosecution arguments more than in the defense arguments. Also, because the prosecution arguments were longer overall (90,340 words compared to 81,464 words), the higher frequency in the prosecution arguments resulted in the defendants being referred to as the agent of more processes. The prosecution included more of the actions that he did, the things he said, the thoughts he had, and his qualities in this context.

Additionally, in most of the cases, there were also significant differences in the semantic features of the verbs the two sides selected. For instance, if the verbs that represented violent, sexual, or illegal processes are tallied, the prosecution across the cases emphasized these, while the defense de-emphasized or even silenced them.[10] This can clearly be seen in the following example from case #10, the sexual abuse case mentioned earlier.

According to the prosecution in this case, during the years the abuse was taking place, the defendant was violent for two reasons: to express his jealousy over the victims' interactions with others and to prevent the victims and their mother from reporting his abuse. As part of the crime narrative, the prosecutor went into great detail about several violent incidents and thus included the defendant of twenty material processes that were [+ violent], as can be seen in (46):

(46) has struck, threatened with a gun, threatening, to kill everybody in that restaurant, pointed a gun at her, when went to Arby's, [threatened], to kill everyone there, punching Pam, first killed the family pets: the ferret, the parrot, the chinchilla, to call Megan at Arby's, threatened, to kill everyone there, threatened, to kill members of the family with guns, punched Pam, killed the family pets, threatened, to kill everyone at Arby's, created just a climate of fear in this family, created through his threatening and violent conduct.

The result was that the prosecution emphasized the defendant's propensity for violence. The defense, in comparison, de-emphasized the violent events by only referring to them in two clauses. Additionally, when a lexical item that was [+ violence] was used, as in (47), the defendant was completely silenced. Only in (48), when the violence was silenced, was the defendant overtly linked to the actions. Furthermore, as can be seen in both (47) and (48), nominalizations/de-activations[11] hid the defendant's agency and the dynamic nature of the events.

(47) . . . the incident of the killing of the animals took place . . .
(48) . . . in response to Mr. Wilder's acts of what he did in May of 2001

Thus, the defense de-emphasized the violent actions and silenced the defendant's role in them, instead of just denying them, while the prosecution emphasized his role in the violence. Ehrlich (2001) described these types of constructions as examples of the "grammar of non-agency" and showed that the defendant's responsibility was hidden through them. To state it in the terms being used in this book, in constructions like this, the defendant's active role in the events is silenced (or at least in the discursive moment).

The same exact pattern held for the defendant's sexual acts. The prosecution highlighted them, going into graphic detail about the alleged abuse, its sexual nature, and the defendant's agency in it. In contrast, the defense silenced the sexual aspects of the abuse and the defendant's role by using the pronoun *it* and nouns such as *the incidents* and *the events*, even in denials and the re-creation of others' discourses. Examples can be seen in (49) and (50).

(49) If this were really going on, all these things happening over this long period of time in this household, in this small household, wouldn't the mother know it was going on?
(50) Michelle Yorkshire said that the events occurred in December of 2000 and 2001.

Even though the jurors were bound to know that the lawyer was discussing the alleged sexual actions of the defendant, the attorney made the violence and sexual nature of the processes irrelevant and not part of the model of reality he was constructing. Thus, silencing, de-emphasizing, and emphasizing were important discursive strategies for this lawyer, as well as for the other lawyers in the corpus.

In two cases, #13 and #14, people other than the defendants were also involved in the crime, and when this occurred, the prosecutor used an additional strategy to emphasize the defendant's criminal actions, they included him or her as the co-agent of violent, criminal, or otherwise negative processes with the other person. The defense, on the other hand, emphasized the other person as the agent of the criminal acts.

For example, in case #13, both the prosecution and the defense admitted that two boys (the defendant will be referred to as Boy #1 and the other boy will be Boy #2) physically attacked the victim, who later died of his injuries. The prosecution emphasized the defendant's punch and how the victim reacted to it, while comparatively de-emphasizing Boy #2 and his actions. In contrast, the defense emphasized both boys and what each had done.[12] In addition to the prosecution de-emphasizing Boy #2 by referring to him much less frequently than they referred to Boy #1, they also diminished his importance by often casting him and Boy #1 as the co-agents of violent processes instead of giving him individual agency. Particularly in the rebuttal, they overtly focused on the defendant and the other boy working together, and the idea that they both could be guilty, despite only Boy #1 being charged. This is reflected in the fact that 31.5% of the times that Boy #2 was the agent of a material process during the crime narrative in the prosecution's main argument, and 75.0% of the times he filled this role in their rebuttal, the defendant was also the agent of the process (in the form of a coordinated noun phrase or a plural pronoun). An example from the prosecution's rebuttal is as follows:

(51) They know that they're up there to give Chris Britt a hard time and they aided each other in getting him up there and they aided each other in the assault that they each committed on him.

In the defense argument, however, this coupling only occurred 10.8% of the times Boy #2 was the agent of a material processes, and importantly, the two boys were never the co-agents of a violent act. By having the two boys work as a single unit, the prosecution was able to argue that the defendant was guilty either if he threw the fatal punch or if he aided and abetted the other boy. Boy #2 was not important, except as an aid to the defendant. The defense de-emphasized their joint actions, and instead focused on the individual responsibility of Boy #2 as they were deconstructing the importance of Boy #1's actions.

While overall the prosecution emphasized the violent, sexual, and/or illegal actions of the defendants, the defense did include them as the agent of one type of process, locative, in these narratives at a higher rate than the prosecution did. This occurred because the defense made more references to where the defendant was when the supposed crime took place. Usually the lawyers claimed he was somewhere else, implying that if he was not present at the crime, he could not have done it. For example, in case #15, the shaken-baby assault case, a neighbor had testified that he had heard screams. The defense attorney then claimed that the defendant was not present in the home when the screams were heard:

(52) I had asked him, "Is that when Kevin was home." And he said, "No. That was when Kevin was at work."

Their argument, then, was that since the defendant, Kevin, was not at home during this period, he could not have caused the screams. The prosecutor, in his closing argument and his rebuttal, silenced this testimony altogether and did not refer to the defendant as the agent of a locative process in the crime narrative. It is here that the difference between overt and implied references to a topic becomes an issue. The prosecution implied that the defendant was in the home since they included him as the agent of processes that occurred there. However, by not referring to his location directly, the prosecution de-emphasized it compared to the defense, who made it an overt issue and topic of discussion. As a result, the two sides did not directly debate this point of contention. Instead, they created opposing and mutually exclusive representations of the same reality.

3.2.2 The Investigation and Trial Narratives

In addition to the emphasis given to the defendants' role in the crime, the prosecution also focused on their role in the investigation and the trial. They were agents of processes 7.3 times per 1,000 words in the prosecutions' investigation narratives in both their original arguments and their rebuttals but only filled this role 5.8 times per 1,000 words in the defense arguments. The differences were a result of the prosecution foregrounding the defendant's verbal and possessive processes in this context significantly more frequently. In other words, the prosecution was foregrounding what the defendants had said during the investigation (to discuss why their statements showed either that they had incriminated themselves or had been lying) and what they possessed during this time (such as *his response*, *his confession*, *his daughter*, *her sister*) more than the defense was. An example of these from case #9 can be seen here:

(53) . . . his statement when he talks about the '98 incident,

The lawyer then went on to argue that this statement was evidence that the victim was telling the truth. In this way, the words of the defendant could be used against him.

The prosecution cast the defendant as the agent of a process in the trial narrative 4.6 times per 1,000 words in their main arguments and 6.4 times per 1,000 words in their rebuttals, while the defense only did so 3.2 times per 1,000 words. The prosecution particularly emphasized the defendant as the agent of verbal processes (2.3 compared to 1.4 times per 1,000 words). However, the prosecution did not reproduce more of the defendant's testimony than the defense did. Instead, they simply emphasized that he was the source of many of the character voices they were creating and discussing. Again, they found ways to use the defendants' words against them.

3.2.3 The Present Context

The only context in which the defense referenced the defendant more frequently than the prosecution did was the present or interlocutory voice. They cast him as an agent of a process in the "here-and-now" 1.0 times per 1,000 words, while the prosecution only did so 0.7 times per 1,000 words. However, as these numbers show, neither side really emphasized the defendant in this context. When the defense did mention the defendant in this context, it was to discuss what the defendants were doing, thinking, and feeling in the current moment as the argument was being presented to the jurors. Part of the difference between the two sides was that the defense was portraying the defendants as the agents of verbal processes in the present. This occurred through the use of *we* to refer to the defendant and the lawyer. The defense lawyers used this pronoun to construct the defendants as co-producers of the discourse when really the lawyer was the only one speaking in each case.

3.2.4 The Future Narrative

The defense also emphasized the material actions of the defendants in the future more than the prosecution did. Part of this difference was the defense lawyer again referring to himself and the defendant as *we* when producing a meta-discourse about the rest of the argument (e.g., *will prove* and *are going to show you*). Also, the defense included what would happen if the defendants were found guilty (e.g., *lose everything*) or innocent (e.g., *go back to his job, back to his family, back to his life*). The prosecution silenced these topics.

3.2.5 Summary

These results show that across the different narratives, the prosecution lawyers were emphasizing the defendants, what they did, and what was done to them significantly more than the defense lawyers were. The only exceptions were in the present and future contexts. The overall result that emerges is that the prosecution lawyers constructed their arguments more around the defendants' roles in the crime, investigation, and trial narratives than the defense did.

Although in many of the cases the differences are clear from examining how often the defendants' processes of different types in the different narratives or analyzing which specific processes were associated with him or her, this does not tell the complete story. In some cases, such as case #17 in which the defendant claimed self-defense against charges of murder and assault, both sides included the defendant doing many of the same processes or having the same processes done to him. Silencing, however, was still a key process in the creation of opposing arguments. The difference was that it occurred at the level of the lawyers' lexical and syntactic choices rather than their choices for the process types to include. This type of phenomenon was seen in the previous discussion of case #10 in which the defense lawyer used de-activations and generalizations to hide the defendant's agency and the violent nature of the processes. It is even better exemplified in the following analysis of how the opposing lawyers in case #17 described the same series of events:

(54) Prosecution—"I had the knife out right there on the step." Defendant's words. And that really takes us to where we are. Defendant got the knife out and used deadly force because he got pushed. He didn't even get pushed very hard. You got the pictures. You can take a look at them. This is a little tiny porch, just three steps. He claims he was pushed several times before he got the knife out. . . . Even in defendant's most favorable version, the version that at times he seemed to be giving to Detective Ingalls, even if you believe that he got the knife out in response to actually being hit, he gets a knife out and uses it to kill Jim Mound because he got a fat lip.

(55) Defense—Yes, Mr. Beardsley acknowledged that after he's been shoved two or three times he's in the process of taking that knife out and he's still on the steps. But folks, this is not a slow-moving movie where things stop and Beardsley takes out his knife and brandishes it and then things start again. I would suggest and I think common sense would perhaps tell you that this is a continuous series of events that yes, he pulls out that knife. He does not go after Mound with it. He doesn't start lunging out and jabbing at that point. He brandishes it. And Jim Mound ignores it and continues to shove Beardsley to the ground and beat him. And it is only at that point, with Mound over him beating him, that he starts lashing out with that knife.

Both had the defendant taking the knife out while he was on the steps. In the prosecution's argument he *used deadly force* and *used* [the knife] *to kill Jim Mound.* Both of these made the defendant the agent of murderous and illegal processes, and the victim was the recipient of one of those processes. In the defense's argument, he *brandishes* [the knife] and *starts lashing out with that knife.* The semantic properties of verbs the defense selected to represent the defendant's actions were different, as they were not [+ murderous] and not illegal. Also, the victim was not the recipient of the defendant's material processes with the knife, so these forms silenced how the defendant's processes affected him. Thus, the defense silenced that the defendant's actions killed the victim and that there was a murderous purpose behind them, two topics the prosecution included through their linguistic choices.

As this example shows, the processes of silencing, de-emphasizing, and emphasizing happen at all levels of a discourse. They happen in the lexical, syntactic, thematic, and topical choices a lawyer makes both in individual narratives and in complete closing arguments. In the discussion that follows, it becomes even clearer that these processes are key means through which the opposing sides create contrastive representations of the defendant's role in the relevant events.

3.3 THREE CASES IN DETAIL

3.3.1 Case #3

In case #3, as discussed above, the prosecution claimed a man had beaten his girlfriend. The defense did not deny that she had been beaten. Instead, they simply claimed that someone else did it. As can be seen in Tables 3.11 and 3.12, the two sides differed in the level of emphasis they gave to the defendant in the different relevant contexts. While these numbers only tell half of the story, the importance of them is that they show that not only did the prosecution emphasize the processes involving the defendant more throughout their arguments, but this was particularly true with regard to the crime, investigation, and crime narratives. Table 3.11 also shows that defense de-emphasized the defendant's role in the investigation almost to the point of silencing it, while the prosecution silenced him in the present, the "here-and-now."

This case is particularly noteworthy within the context of entire corpus because while the prosecution included the defendant as both the agent and the recipient of significantly more processes during the alleged crime than the defense did, the defense referred to him as an agent in this context more frequently than was average (19.9 times per 1,000 words, compared to 15.0 times per 1,000 words in the corpus as a whole). This was a result of their providing an alternative interpretation of the events rather than simply ignoring the prosecution's claims of what took place.

The prosecution constructed the defendant as the agent of more processes during the crime than the defense did because the prosecution included him as an agent of more material (14.1 times per 1,000 words for the prosecution, 7.9 times per 1,000 words for the defense) and verbal processes (2.5 times per 1,000 words for the prosecution, 0.4 times per 1,000 words for the defense). What the defendant did and said during the crime was not only different in the two cases, but it was more emphasized in the prosecution's argument.

The prosecution's narrative involved the defendant coming home from rehab, drinking, going into his bedroom, seeing his girlfriend in his bed with another man, beating his girlfriend, answering the door when the neighbors came to check on them, and then continuing to beat her. An example of their crime narrative, in this case a re-voicing of the story told by the victim, is as follows:

> (56) That around 7:00 A.M. he, Steven, came back and came in and grabbed me out of bed. He was holding me by my hair. Then with his fist he punched me in my left eye and temple.

They claimed the defendant drank, went into his room, beat up the man who was in the room, escorted him to the door, and then came back and comforted

TABLE 3.11

Distribution of Processes with the Defendant in Case #3 as the Agent

		Prosecution	Defense	Rebuttal
Crime	Material	14.1[1,2]	7.9[1]	2.2[2]
	Verbal	2.5[3]	0.4[3]	—
	Behavioral	1.4	0.8	—
	Mental	1.7	2.1	—
	Quality	0.8[4]	3.9[4]	2.2
	Location	1.5	1.7	—
	Possessive	2.9	2.5	1.1
	Existential	0.2	—	—
	Total	25.2[5]	19.3[6]	5.5[5,6]
Other	Material	2.0	0.8	—
	Possessive	0.2	—	—
	Total	2.2	0.8	—
Investigation	Material	1.2[7]	—[7]	—
	Verbal	3.7[8]	0.2[8]	—
	Mental	2.0[9]	0.2[9]	—
	Quality	0.8	—	—
	Possessive	1.5[10]	—[10]	—
	Total	9.0[11,12]	0.4[11]	—[12]
Trial	Material	1.7	0.8	—
	Verbal	3.1	1.2	2.2
	Mental	0.5	0.6	—
	Quality	0.8	0.8	—
	Location	0.2	0.2	—
	Possessive	0.3	0.8	—
	Total	6.6	4.4	2.2
Present	Material	—	0.4	—
	Verbal	—	0.4	—
	Possessive	—[13]	1.5[13]	—
	Total	—[14]	2.3[14]	—
Future	Material	—	0.8	—
	Verbal	—	0.6	—
	Quality	0.2	—	—
	Possessive	0.5	0.4	—
	Total	0.7	1.9	—

Note: Differences that are statistically significant are given matching superscripts.

his girlfriend. In the defense's story, the other man in the room had already beaten the victim by the time the defendant arrived. To support this story, they included quotations from the victim that contradicted those reproduced in the prosecution's argument.

(57) Mr. Hills did not assault me.

TABLE 3.12

Distribution of Processes with the Defendant in Case #3 as the Recipient

		Prosecution	Defense	Rebuttal
Crime	Material	0.2	0.2	—
	Verbal	0.3	—	—
	Behavioral	0.2	—	—
	Mental	0.2	0.2	—
	Relational	0.7	0.4	—
	Total	1.5	0.8	—
Investigation	Material	0.8	—	—
	Verbal	0.7	0.2	—
	Relational	0.2	0.2	—
	Possessive	—	—	—
	Total	1.7	0.4	—
Trial	Material	0.3	0.2	—
	Verbal	0.3	—	—
	Mental	—	0.2	—
	Relational	0.3	—	—
	Total	1.0	0.4	—
Future	Material	—	0.6	—
	Mental	—	0.2	—
	Total	—	0.8	—

Note: Differences that are statistically significant are given matching superscripts.

Interestingly, the same person said both (56) and (57), and unsurprisingly, the two sides each chose to use the quotation that supported their narrative and silenced the other.

Also, as is shown in (57), the defense did not ignore the prosecution's accusations against the defendant. They falsified them, meaning they argued that the charges were not true. However, when doing so, they used generalizations that silenced the details the prosecution discussed. In contrast, the defense used specific verbs to represent the processes that they claimed the defendant did while someone else committed the crime (e.g., *cuts this guy* and *gets rid of the assaulter*). For their part, the prosecution silenced this fight between the defendant and the other man by simply denying that this other man existed.

As mentioned above, in the two side's alternative narratives, the prosecution also cast the defendant as the agent of verbal processes during the crime more frequently. The reason for this was that the prosecution included in their narrative the defendant answering the door and talking to people who came to check what was going on. They also constructed the defendant as talking to the victim while he physically assaulted her as in example (58):

(58) I'm not going to hurt you. I just want to know why.

The defense silenced his going to the door so did not include those verbal processes, and they silenced what he supposedly said to the victim during the abuse as they simply denied that he had abused her.

The defense did discuss the defendant's qualities during the crime significantly more frequently than the prosecution did (3.9 times per 1,000 words for the defense, 0.8 times per 1,000 words for the prosecution). This was because defense lawyers claimed the witnesses at the crime scene mistakenly decided that the defendant *was guilty* or *was the attacker*. The defense lawyer argued that the witnesses were wrong and the defendant *was not responsible*. The prosecution silenced the witnesses' evaluations of the defendant during the crime (although they did, as the defense did, include that he was drunk). Because of these dissimilar choices for which topics to include, the defense constructed the defendant as the agent of quality processes significantly more frequently.

The investigation story was another site in the closing arguments in which the two sides differed with regard to the processes of the defendant that each included. In fact, the defense almost completely silenced the defendant's role in this narrative, as they only referenced him as the agent of a process in this context 0.4 times per 1,000 words and as the recipient of a process another 0.4 times per 1,000 words. In comparison, the prosecution, who referred to him as the agent of a process during the investigation 9.2 times per 1,000 words and as the recipient of a process 1.5 times per 1,000 words, emphasized his active role in these particular events.

Specifically, the defense only included the defendant as the agent of a verbal and a mental processes during the investigation once, and it was in the same sentence, which can be seen in (59):

(59) Mr. Hills told the police that he didn't think he cut this guy or the guy was bleeding.

In contrast, the prosecution included many material processes (*sit*, *do anything*, *help*, and *locate*) that the defense silenced as they discussed how the defendant did not try to help the police find the other man. The prosecution also included significantly more of his mental and verbal processes than the defense did. For example, they said that he lied to the police about his alcohol consumption and that he frequently said *I really don't remember* and *I don't know*. The defense silenced his alleged lies and his lack of memory. As with the crime narrative, the silencing of different topics and processes by the prosecution and the defense was an important means through which they created opposing arguments.

The only statistically significant difference between the prosecution's and the defense's inclusion of the defendant in the trial narrative was that the prosecution included verbal processes with the defendant as the agent significantly more frequently (3.1 times per 1,000 words for the prosecution,

1.2 times per 1,000 words for the defense). The reason for this was that the prosecution was emphasizing how the defendant *lied* and how *he admitted* to several of the prosecution's assertions about the crime. The defense silenced these parts of his testimony.

The defense, however, did include the defendant in the discourse in the "here-and-now" (2.7 references per 1,000 words) while the prosecution silenced him in this context. This was in part due to the meta-discourse the defense lawyer created, in which the defendant and the lawyer were agents of material and verbal processes together, through first-person plural pronouns, instead of the lawyer being the agent on his own. By using these pronouns, the lawyer emphasized the fact that he and the defendant were a single unit working together and silenced the differences between himself and his client. This can be seen in the following examples:

(60) We admit . . .
(61) We don't deny . . .

The defense also cast the defendant as the recipient of processes in the future when discussing the jurors' agency in future processes (0.8 times per 1,000 words). The prosecution silenced the defendant in this role in this context. For example, the defense told the jurors that reasonable doubts meant they had to find the defendant not guilty:

(62) And if there is a reasonable doubt in your mind then you can't find my client guilty.

As will be discussed in Chapter 5, the defense lawyers tended to instruct the jurors on what to do in the future more frequently than the prosecution lawyers did, so this pattern was a result of that. The prosecution silenced the effects of the jurors' future processes on the defendant.

In summary, the two sides presented completely different narratives and arguments. The prosecution focused on the violent behaviors of the defendant during the crime, including his threatening statements to the victim, as well as his behaviors during the investigation and trial. The defense silenced or de-emphasized these issues by either not talking about them or by referring to them with generalizations. They replaced them with other topics and for those, they included the defendant doing specific processes that the prosecution silenced.

3.3.2 Case #6

According to the prosecution in case #6, a young girl died as the result of the defendant losing her temper and shaking the child to death. Interestingly, the defense acknowledged that the defendant had shaken the victim, but they argued that she had not done it in anger. Instead, she had been trying to revive the little girl, whom she had found unconscious. Due to the nature of these arguments, the case revolved around the testimony of medical experts more than the average case, and this was given the most focus in the closing arguments.

As shown in Tables 3.13 and 3.14, the distribution of processes with the defendant either as an agent or as a recipient is very different in this case compared to the corpus as a whole. The first difference is in the crime narrative. There was much less emphasis placed on it in both the prosecution and the defense arguments because of the attention given to the medical testimony. In fact, the prosecution only included the defendant as the agent of a process in this context a little more than half as often in this particular case compared to in the corpus as a whole (13.0 compared

TABLE 3.13

Distribution of Processes with Defendant in Case #6 as the Agent

		Prosecution	Defense	Rebuttal
Crime	Material	8.6	6.4	2.7
	Behavioral	0.2	0.7	0.9
	Mental	2.0	1.0	2.7
	Quality	0.9	0.7	0.9
	Location	0.1	0.5	—
	Possessive	1.2	0.7[1]	3.6[1]
	Existential	—[2]	—[3]	0.9[2, 3]
	Total	13.0	10.1	11.6
Investigation	Material	1.8	2.0	3.6
	Verbal	4.9	7.2	4.5
	Behavioral	0.7	1.1	—
	Mental	0.9[4]	2.7[4]	—
	Quality	0.2	1.0	0.9
	Possessive	3.1	1.4	3.6
	Total	11.7	15.5	12.5
Trial	Material	0.8	0.2	—
	Verbal	0.4	—	—
	Mental	0.2	—	—
	Quality	0.4	—	—
	Location	0.1	—	—
	Possessive	0.2	—[5]	0.9[5]
	Total	2.2[6]	0.2[6]	0.9
	Mental	—	0.1	—
	Possessive	1.3	0.2	1.8
	Total	1.3	0.4	1.8
Future	Material	—	0.1	—
	Possessive	0.5	—	—
	Total	0.5	0.1	—

Note: Differences that are statistically significant are given matching superscripts.

TABLE 3.14

Distribution of Processes with the Defendant in Case #6 as the Recipient

		Prosecution	Defense	Rebuttal
Crime	Material	0.1	0.2	0.9
	Relational	0.3	—[1]	0.9[1]
	Total	0.4	0.2	1.8
Investigation	Material	0.7	1.6	1.8
	Verbal	0.7	1.5	—
	Mental	0.1	—	—
	Relational	0.5	0.4	1.8
	Total	2.1	3.5	3.6
Trial	Material	1.3[2]	—[2, 3]	0.9[3]
	Total	1.3[3]	—[3, 4]	0.9[4]
Present	Relational	0.1[5]	0.6[5]	1.8
	Total	0.1[6]	0.6[6]	1.8
Future	Material	0.1	0.4	0.9
	Mental	0.1	—	—
	Total	0.2	0.4	0.9

Note: Differences that are statistically significant are given matching superscripts.

to 25.2 times per 1,000 words in the main arguments). The defense referred to her as an agent of a process during the crime only two-thirds as often as usual (10.1 to 15.0 times per 1,000 words). Another difference in this particular case was the foregrounding of the investigation narrative, particularly in the defense argument. Not only did both sides refer to the defendant as an agent in this context significantly more frequently than in the corpus as a whole, but the defense actually emphasized her role in this context even more than the prosecution did. Finally, both sides de-emphasized the processes of the defendant while on the trial, in the present, and in the future.

The crime narratives in this particular case were, in actuality, very similar. In fact, both had the defendant as the agent of the verb *shake* with the victim as the recipient of it. However, the prosecution emphasized it more, repeating it thirty-two times in their main argument and two more times in their rebuttal, compared to the defense who said it only sixteen times. While it cannot be claimed that the defense de-emphasized the fact that their client had done this, they also did not emphasize it as much.

While the prosecution and the defense agreed on that one point, it was in what they included/excluded for the rest of the details of the crime narratives that the two sides created their opposing representations of what occurred. The prosecution focused on the violence the defendant used and the length of time for which she shook the victim, as in the following examples:

(63) She had shaken Serena Hu, shaken her violently for up to a minute.
(64) She shook her up and down, by her own estimation, up to a minute.

Additionally the prosecution referred to her as the agent of either *killed Serena Hu* or *caused Serena Hu's death* fifteen times. The defense, as could be expected, silenced the violence and the claim that the victim had died as the result of it. In fact, they never once referred to the defendant as the agent of a verb that stated or inferred that she was the cause of the victim's death, not even in a denial or in a quotation of another person's claim. Instead, the lawyer focused on how the defendant's actions were an attempt to save the child, who had been somehow knocked unconscious:

(65) The shaking that she did . . .
(66) Carolyn Jakobson made those injuries worse by shaking Serena Hu when she was trying to revive her.
(67) She contributed to the damage inadvertently.

The example in (65) is very interesting because the victim is completely silenced in this particular utterance, and the lawyer used this construction several times. Then, in (67), the defense again silenced the victim and only gave partial responsibility to the defendant. Most important, though, in all of them they silenced the violence the prosecution had associated with the defendant's actions.

An additional difference between the two sides' inclusion of the defendant in the crime narratives was that the defense repeatedly said that the defendant was washing dishes during the alleged crime, but the prosecution silenced this. The importance of this is that it is much like the pattern in the corpus as a whole in that the defense often referenced the defendant's location during the alleged crime when they claimed that the defendant was elsewhere. In this case, the defense did not have that option so, instead, they focused on her doing something else. This process was irrelevant to the prosecution's case, so they ignored it in their arguments.

Overall, this crime narrative is a perfect example of the importance of silencing, de-emphasizing, and emphasizing. The prosecution and the defense both said that the defendant had shaken the victim, but the prosecution emphasized this point more than the defense did. Additionally, the prosecution emphasized the violent nature of the shaking and that the defendant was the cause of the victim's death. The defense silenced this completely. Instead, they focused on the defendant's claims that she had been trying to help the young girl who had been hurt when the defendant's attention had been directed at the dishes. Interestingly, the prosecution in this case actually addressed the defendant's claim that she had been trying to revive the victim when shaking her. However, they did not even bother to negate this as it was simply mentioned in a list of stories that the defendant had told detectives during the investigation. The implication was that since it was not even the final story that she told, it could not be believed. By only referring to it once in a larger list, they de-emphasized it. Thus, silencing, de-emphasizing, emphasizing were once again key strategies for creating opposing representations of the defendant's role in the crime.

These strategies were again evident in the competing investigation narratives. To start with, the defense emphasized the victim in this context by having her as the agent or the recipient more often for almost every type of process. Basically, they claimed that the defendant had been consistent during her police interviews and that the police had broken her down emotionally in order to obtain some of her inconsistent statements. The first part of this argument was made by exaggerating how often she had given the same statement, as in the following example:

(68) She gave her explanation over and over, probably in excess of seventeen times, and that's about all she can do.

In the prosecution's argument, they said that the defendant only explained what happened three times (instead of seventeen). The bigger difference between the two sides was in whether she changed her story or not. In the prosecution's case, she did because her statements differed in terms of how the child got hurt originally, how angry the defendant was, how long and hard she shook the victim, and how she had not done it to revive her. In the defense argument, they said there were no significant differences in the stories, and in fact, when they explicitly denied that she has changed it, the lawyer silenced the details by referring to them with a generalization:

(69) Her explanation had the same basic elements.

As there was no mention of the parts that did change, the implication was that they were unimportant.

The second part of the defense's investigation narrative, that the defendant had been emotionally manipulated by the police officers, revolved around the strategies the police had used and her response to them. In other words, the defense emphasized what the police said to the defendant, what she said in response, and what she thought/felt during this time. Their increased focus on these topics is reflected in the quantitative results. In the defense argument, the defendant was the recipient of more processes in this context (3.5 compared to 2.1 times per 1,000 words) and was the agent of more verbal and mental process (7.2 compared to 4.9 times per 1,000 words for verbal processes and 2.7 times per 1,000 words, compared to 0.9 times per 1,000 words for mental processes).

These differences are even more striking when the actual discourse is examined qualitatively. The defense constructed a narrative in which the police officer treated the defendant horribly, breaking her down emotionally and mentally until she believed that she had caused the victim's death. This can be seen in the following examples:

(70) He told her over and over and over that she was responsible for the injuries.

(71) And after brainwashing her, convincing her that her act caused the injury, he left her alone in that room for an indeterminate amount of time. Didn't tell her when he was going to be back, just closed the door. Maybe it locked. No windows. In the law enforcement center, and there she sits. When he comes back, she's sobbing.

(72) He would have told her she did it a different way, and she probably would have adopted that.

The defense claimed that the police caused the defendant to admit to something she did not do because of their verbal and physical (in)actions.

In contrast, the prosecution denied that the police *threatened* the defendant (something the defense never claimed) or *coerced* her (a term the defense never used). In their version, the police officer did only three things: he checked on the defendant on his way out the door to serve the search warrant, *obtained* her confession, told her that the victim had died. They silenced all of the actions of the police that the defense included. Of these three actions, the most time was spent on the last topic, the announcement of the victim's death, and the victim's reaction to it.

(73) When Investigator Halford informed the defendant that Serena Hu had died, she showed absolutely no emotion. She didn't cry. She didn't act shocked. She didn't act surprised. Nothing at all, even though she had just been informed that an almost 18-month old child, who she had been caring for, was now dead.

The significance of this is that while the prosecution emphasized this event, referring to it four times, the defense completely silenced it.

The result of these contrasting patterns was that two very distinct representations of the investigation were created. Unlike in many cases, the prosecution did provide a sweeping general denial of the defense claims, but for the most part, the two sides simply represented the defendant and the police doing different actions. They ignored the processes the other side included.

To summarize all of the results for case #6, the differences between the representations of the defendant and her processes were mainly found in the crime and investigation narratives. While the stories they told were actually quite similar, the contrasting details they provided were essential in creating their arguments. The prosecution emphasized the defendant's violent shaking of the victim as well as her lack of response to the news the victim had died, topics the defense de-emphasized or silenced. Instead, the defense centered their argument on the defendant having been distracted from the victim during the incident and on her being manipulated by the police. In this particular case, direct denials of the other side's claim did occur (e.g., the prosecution said the police did not coerce the defendant) through generalizations;

nevertheless, silencing, de-emphasizing, and emphasizing played key roles in the creation of these contrasting versions of reality.

3.3.3 Case #7

Case #7 was the "he said–she said" case in which a man was charged with sexually touching a woman against her will while she was sleeping at a party. The defendant claimed the act was consensual. This was the only case in the corpus in which the defense referenced the defendant significantly more frequently than the prosecution did. As can be seen in Tables 3.15 and 3.16, in this case, unlike in cases #3 and #6 and the corpus as a whole, the defense emphasized the crime, investigation, and trial narratives significantly more than the prosecution did. The prosecution referenced the defendant in the crime narrative just as frequently as was average, but the defense simply included him even more times than the average defense did. This inverse pattern resulted from the defense admitting that many of the events described in the prosecution argument had occurred and adding additional events in order to redefine the narrative the prosecution had presented. The prosecution silenced the additional processes for which the defendant was the agent or the recipient that the defense included. As a result, the defense referred to the defendant as the agent of material, verbal, quality, and possessive processes significantly more frequently than the prosecution did. Importantly, the defense also included him as the recipient of material processes in this context more frequently.

The prosecution's narrative was that the defendant came to the party, flirted with the victim, inappropriately touched her while she was asleep, took money from her purse, and then called someone to pick him up. The defense's narrative was similar except that the victim was not asleep in theirs. They included more details that the prosecution omitted, such as the defendant helping the victim to the bathroom when she felt sick, comforting her and her sister, and unbuckling his belt before they got into the bed. It was the inclusion of this extra information that caused the defense to reference the defendant as the agent of processes during the crime more frequently than the prosecution did. Also, since the defense did not deny that the defendant had done any of the actions that the prosecution had included, they argued that these additional material processes proved he was not guilty. They were evidence for (1) the actions and qualities of the defendant that would have made him attractive to the victim and (2) why the victim would have been aware that the defendant's intentions were sexual in nature. An example of #1 can be seen in (74) and example of #2 is in (75):

(74) He was trying to console her.
(75) He had unbuckled his pants.

While the defense included (74) to illustrate the relationship the two had created and (75) to demonstrate that the defendant had been overtly sexual in his

TABLE 3.15

Distribution of Processes with the Defendant in Case #7 as the Agent

		Prosecution	Defense	Rebuttal
Crime	Material	15.7[1]	26.6[1]	21.8
	Verbal	1.7[2]	5.2[2]	1.7
	Behavioral	0.4	1.6	—
	Mental	1.3[3]	2.7	6.7[3]
	Quality	0.6	2.5	1.7
	Location	1.5	2.2	—
	Possessive	5.4	9.0	1.7
	Existential	—	0.3	—
	Total	26.9[4]	51.0[4]	33.5
Other	Mental	—	0.3	—
	Quality	—	0.5	—
	Total	—	0.8	—
Investigation	Material	0.4	0.3	—
	Verbal	2.8	6.0	8.4
	Behavioral	—	0.3	—
	Mental	0.6	1.9	—
	Quality	0.2	0.8	—
	Possessive	0.9	0.3	—
	Total	4.9[5]	9.6[5]	8.4
Trial	Material	0.2	0.8	—
	Verbal	2.4[6]	6.3[6]	5.0
	Mental	—	1.1	—
	Quality	1.1	1.6	—
	Location	0.4	—	—
	Possessive	—	0.8	—
	Total	4.1[7]	10.7[7]	5.0
Present	Mental	—	0.5	—
	Possessive	0.2	0.5	—
	Total	0.2	1.1	—
Future	Mental	0.2	—	—
	Possessive	—	0.5	—
	Total	0.2	0.5	—

Note: Differences that are statistically significant are given matching superscripts.

actions leading up to the physical encounter, the prosecution silenced these types of material processes.

Similarly, the defense also included the defendant's sexual verbal processes that would have alerted the victim to the nature of their encounter. An example of sexual verbal process is in (76):

(76) He talked to her about becoming aroused.

TABLE 3.16

Distribution of Processes with the Defendant in Case #7 as the Recipient

		Prosecution	Defense	Rebuttal
Crime	Material	0.4[1]	1.9	5.0[1]
	Verbal	0.2	0.3	1.7
	Behavioral	0.2	—	—
	Mental	0.2	1.1	—
	Relational	1.1	2.7	1.7
	Total	2.1[2, 3]	6.0[2]	8.4[3]
Other	Material	—	1.1	—
	Total	—	1.1	—
Investigation	Material	0.9	—	—
	Verbal	0.4	1.4	—
	Relational	0.2	—	—
	Total	1.5	1.4	—
Trial	Material	1.1	—	—
	Behavioral	0.2	—	—
	Relational	1.1	—[4]	1.7[4]
	Total	2.4[5]	—[5, 6]	1.7[6]
Present	Relational	—	0.3	—
	Possessive	—	0.3	—
	Total	—	0.5	—
Future	Material	0.2	0.3	—
	Mental	0.4	—	—
	Relational	0.4	—	—
	Total	1.1	0.3	—

As with the other sexual processes, the prosecution did not include these sexual verbal actions in their narrative of the crime.

Additionally, the defense included more quality processes with the defendant as the agent. These occurred when the lawyer was discussing either the qualities of the defendant that would have made the victim a willing partner, as in (77), and his sexual state, as in (78).

(77) She was a little tipsy but friendly, flirtatious. Gawking at him. She said, "You're cute."

(78) He became aroused.

Compared to the defense, the prosecution de-emphasized his qualities and sexual states.

The final key finding for the defendant's role in the crime narrative is that the defense included him as the recipient of more material processes than the prosecution did with the victim as the agent. In fact, this is perhaps the most important difference because it represents that the defense was portraying the victim as a willing participant who did these sex acts to the defendant. The defendant was not the only one acting physically, as she was kissing and touching him as well. Since she was sleeping in the prosecution's version of the crime, the defendant was the agent rather than the recipient in theirs.

As can also be seen in Table 3.15, the defendant also played a more active role in the defense's investigation and trial narratives compared to the prosecution's. Specifically, he was the agent of a process 9.3 times per 1,000 words in the defense's investigation narrative and 10.7 times in their trial narrative. However, he was only the agent of a process 5.2 times per 1,000 words in the prosecution's investigation narrative and 3.9 times per 1,000 words in their trial narrative. The only exception to these findings was that the defendant was the recipient of more processes during the trial in the prosecution's argument (2.4 times per 1,000 words) because the defense silenced these processes.

The differences in the investigation and trial narratives were the result of the defense including the defendant as the agent of significantly more verbal processes in both narratives. The prosecution presented their crime narrative based on the statements and testimony of the defendant while the prosecution based theirs on what the victim had said. Thus, the defense referred to the defendant's verbal processes in these contexts more frequently. The defense also included the defendant as the agent of more mental processes during the trial because they introduced some of his testimony that they re-voiced with *he remembered that. . . .* The prosecution de-emphasized the defendant's verbal and mental processes in this context compared to the defense.

The prosecution constructed the defendant as the recipient of material processes during the investigation and the trial. The defense did not. This was when the prosecution referenced how the defendant *was caught* and *was charged with a crime*. The defense silenced these topics.

In conclusion, case #7 was different from the other trials in the corpus because the defense referred to the defendant significantly more frequently in the crime, investigation, and trial narratives than the prosecution did. As in the previous case, the mechanisms through which the differences between the two sides were created included each side emphasizing the defendant as the agent or recipient of different processes and process types and silencing events that supported the other side's argument. Interestingly, not only was this case unusual in terms of the quantitative patterns, but it was also one of the only cases in which the defendant was found not guilty. However, a causal link cannot be claimed with such little evidence.

3.4 CONCLUSIONS

This study is the first of its kind in terms of the depth at which it analyzes how lawyers represent the defendants as participants in events and contexts. However, the results are not completely without precedent, as several studies have examined the semantic properties of the lexical items lawyers use to refer to defendants' processes. What this book has added is (1) that silencing or de-emphasizing entire events and processes is a common way in which lawyers create opposing arguments and (2) that regardless of the specific linguistic strategies lawyers use, the common thread is that they are utilizing the power of silencing, de-emphasizing, and emphasizing.

Studies including this one have consistently shown that one method lawyers use for controlling the representation of the defendants' and the victims' processes is to select lexical items with semantic properties that *highlight* (Goodwin 1994) helpful characteristics of the processes for that side's case. For instance, Cotterill (2001, 2004) described prosecution lawyers using verbs with more violent connotations than the defense did. When a defense lawyer used *push*, for instance, prosecution used *lash out*, which suggests more aggression and less emotional control. Goodwin (1994) argued that in the first trial for the police officers who beat Rodney King, the prosecution simply argued that King's actions on the videotape of the incident were not violent. In the second case, they actually used nonviolent terms to describe his actions as the images on the tape were shown, and it was in this trial that the prosecution won. One explanation is that through the second prosecution's use of a linguistic coding scheme that highlighted certain nonviolent aspects of King's actions, the lawyers were able to shape how the jurors viewed the tape. The potential impact of such semantic choices has led to cases in which the judge bans certain terms from being used, because of the additional meaning they bring. In Danet (1980b), the judge accepted the defense lawyer's petition to bar such terms as *suffocate* and *smother*, so the prosecution was not allowed to use terms that focused on the more violent or murderous nature of the actions of the defendant. The common thread among these results is that the words that lawyers choose include and exclude different details and thus allow the lawyers to silence, de-emphasize, and emphasize. Given the consistency of this finding across a variety of speech communities and cases, it is clear that lexical selection is important for lawyers. However, as this chapter has shown, this is only a limited means through which lawyers control the representations of reality they create.

Another finding from this chapter is that lawyers use de-activations and generalizations to silence or at least de-emphasize the details of the crime and the defendant's agency. This is consistent with two other related studies. Amsterdam and Hertz (1992) analyzed a pair of closing arguments from a murder trial in which the defendant admitted committing the crime but that it was manslaughter not murder. The prosecution in that case used more verbs to describe the defendant's actions, while the defense used nouns, adjectives, and adverbs. Aldridge and Luchjenbroers (2007) also showed that during the cross-examination of a witness in a sexual assault case, the defense lawyer minimized the violence and abuse that the victim experienced by referring to the events as *a sexual encounter* rather than going into detail about the actual processes involved. While Aldridge and Luchjenbroers and Amsterdam and Hertz did not refer to these processes as silencing and de-emphasizing, that is what they are. It is a key strategy that lawyers use when discussing topics that are contrary to their case. They ignore the details that the other side included, even in negations, quotations, and other constructions that diminish their responsibility for the claim.

Another way that lawyers silence the responsibility of the defendant is through syntax such as passives and de-activation/nominalization. This occurred in this corpus and has been described in the literature. Tiersma (1999) argued that in the defense closing argument in the OJ Simpson case, the lawyer used passives and nominalizations to hide the agent of the crimes. Ehrlich (2001) and Aldridge and Luchjenbroers (2007) both argued that defense lawyers describe sexual events in a rape trial by including both the victim and the defendant as the co-agents of sexual actions, much as in case #7 in this book. This hides the unwilling nature of the victim's participation. Ehrlich (2001) also previously described "the grammar of non-agency" (38), which is seen in this corpus. She claimed that while criminal sexual behaviors are sometimes denied by defense lawyers, they are more often obscured and mitigated with modals to insert uncertainty, passives that ignore the agent, and nominalizations for sex acts that deny not only the agent, but also the dynamic nature of the process.[13] Danet (1980a) described these same syntactic processes being used by the defense lawyer in a manslaughter case. Importantly, these results are confirmed in this corpus, showing that the processes described in this chapter are not specific to the lawyers in this community but are strategies used across cases, individuals, and localities.

The finding that dominated this analysis, however, has not been discussed in detail previously, except in Felton Rosulek (2008). The lawyers often did not need to use semantics, lexical choice, or syntax to make their case. Instead, they simply included different processes involving the defendants and silenced or de-emphasized those described in the other side's narratives. In each case, it was as if two completely different realities were being represented because each side said that different events had occurred. Thus, the lawyers did not have to spend much time issuing denials or addressing the logical flaws in the other side's arguments. They just said that the defendants had done different processes as they utilized the power of silencing, de-emphasizing, and emphasizing.

4 Discussion

Previous studies have taught us that throughout a trial, lawyers for each side try to create their own version of the defendants and their actions through lexical and syntactic choices (e.g., Drew 1985, 1992; Eades 2008; Ehrlich 2001; Matoesian 2005). This chapter showed that these selections function in the closing arguments as means of silencing, de-emphasizing, and emphasizing certain information. While earlier work has tended to focus on single words or phrases in individual cases, this chapter has shown that all types of linguistic forms are part of wider patterns. Additionally, this chapter has shown that silencing, de-emphasizing, and emphasizing also are key to understanding lawyers' topic choices, particularly in terms of the level of focus given to the defendants and the roles they are depicted in playing during the different narratives and voices included in the arguments. All of the linguistic and discursive selections lawyers make all work together to construct distinct representations of these men and women.

Defense lawyers call their clients by name and include their mental processes, their internal workings, while describing their positive qualities. At the same time, the lawyers ignore accusations that these people were involved in violent, sexual, or illegal acts, or at least silence the details of them. As they do so, they create more personal and sympathetic depictions of the defendants. On the other hand, prosecutors limit the defendants' identities to their roles in the crime, investigation, and trial by referring to them as *the defendants*, ignoring their names, and focusing on their active participation in the crime, investigation, and trial. They go into detail when describing violent, sexual, and illegal acts.

To put this another way, while the general public may assume that the representations of defendants are created through name-calling, metaphors, and sympathetic and dramatic stories, the reality is much more mundane, complex, and nuanced. By silencing or de-emphasizing the traits and behaviors that support the other side's depiction of the person and by emphasizing those that fit their case, each lawyer constructs a unique representation of the person on trial. The lawyers do not have to deny the identity created for the defendant by the other side, as they simply represent the person as being someone very different.

4

The Victims

While the terms used to refer to the defendant that were described in previous chapter are rarely challenged (although in some cases the lawyers do point out the linguistic strategy of the opposition in their own arguments as Johnnie Cochran did in the OJ Simpson case), the terms used to refer to the other person directly involved in the crime, the victim, have been debated in more formal ways. In various courtrooms across the United States, prosecution and defense lawyers have argued over the proper term to refer to the person who allegedly suffered from the crime. The law, as mentioned in the last chapter, refers to this person as the *victim*, and this term is commonly used in many cases. However, in some, such as the high-profile legal proceedings that occurred when American basketball player Kobe Bryant was charged with rape (*People v. Bryant*, No. 03-CR-204 (Dist. Ct., Eagle Cty., June 24, 2004)), the defense lawyers have argued that the term *victim* is prejudicial in that it presupposes that the crime was committed and the person suffered because of it. While not all judges have ruled in favor of the defense on this matter, at least in the case of *People v. Bryant*, the judge accepted the defense's argument and decided that although the woman was legally a victim, she would not be referred to as such in the courtroom because of the implications it may carry for the general public (McDonald 2005). As in other cases like it, the person's name or the terms *alleged victim*, *accuser*, and so on, had to replace it.

Appellate courts have produced mixed results on this issue. In both *Talkington v. State*, 682 S.W.2d 674 (Tex. Ct. App. 11 Dist. 1984) and *State v. Cortes*, 84 Conn. App. 70, 851 A.2d 1230 (2004) the states' (Texas's and Connecticut's) Appellate Court ruled that the judge's frequent use of the word *victim* denied the victim the right to due process and was thus a reversible error. However, in *State v. McCarroll*, 336 N.C. 559, 445 S.E.2d 18 (1994) and *Jackson v. State*, 600 A.2d 21 (Del. 1991) the courts ruled that the prosecutors' and the judges' use of this term had not been an error.

Regardless, the important point is that it is an issue that has become contested in courts across the country, and that makes it extremely relevant for this book. First, it demonstrates that lawyers are consciously aware of the lexical properties of at least some of the terms that both sides use and try to silence those that might hurt them. Second, it begs the question of whether or not prosecution lawyers are really using the term *victim* with any frequency. Third, it does not address the issue of the other linguistic and discursive means through which the prosecution, regardless of their use of this term, accomplish the same task.

In the previous chapter, it was shown that the prosecution used multiple linguistic means to portray the defendant as guilty and dislikeable. In this chapter, we see that the prosecution used similar strategies to construct the victim as being negatively affected by the crime, and the defense used them to do the opposite. Interestingly, the use of the term *victim* was a small and rather inconsequential part of the closing arguments.

1 Frequency of Reference

At the beginning of the previous chapter, Table 3.1 showed that there were significant differences between the prosecution and the defense in terms of how frequently they referenced the different social actors. For the victims, the situation was slightly complicated, as can be seen more clearly in Table 4.1. On one hand, the prosecution lawyers mentioned the victims by name, pronoun, or another noun phrase significantly more frequently than the defense did, both in terms of the number of references per 1,000 words and in the total number of references (since the prosecution arguments were longer on average). On the other hand, while the prosecution in both their main arguments and their rebuttals emphasized the defendants over the victims, the defense emphasized the victims over everyone else.

TABLE 4.1
Frequency of Reference

	Prosecution	Defense	Rebuttal
Victims (excluding cases with more than one victim)[1]	35.0 (2,179)[1, 2]	30.1 (1,993)[1]	27.3 (397)[2]
Defendants	38.6 (3,490)[3, 4]	27.5 (2239)[3, 5]	34.5 (634)[4, 5]
Jurors	23.8 (2,146)[6, 7]	28.3 (2307)[6]	27.4 (516)[7]
Opposing side	2.3 (207)[8, 9]	7.2 (590)[8, 10]	8.2 (155)[9, 10]
Lawyer who is speaking	15.1 (1,366)[11, 12]	18.0 (1,469)[11]	20.3 (382)[12]

Note: The first number in each square is the number per 1,000 words; the actual number of tokens follows in parentheses. For this analysis, cases with more than one victim (cases #10, #11, and #17) were excluded from the totals for the victims because these numbers skewed the totals toward higher numbers. This means that the numbers of actual tokens are not easily comparable. Differences that are statistically significant are given matching superscripts.

In this chapter, we will discuss in detail what these conflicting patterns mean and how the lawyers for both sides used these and other linguistic and discursive choices to create opposing representations of the victims. Silencing, de-emphasizing, and emphasizing will once again be shown to have been key processes.

To better understand the general patterns described above, we first turn to Table 4.2, which shows the quantitative data from the individual cases in the corpus. The results in this table demonstrate that the prosecution consistently referred to the victim more frequently than the defense did.

For eighteen of the twenty-three victims in the corpus (the non-italicized entries), the pattern held that the prosecution, at least in their main argument, explicitly mentioned the victim more frequently than the defense did and thus emphasized him or her. In many of the cases, the differences were quite large. For instance, eight of the victims were referred to more than ten additional times in every 1,000 words in the prosecution arguments, and seven of the victims were referred to more than twice as frequently in the

TABLE 4.2
References to the Victims

Case	Prosecution	Defense	Rebuttal
1	47.1 (74)[1]	14.5 (40)[1, 2]	49.2 (45)[2]
2	31.6 (228)[3, 4]	22.2 (195)[3]	20.9 (44)[4]
3	32.8 (192)[5]	28.4 (137)[6]	10.0 (9)[5,6]
4	*46.4 (108)*[7]	*90.2 (302)*[7, 8]	*41.5 (8)*[8]
5	21.4 (57)	13.8 (52)	17.9 (13)
6	21.7 (207)[9, 10]	14.5 (116)[9]	9.8 (11)[10]
7	*47.7 (222)*[11, 12]	*69.4 (253)*[11, 13]	*23.5 (14)*[12, 13]
8	90.2 (129)[14]	41.5 (151)[14, 15]	67.5 (45)[15]
9	48.0 (245)[16]	31.6 (114)[16]	—
10: older victim	50.6 (382)[17, 18]	10.5 (17)[17]	12.0 (18)[18]
10: young victim	26.5 (200)	20.4 (33)	16.6 (25)
11: victim #1	26.6 (134)[19]	2.5 (5)[19]	—
11: victim #2	18.7 (94)[20]	4.5 (9)[20]	—
11: victim #3	10.1 (51)[21]	3.0 (6)[21]	—
11: victim #4	18.1 (91)[22]	9.1 (18)[22]	—
11: victim #5	*8.9 (45)*	*9.1 (18)*	—
11: victim #6	10.9 (55)[23]	2.5 (5)[23]	—
12	49.2 (144)[24]	28.4 (132)[24]	39.5 (47)
13	*27.7 (238)*[25]	*39.0 (158)*[25]	*23.4 (23)*
15	25.4 (205)[26, 27]	14.4 (180)[26]	13.2 (47)[27]
16	*57.1 (130)*	*56.8 (156)*	*44.5 (94)*
17: murder victim	22.0 (189)	18.8 (85)[28]	28.5 (65)[28]
17: assault victim	*2.0 (17)*[29, 30]	*21.7 (98)*[29, 31]	*12.7 (29)*[30, 31]

Note: The first number in each box is the number per 1,000 words; the totals are in parentheses.

prosecution arguments. The effect of these quantitative differences was that the prosecution either gave the jurors a lot more information about the victims and the processes they were involved in, or else the prosecution repeated the same message about the victims more often. Either way, the prosecution tended to keep the focus of their arguments more on the victims than the defense did.

These effects of these data can be clearly seen in an example from case #11. In this case, six women were attacked by the defendant during a crime spree. The first victim was kidnapped, raped, assaulted, and robbed, while the others were assaulted and robbed. In the defense lawyer's closing argument, she ignored the first victim despite the fact that this woman had experienced the most violent crimes that the defendant was charged with and that she was the most referenced victim in the prosecution's argument. The defense lawyer never referred to her as an individual, and the only possible references to her came when the lawyer discussed *the women* and *the victims*. However, she only made five such references in her argument, and they all occurred during the investigation and trial narratives as in this example:

(1) I submit to you that the photographic lineup was unduly suggestive to the women who were shown the photographic lineup.

To use van Leeuwen's (2002) terminology, they used the process of assimilation to erase her as an individual and replace her with the undifferentiated group of victims. By omitting any references to the victim as an individual, particularly in the context of the crime, the defense lawyer silenced her and what had happened to her.[1] Additionally, the attorney avoided discussion of the defendant's alleged role in the more violent and abhorrent acts and effectively separated those events from the robberies he was also charged with. As a result of the two sides' divergent patterns of reference to the first victim, the prosecution created a discourse about a man who committed violent actions against a woman and who also robbed some others, while the defense's argument was about a man who may have robbed some women. Thus, the silencing of this victim had a major impact on the versions of reality that were created.

While most of the cases followed the pattern of the prosecution referring to the victim(s) more often than the defense did, the cases in the table that were italicized were inconsistent with the others. However, the results in these cases are easily explainable. For case #13, the prosecutor did not ignore the victim; in fact, he referred to the victim more times than the defense did, but he included many additional topics in his argument (e.g., the legal definition of aiding and abetting), which made it quite long (8,581 words compared to the average of 5,314.1 in prosecution arguments). Thus, the victim's role in the crime narrative was included, but it was given less focus overall. In case #11, not only did the defense silence one victim, as discussed previously, but the lawyer also emphasized the victim whom the prosecution had mainly ignored because she had suffered the least in terms of violence or loss of property.

Then, there were cases #4, #7, #16, and #17. In each of these, the defense presented an alternative version of the crime or investigation narratives rather than simply ignoring the prosecution's. For example, in case #4, the defense focused on the victim having recanted her allegation that the defendant had beaten her. Because they emphasized this second narrative, the defense emphasized the victim more than most lawyers did, but they included her in a different series of events than the prosecution did (since the prosecution was focusing on the original crime narrative). In case #17, the prosecution claimed that the defendant killed a man during a fight, and then, when the victim's nephew came out after the fight was completed, he, too, was assaulted by the defendant. In comparison, the defense argued the defendant had acted in self-defense while being attacked by both men at the same time. As a result of these contradicting narratives, the prosecution's argument de-emphasized the nephew/assault victim almost to the point of silencing him, while the defense emphasized him as an active participant. In fact, the defense actually included this victim even more than they did the murder victim (as they included the nephew in the investigation and trial narratives). Thus, the defense lawyers in these cases emphasized the victims because they included narratives in which the behavior of the victim exonerated the defendants. These were versions of reality that the prosecution ignored. Thus, despite these cases differing from the norm, the processes of silencing, de-emphasizing, and emphasizing information were still key.

While this pattern of the prosecution including the victim more often in their arguments is important, it does not negate the fact that the victims were the most emphasized social actors in the defense arguments. The explanation is the defense lawyers de-emphasized the defendants and their roles in the crime narrative. Even in denials, they made general sweeping statements that took one or two clauses, and then they spent the rest of their arguments on other topics. However, they still attacked the victims by either dismissing their credibility or giving alternate explanations for what occurred, as in the following examples:

(2) Jim Mound was drunk and drugged out of his mind.
(3) Ms. Benneton gave numerous conflicting statements.
(4) She was mistaking Hills for the assaulter.
(5) The child fell from the high chair.

As a result of the defense including these topics, they focused on the victims in order to construct a very different identity for them from that of the prosecution, and they tended to focus on this more than they built up the defendant. However, they still spent less of their arguments discussing them than the prosecution spent focused on the victim.

2 Terms of Reference

2.1 RESULTS FOR THE ENTIRE CORPUS

Given the research discussed in Chapter 2 showing that speakers in general, and lawyers in particular, use lexical items based on their understanding of reality and their discursive goals, it is not surprising that lawyers have distinct patterns of reference for victims depending on what side of the case they are on. However, in general, very little is known about these patterns. The one key study on this topic is Danet (1980a), which analyzed the trial of a doctor charged with manslaughter after performing a late term abortion. The author found that the prosecution, in order to humanize the victim for the jurors, used terms like *baby boy*. The defense, on the other hand, used terms such as *fetus* and *product of conception*. As the defense argument was that the alleged victim was not in fact a person and therefore could not be a legal victim of manslaughter, they limited him to being a scientific or medical object and erased his personhood. Expanding on this work, in Felton Rosulek (2008, 2009), I argued that the lexical differences can be much more subtle, such as the two sides simply using unique forms of the victim's name. In this section, we explore this issue in more depth, and to start, the breakdown for each side's terms of reference for the victim can be seen in Table 4.3.

As the numbers show, the prosecution and the defense lawyers selected nominations more frequently than the other types (except for pronouns). In fact, the prosecutors used the victim's name 29.7% of times they referred to him or her[2] in their main argument and 32.4% of times in their rebuttals. The defense rate was almost as high: 26.1%. While the prosecution did use the victims' names more often and thus pointed to their unique identity a bit more, the difference was relatively small. The defense was definitely not silencing the victims' names, as the prosecution had done to the defendants. Functionalizations (including *the victim*) were very rare, as they only accounted for

TABLE 4.3

Non-Pronominal Terms of Reference for the Victim

		Prosecution	Defense	Rebuttal
Nominations	Percent of references	*29.7%*[1]	*26.1%*[1, 2]	*32.4%*[2]
	Number per 1,000 words	11. 4[3, 4]	7.7[3]	8.8[4]
	Total number	951	570	166
Functionalizations	Percent of references	*1.9%*	*2.6%*	*2.3%*
	Number per 1,000 words	0.7	0.8	0.6
	Total number	60	56	12
Identifications	Percent of references	*3.8%*[5]	*10.1%*[5, 6]	*4.5%*[6]
	Number per 1,000 words	1.5[7]	3.0[7, 8]	1.2[8]
	Total number	123	221	23

Note: Differences that are statistically significant are given matching superscripts.

1.9% of the prosecutors' references to the victims in their main arguments and 2.6% of the defense lawyers.' While neither side used identifications very frequently, the defense did use them more often, as 10.1% of the defense references to the victims were in this category (e.g., *the young girl*). Overall, though, unlike for the defendants, the distribution of the types of references gives few clues into how the two sides created opposing representations of these individuals.

2.1.1 Nominations

While the use of nominations for the defendants proved to be key in the creation of opposing representations of these men and women, they are not quite as important for the victims. However, they do still play a significant role.

As Table 4.4 shows, while both sides tended to use a semi-formal nomination for the victims, just as they had for the defendants, the second most frequent type for the victims was informal nominations.[3]

The main difference shown in this table is that the defense lawyers used formal nominations more for the victims than the prosecution lawyers did. Thus, just as they had for the defendants,[4] the defense overtly recognized the formality of the context with their terms of reference, rather than simply using the semi-formal terms as the prosecution did. While this may seem like a minor detail, in some cases it was used to help create very different types

TABLE 4.4

Distribution of Nominations for Victims

		Prosecution (*n* = 951)	Defense (*n* = 570)	Rebuttal (*n* = 165)
Informal (given name)	Percent of nominations	*28.5%*[1, 2]	*34.9%*[1, 3]	*63.0%*[2, 3]
	Number per 1,000 words	3.2[3]	2.7[4]	6.3[3, 4]
	Total number	271	199	104
Semi-formal (given name and surname)	Percent of nominations	*67.1%*[5, 6]	*40.9%*[5, 7]	*27.9%*[6, 7]
	Number per 1,000 words	7.7[8, 9]	3.1[8]	2.4[9]
	Total Number	639	233	46
Formal (surname)	Percent of nominations	*2.1%*[10]	*5.3%*[10, 11]	*0.0%*[11]
	Number per 1,000 words	0.2	0.4[12]	—[12]
	Total number	20	30	0
Formal (title and surname)	Percent of nominations	*4.1%*[13, 14]	*19.1%*[13, 15]	*9.1%*[14, 15]
	Number per 1,000 words	0.5[16]	1.5[16]	0.8
	Total number	39	109	15

Note: Differences that are statistically significant are given matching superscripts.

of identities for the victims. For instance, in case #1, 81.8% of the prosecution references to the victim were in the form of just her first name. The rest were semi-formal nominations. In contrast, 66.7% of the defense nominations were *Ms. Gutteridge*, and the rest were semi-formal nominations. Because these two sides had such distinct patterns, the prosecution emphasized the victim's youth and helped develop a sense of a personal relationship with her, while the defense created social distance and a formal atmosphere while de-emphasizing her age.

One difference that this table does not reveal is that when the two sides used the same types of nominations, they did not always use the same name for the victim. For instance, in two cases, the prosecution used the victims' nicknames (both were children) rather than their full given names. One such case, #12, was discussed in Felton Rosulek (2008). In it, the prosecution referred to the victim by her diminutive nickname *Lizzy*, although in a few instances they also included her surname. The defense usually used both her first and last name, and they always used her full first name, *Eliza*. A similar pattern is found in case #9. The prosecution tended to use the diminutive form of the victim's first name, *Nicki* (seven out of twelve nominations), while the defense tended to use the full form of her name, *Nicole* (four out of six nominations). The result in both of these cases was that the prosecution once again emphasized the victim's youth and the lawyer's personal relationship with her.

Another important finding not shown in the table is revealed in a comparison of the results for the victims and the defendants. While the prosecution referred to the defendant by name only 2.4 times per 1,000 words, or 6.1% of the time, they used the victim's name 11.4 times per 1,000 words (29.7% of references). One result of this was that there were many times, as in (6), where the victim was referred to by name but the defendant was not:

> (6) The State alleges that the defendant ordered Mr. Harrison into a car which was driven back up to ___ Avenue, and someplace near ___ Avenue, Mr. Harrison bailed out of the car.

By using the victims' names, the prosecutors called attention to their unique identities and showed them respect. By consistently doing this while not doing it for the defendants, the prosecution set the victim and the defendant apart linguistically and emphasized their different roles in the case. The defense did not do this.

Finally, it must be noted that while that the defense usually used nominations for the victims, this hides the fact that in some cases, this was not true. For instance, in cases #10 and #11, both of which were discussed in detail in Felton Rosulek (2009), the defense silenced the unique identity of the main victim (there was more than one in both of these cases) by never or almost never referring to her by name. In case #10, although the prosecution referred to the victim by name 96 times, or 25.1% of the times they referenced her, the defense lawyer referred to her using her name in only one utterance, which is presented here:

(7) You had the Yorkshire family: Megan, Michelle, Pam.

The lawyer only referred to the second victim by name two other times, so they also de-emphasized her unique identity. In case #11, the defense never referred to the main victim by name, or as an individual for that matter, instead only linguistically pointing to her as part of the *women* who testified. In these particular cases, the lawyers linguistically erased these women's personal identities from their arguments, just as the prosecution had done to the defendants.

To conclude, patterns of nominations for the victims did not necessarily play as large a role in the creation of opposing representations, but that does not mean they were not important in individual cases and in separating the victims from the defendants.

2.1.2 Functionalizations

Interestingly, despite defense lawyers' attempts in some cases to ban the word *victim*, at least in the cases in this corpus, it was mostly a non-issue. As stated above, functionalizations in general were rarely used for the victims. If one was used, most of the time it was *the witness* (or the equivalent forms, such as *people who testified*). These terms often occurred during the trial narratives when the lawyers were describing the commonalities among people's testimony. While in several of the cases, the prosecution did use the term *the victim*, it was never used frequently (the maximum was six times in one argument). The defense lawyers, as could be expected, never used this term, but in one case the defense lawyer did call the person *the alleged victim* and in another there was a use of *purported victim*. Overall though, the term *victim* did not have the same role as *the defendant*.

There was only one exception in the corpus to the infrequent use of a functionalization for the victim. Case #9 involved a girl who accused her brother-in-law of inappropriate touching. The defense lawyer referred to her as *the complainant* 5.8 times per 1,000 words or 18.4% of the times he referenced her. He used it in the interlocutory voice as well as in the crime, investigation, and trial narratives:

(8) The complainant was well past six when she began telling her story about Jakob Bergestad and changing it.

By using this term instead of her name (they only used a nomination 1.7 times per 1,000 words), the defense de-emphasized the unique identity of the victim and emphasized her role in the case, just as the prosecution consistently did to the defendants in each case. As might be expected, the prosecution never used this term. The selection of this particular functionalization is noteworthy. On one hand, it is a term that was less biased toward guilt than *victim* for the girl's role in the context, for it did not assume that the abuse happened, only that she said it did; and it plays on the negative connotations of the act of complaining. These factors make it beneficial for the defense. However, none of the other lawyers in the corpus used it, and although it is not wrong to use it in this context in American English, it usually is used in civil rather than criminal courts (Garner 2011). Regardless, the important fact is that the lawyer used it for the purposes of emphasizing the girl's role in the case and de-emphasizing her other features, including her age and status as a possible victim.

2.1.3 Identifications

Although the prosecution rarely used identifications for the victims, the defense used them more often.[5] Even though the numbers are small, it is still important that the defense was using these terms more often to focus on specific characteristics of the victims rather than their unique individuality. Additionally, as Table 4.5 shows, while both sides used more classifications (by age, gender, etc.) than relational identifications, this was particularly true of the defense. Neither side used any physical identifications.

Many of the classifications for both sides were references to the victims by their age and/or gender. The most extreme example of this was in case #16. The victim had been an infant at the time of the alleged crime, and the defense limited her identity to this fact. In fact, the attorney referred to her as *the child* or *the baby* 87 times, or 48.3% of the times he referred to her in the closing argument, as in the following example:

(9) She's with the child alone again around approximately eight and a half hours

To put this in perspective, he referred to the victim by name only forty times (twenty-seven of the forty occurred in the first half of the argument). In comparison, the prosecution in their main argument referred to her as *the child/baby* only six times. Instead, they used her name ninety-five times. The

TABLE 4.5
Distribution of Identifications for the Victim

		Prosecution	Defense	Rebuttal
Classifications	Percent of identifications	*66.4%*[1]	*91.1%*[1]	*77.3%*
	Number per 1,000 words	1.0[2]	2.6[2, 3]	0.9[3]
	Total number	81	195	17
Relational identifications	Percent of identifications	*33.6%*[4]	*8.9%*[4]	*22.7%*
	Number per 1,000 words	0.5[5]	0.3[5]	0.3
	Total Number	41	19	5

Note: Differences that are statistically significant are given matching superscripts.

difference was that the prosecution emphasized the fact that the victim was a unique individual, while the defense completely de-emphasized this. They constructed a much more impersonal and abstract version of her that centered only on the fact she was a young human being.

In other cases, identifications were used less frequently but with the purpose of drawing the jurors' attention to a specific characteristic of the victim. As was discussed in Felton Rosulek (2008), lawyers made references to a person by his or her age if this was relevant to the point they were making. In case #12, which was about the sexual abuse of the child, both the prosecution and the defense focused on the victim's young age. The prosecution emphasized that the crime had happened to a vulnerable young girl, while the defense used her age to reference societal expectations of young people, as in these examples:

(10) The State's case is based upon the statements of a young girl.

(11) Wouldn't it be more reasonable that a young girl of that young age, being subject to that extensive sexual abuse over a 200-day period, show some signs of mental or emotional problems?

They pointed to her age as a reason for her not to be believed in (10) and as an indicator of how she should have been behaving but was not in (11). They made her age her only relevant feature in these particular clauses by using these terms. While not given emphasis overall, her age was made salient in these particular instances by the use of these terms of reference.

In addition to these individualizing forms, the defense in case #17 used identifications to strategically assimilate the two victims into a single unit. This is the case in which the prosecution claimed that the two victims fought the defendant separately, while the defense argued that the defendant had been forced to fight them both simultaneously. Thus, the prosecution only linked the victims linguistically 0.3 times per 1,000 words (three), while the defense did it 3.8 times per 1,000 words (seventeen). Many of the defense terms were plural classifications that eliminated the individuality of the two men:

(12) He used it as an equalizer against tougher, stronger, younger men who thought that they could take advantage of him.

Thus, linguistically, the defense was able to de-emphasize the distinctions between the victims during the crime narrative.

With regard to relational identifications, the prosecution used them more often, but these results are deceiving because twenty-three of the prosecution's forty identifications for the defendants were in case #10. Without that case, both sides used roughly the same number of relational identifications for the defendant (0.2/1,000 words to 0.1/1,000 words, 0.5% of references). It is still important, though, that this case had such a high frequency of relational terms. Since the defendant in this case was the victims' stepfather, the prosecution emphasized this relationship by frequently referring to the victims by how they were related to each other and to the defendant. This can be seen in the following excerpt:

> (13) The defendant repeatedly and over a long period of time touched the intimate parts of the two daughters of his girlfriend.

The defense only pointed to the relationship the defendants and the victims had by referring to them all as a *household*. Thus, the prosecution emphasized their familial relationship with these terms while the defense silenced it.

In summary, despite the relatively rarity of identifications, they still were used for silencing, de-emphasizing, and emphasizing in several cases. They, along with the results for nominations and functionalizations, demonstrate that the terms of reference for the victims are much more nuanced and case specific than those used for the defendants.

2.2 THREE CASES IN DETAIL

In order to better describe how forms of reference were used to create opposing representations of the victims, the specifics of three cases will now be discussed.

2.2.1 Case #3

In case #3, unlike in many of the cases, the defense used a nomination for the defendant more frequently (5.8 times per 1,000 words) than the prosecution did (4.1 times per 1,000 words), and despite the prosecution referring to the victim more frequently overall (32.6 times/1,000 words compared to 28.4 times/1,000 words), a higher percentage of the times the defense referred to the victim were nominations (20.4% to 12.5%). As shown in Table 4.6, the defense mostly used the formal *Ms. Benneton*, but the prosecution never used it. The prosecution instead used her first name only, despite her being an adult, or her first and last name together.

In this case, the defense agreed that the victim had been assaulted, but they argued that she was not assaulted by the defendant. Thus, the defense

TABLE 4.6

Nominations for the Victim in Case #3

	Prosecution (n = 192)	Defense (n = 137)	Rebuttal (n = 9)
Nomination	12.5% (24)[1]	20.4% (28)	44.4% (4)[1]
Suzanne	6.3% (12)	2.3% (3)	—
Suzanne Benneton	6.3% (12)[2]	2.3% (3)[3]	44.4% (4)[2, 3]
Benneton	—	0.8% (1)	—
Ms. Benneton	—[4]	16.2% (21)[4]	—

Note: Differences that are statistically significant are given matching superscripts.

attorney acknowledged that the jurors could feel sympathy for her, and by using her name, he furthered this sentiment by indexing her unique identity. What is particularly noteworthy about the attorney's use of nominations is that, just as he had done for the defendant, he mainly used formal nominations for the victim. In contrast, he referred to the other witnesses more informally, using their first names only or their first and last names and never giving them a title.[6] The contrasting patterns of nominations set the defendant and the victim apart from the other people who testified. This was important, as these were the only two people whose testimony the lawyer wanted the jurors to believe. In this case, the victim had changed from her original story and had said on the stand that the defendant was not responsible for her injuries, a claim that the other witnesses contradicted. By making the defendant and the victim different and giving them a level of respect, the lawyer cast them as believable and emphasized their separateness from the others who had been present during the criminal acts.

In the prosecution's argument, the lawyer used informal and semi-formal nominations at an equal rate for the victim. Six of the twelve instances in which an informal term was used were in the voices of characters, but six (or half) were in the voice of the lawyer as the narrator of either the crime story (five) or the trial (one) story. Since all of this lawyer's references to the defendant with an informal nomination were in the voice of a character or associated with one, it is striking that he referred to the victim by her first name six times in his own voice. This perhaps indexes their more personal relationship or the relationship the lawyer wanted the jurors to feel they had with the victim.

Neither side used a functionalization frequently. The prosecution referred to the woman as *the victim* twice and the defense used *the witness* once in their trial narrative. However, both sides used an identification relatively often. In fact, the prosecution used one more than they used a nomination (14.1% compared to 12.5%). The defense used an identification only 7.3% of the times they referred to her. Most of the terms of this type for both sides were relational identifications, either *mom/mother* or *girlfriend/fiancé*. For the prosecution, the use of *his mother* occurred when the lawyer was presenting the crime narrative by describing the testimony of the victim's son. Since they were focusing on his perspective of the events and his testimony, they highlighted this relationship. The use of *girlfriend* or *fiancé* was used to mark the discrepancy between how the defendant had acted and how he had been expected to behave, given his relationship with the victim. This can be seen in example (14).

(14) May I suggest a more-appropriate answer? How about "Yeah! Because somebody beat the daylights out of my girlfriend. And while you're wasting your time talking to me, he's out there in a

gray Ford Tempo driving around. And let me tell you what he looks like and let me do anything I can to help you find him."

Thus, these references were as much about the defendant as the victim in that it was the defendant's role and relationship being pointed to when the noun phrase pointed to the victim.

In the defense's argument, the relational identifications for the victim once again focused on other people's relationships with her, rather than her as an individual. The use of *mother* occurred in quotations from the victim's son's testimony. Unlike in the prosecution argument, it was also used when the lawyer insinuated that the son was not honest because of his relationship with the victim:

(15) Remember he is the son of the injured mother. He is well meaning. I have no doubt about that, but he is protective of his mother.

Bennett (1978) described an extremely similar scenario when he discussed a lawyer referring to the defendant as *your son* when cross-examining the defendant's mother on the witness stand. The point was to infer that she was in a position to lie to protect him, and this is the exact same thing the lawyer was doing in this case—pointing to the relationship through a term of reference in order to call attention to the social properties and expectations of it.

Overall, this case was slightly different from many in the corpus in that the defense wanted the jurors to believe the victim's testimony, while the prosecution wanted the jurors to believe her initial statements to the police, not what she had said on the witness stand. This resulted in both sides using nominations to refer to her, although the defense strategy was to use her title and last name, while the prosecution used only her first name frequently. Both sides used relational identifications to take the focus off the victim and to place it on the other people's relationships with her. Who she was as an individual did not matter in these instances, just that she had a certain role and others were expected to behave a certain way because of it.

2.2.2 Case #6

In case #6, we find a very different pattern, except that once again, the prosecution referred to the victim more frequently than the defense did (21.7 times/1,000 words and 14.5 times/1,000 words).

In this case, the prosecution went out of their way to refer to the victim by name (62.3% of the time, 13.5 times per 1,000 words), instead of using another term such as a pronoun. The defense, in comparison, used her name much less often (25.9% of the time, 3.7 times per 1,000 words). These contrasting patterns between the two sides meant that the prosecution emphasized the unique identity of the victim and kept her as an individual in the forefront of the juror's minds. The defense de-emphasized this to some extent and definitely did not foreground it.

TABLE 4.7
Nominations for the Victim in Case #6

	Prosecution (*n* = 207)	Defense (*n* = 116)	Rebuttal (*n* = 11)
Nomination	62.3% (129)[1]	25.8% (30)[1]	54.5% (6)
Serena	0.5% (1)[2, 3]	20.7% (24)[2]	9.1% (1)[3]
Serena Hu	61.8% (128)[4]	5.2% (6)[4,5]	45.5% (5)[5]

Note: Differences that are statistically significant are given matching superscripts.

Instead, the defense used more identifications, which accounted for 32.8% of their references to her.

Not only did the prosecution use significantly more nominations than the defense did, but the two sides used different forms of them as well. As can be seen in Table 4.7, the prosecution used both the victim's first and last name almost exclusively, while the defense tended to her first name only.

The fact that the prosecution did not use the victim's first name only is particularly interesting considering the findings of case #3 and the analysis presented in Felton Rosulek (2008), which showed that prosecution tended to use more informal terms for the victim than the defense did, presumably to lessen the social distance between the lawyer and the victim and between the jurors and the victim. One explanation for this case is that the victim was deceased, and in Felton Rosulek (2009) and in case #3, when a person had passed away, the lawyers tended to avoid the less formal terms. However, this does not explain the defense using informal nominations in this case. In general, they tended not to use informal nominations for the victims presumably because these lawyers did not have a personal relationship with them and did not want the jurors to feel like they did either. In this case, though, the victim was a child and, as was discussed in Felton Rosulek (2009), for children, the use of the first name only is quite common. Thus, these competing factors—the youth of the child and her being deceased—may have led to these unique patterns.

Both sides also referred to the victim as *the child*, although the defense did so much more frequently (2.5 times per 1,000 words for the defense, compared to 0.9 times per 1,000 words for the prosecution). Also, this phrase was a much higher percentage of the defense's terms (17.2%) than the prosecution's (4.3%). The defense also used *the kid* and *the toddler*, which also limited the victim's identity to her age and humanness, quite frequently.

There were three reasons that the prosecution used *the child*. First, two of the tokens occurred when they were describing the victim as being normal for her age, so her youth was her most relevant characteristic. Second, other instances were during the discussion of information found in medical reports, so the use of this term was a clue that the lawyer had shifted genres. Third, this form occurred when the lawyer was constructing the message that the victim had a unique set of properties that separated her from the other children whom the defendant had not hurt, as in the following example:

(16) They testified to seeing the defendant interacting with her nieces, not someone else's child, not a child that the parents had already expressed concern about not wanting the defendant left alone with her, not a child that the defendant had become mad or angry with by her own admission.

Thus, the general pattern was that the prosecution used this identification rarely but for very specific purposes. Also, since they used her name so frequently overall, her status as an individual person was still emphasized in the argument as a whole.

The defense used these identifications very differently. While a few were in the medical portion of the investigation narrative, almost all of them were in the crime narrative, as in the following example:

(17) We don't exactly know how the child fell.

This is important for two reasons. First of all, the fact that the defense used this term more than the victim's name de-emphasized her unique identity. This is especially true when we compare how frequently the prosecution referred to her by name. In the defense argument, the personal connections the hearers may have felt for her were backgrounded, and she became a more abstracted entity. Second, this is the very same pattern as discussed earlier in case #16, although not to the same extreme as in that case. Both of these cases involved charges of shaken baby syndrome, and although different lawyers gave the arguments, the strategy was the same, to de-emphasize that this was an individual baby, someone people are naturally drawn to, who was injured or killed.

The contrasting patterns of terms of reference in this case resulted in very different representations of the victim being created. In the prosecution's case, she was a normal, happy, individual, while in the defense case, she was simply a young person.

2.2.3 Case #7

Case #7 is a bit different in that the defense actually referred to the victim more frequently than the prosecution did (69.4 times per 1,000 words compared to 47.7 times per 1,000 words). Importantly, this was the same defense argument discussed in the previous chapter that also emphasized the defendant. The prosecutor in this case did not de-emphasize or silence the victim, but instead, she just was emphasized to an extreme degree in the defense argument.

As shown in Table 4.8, both sides referred to the victim by name with roughly the same frequency, 6.4 times per 1,000 words for the prosecution

TABLE 4.8
Nominations for the Victim in Case #7

	Prosecution (n = 222)	Defense (n = 253)	Rebuttal (n = 14)
Nomination	13.5% (30)	9.1% (23)	21.4% (3)
Bridget	0.9% (2)	2.0% (5)	—
Bridget O'Day	9.5% (21)	6.7% (17)	14.3% (2)
Ms. Bridget O'Day	0.5% (1)[1]	0.4% (1)[2]	7.1% (1)[1, 2]
Ms. O'Day	2.7% (6)[3]	—[3]	—

Note: Differences that are statistically significant are given matching superscripts.

and 6.3 times per 1,000 words for the defense. Because the defense referred to her more often, a smaller percentage of their terms were nominations.

Both sides used mostly the semi-formal constructions, but the prosecution did use a formal title seven times. Four of the seven instances of a formal nomination in the prosecution's argument were in the crime narrative, and the other three were in the investigation narrative. In the crime narrative, two were used when the lawyer was discussing a formal topic: how the events fit into the legal definition of the crime:

(18) The defendant knew or had reason to know that Ms. O'Day was asleep or unconscious.

Contrastively, in the defense argument, the use of the formal term was in the interlocutory voice. This is noteworthy only in that in cases like #3, when the defense lawyer wanted the jurors to believe the victim, they showed her respect with a formal nomination, but they did not do the same when they did not want the jurors to believe her. As in the other cases in which the victims were adults, the informal nominations in both sides' cases tended to be in the witnesses' voices.

In this particular case, neither side used a functionalization or an identification very often. The only such term used more than two times by either side was *victim*, which the prosecution used five times, but three of the instances were in lists of people who were all being referred to by functionalizations, as in the following:

(19) You, not the judge, not the prosecutor, not the defense lawyer, and the victim, not the law enforcement officers, you are the sole judges.

The lawyer was discussing the role of the jurors in these utterances and thus the roles of the others involved in the case, including the victim, were relevant. Other than the few instances like this, however, neither side used forms other than nominations and pronouns consistently for this young woman.

To summarize, the differences in the representations of this victim created by the two sides were mostly not created through the terms of reference the lawyers used. While there were differences between the two sides, particularly in the use of informal and formal nominations, these were often minor contrasts. The means through which the two sides created opposing representations of this woman came in their other linguistic and discursive choices, as will be discussed later in this chapter.

3 The Roles of the Victims in Clauses

We turn now to the distribution of the processes involving the victims as agents or recipients. The analysis shows that these were the most important ways in which the lawyers separated their arguments from the other side's, and once again the lawyers made linguistic and discursive choices that harnessed the power of emphasizing, de-emphasizing, and silencing to construct opposing representations. For instance, compared to the defense, the prosecution tended to emphasize processes involving the victim during the crime and investigation. Additionally, regardless of the narrative or type of process, the two sides included the victims in different processes and mainly silenced those that the other side included. In other words, they often did not contradict each other or directly argue that the other was wrong. Instead, they simply discussed different topics or talked about the same topics with different linguistic options.

3.1 RESULTS FOR THE ENTIRE CORPUS

Table 4.9 presents the distribution of processes for which the victims were the agents in each narrative in the closing arguments when the entire corpus was examined, and Table 4.10 shows the distribution of the processes with the victims as the recipients. In each box, there are two numbers; the first is when cases with more than one victim are included,[7] and the second number, the one in parentheses, excludes the three cases in which there were more than one (to ensure that the numbers are comparable to those for the defendants). The results show that the prosecution lawyers included significantly more processes from the crime and trial with the victim as the agent. Thus, compared to the defense, the prosecution emphasized the victim's active role in these events. However, as the ensuing discussion will indicate, the differences with regard to the victim between the prosecution's and the defense's arguments went beyond this. The opposing constructions of reality also developed from the contrasting patterns for the types of processes they tended to emphasize for the victims, the specific processes they included, and the actual linguistic forms they used to refer to those processes. Thus, through

TABLE 4.9

Distribution of Processes with the Victim as the Agent

		Prosecution	Defense	Rebuttal
Crime	Material	5.6 (4.5)	5.2 (4.9)[1]	4.3 (3.3)[1]
	Verbal	1.3[2] (1.4)[3]	0.7[2] (0.7)[3]	1.0 (1.0)
	Behavioral	2.6[4] (2.9)[6]	2.2[5] (2.3)[7]	1.1[4, 5] (1.2)[6,7]
	Mental	1.0 (1.0)	1.0 (1.0)	1.5 (1.4)
	Quality	1.8 (1.6)[8]	1.5 (1.2)	1.2 (0.7)[8]
	Location	0.7 (0.6)	0.6 (0.6)	0.5 (0.5)
	Possessive	6.5[9, 10] (6.2)[12, 13]	3.8[9, 11] (4.1)[12, 14]	2.5[10, 11] (2.0)[13, 14]
	Existential	0.0 (0.0)	0.0 (0.0)	—
	Total	20.0[15, 16] (18.3)[18, 19]	15.1[15, 17] (14.9)[18, 20]	12.1[16, 17] (10.0)[19, 20]
Other	Material	0.3 (0.3)	0.6[21] (0.4)[22]	—[21, 22]
	Total	0.3 (0.3)	0.6[23] (0.4)[24]	—[23, 24]
Investigation	Material	1.1 (1.0)[25]	1.0 (1.0)[26]	1.6 (1.9)[25, 26]
	Verbal	1.7 (1.6)	1.4 (1.3)	1.2 (1.3)
	Behavioral	0.1 (0.1)	0.1 (0.1)	—
	Mental	0.7 (0.9)	0.8 (0.8)	1.0 (1.1)
	Quality	0.3 (0.4)	0.5 (0.6)	0.3 (0.3)
	Location	0.1 (0.1)	0.1 (0.1)	0.1 (0.1)
	Possessive	1.1 (1.2)	0.9 (1.0)[27]	1.5 (1.9)[27]
	Total	5.0 (5.1)	4.7 (4.9)	5.6 (6.5)
Trial	Material	1.0[27] (1.1)[28, 29]	0.4[27] (0.4)[28]	0.5 (0.4)[29]
	Verbal	3.1 (2.5)	3.1 (3.0)	2.8 (2.9)
	Behavioral	0.1[30] (0.1)[31]	—[30, 31]	0.0 (0.0)
	Mental	0.6 (0.5)	0.6 (0.6)	0.7 (0.9)
	Quality	0.3 (0.3)	0.3 (0.4)	0.6 (0.5)
	Location	0.1 (0.0)	0.0 (0.0)	0.1 (0.1)
	Possessive	1.2[32] (1.0)	0.7[32] (0.7)	1.0 (0.5)
	Total	6.4[33] (5.6)	5.2[33] (5.1)	5.7 (5.5)
Present	Material	0.0 (0.0)	0.0 (—)	—
	Quality	0.3[34] (0.4)[35, 36]	0.1[34] (0.1)[35]	—[36]
	Possessive	0.4 (0.05)	0.3 (0.3)	0.5 (0.5)
	Total	0.7 (0.9)[37]	0.5 (0.4)[37]	0.5 (0.5)
Future	Material	0.0 (0.0)	0.0 (0.0)	—
	Mental	—[38] (0.0)[40]	—[39,41]	0.2[38, 39] (0.2)[40, 41]
	Quality	0.1 (0.1)	—	—
	Possessive	0.3 (0.3)	0.4 (0.3)	0.4 (0.5)
	Total	0.4 (0.4)	0.4 (0.4)	0.6 (0.7)

Note: Differences that are statistically significant are given matching superscripts.

TABLE 4.10

Distribution of Processes with the Victim as the Recipient

		Prosecution	Defense	Rebuttal
Crime	Material	5.9[1, 2] (5.2)[4]	4.2[1, 3] (4.4)[5]	2.0[2, 3] (2.5)[4, 5]
	Verbal	0.4 (0.3)	0.2 (0.3)	0.1 (0.1)
	Behavioral	0.1[6] (0.1)	0.3[6] (0.3)	0.1 (0.1)
	Mental	0.1 (0.0)	0.0 (0.0)	—
	Relational	2.6[7, 8] (2.0)	1.5[7] (1.5)	1.6[8] (1.7)
	Possessive	0.0 (0.1)	0.1 (0.1)	—
	Total	9.0[9, 10] (7.7)[12, 13]	6.4[9, 11] (6.5)[12, 14]	3.8[10, 11] (4.3)[13, 14]
Other	Material	0.1 (0.1)	0.1 (0.1)	—
	Total	0.1 (0.1)	0.1 (0.1)	—
Investigation	Material	0.3 (0.2)	0.3 (0.3)	0.3 (0.3)
	Verbal	0.2 (0.1)	0.1 (0.2)	0.2 (0.2)
	Behavioral	0.0 (0.1)	0.0 (0.1)	—
	Mental	0.0 (0.0)	—	—
	Relational	0.2 (0.2)	0.1 (0.1)	0.3 (0.3)
	Total	0.6 (0.5)	0.6 (0.6)	0.8 (0.8)
Trial	Material	0.2 (0.2)	0.1 (0.1)	0.3. (0.3)
	Verbal	0.1 (0.1)	0.1 (0.1)	0.2 (0.1)
	Behavioral	0.1 (0.1)	0.0 (0.1)	—
	Mental	0.0 (0.1)	0.0 (0.1)	—
	Relational	0.3 (0.2)	0.1 (0.2)	0.2 (0.1)
	Possessive	0.0 (0.0)	0.1 (0.1)	0.1 (0.1)
	Total	0.8 (0.7)	0.5 (0.6)	0.7 (0.5)
Present	Material	0.0 (—)	—	—
	Relational	0.2 (0.0)	0.2 (0.1)	0.1 (—)
	Possessive	0.0 (0.0)	0.0 (0.0)	—
	Total	0.2 (0.0)	0.2 (0.1)	0.1 (—)
Future	Material	0.0 (0.1)	0.0 (—)	—
	Mental	0.1 (0.1)	0.1 (0.1)	0.1 (0.1)
	Relational	0.1 (0.1)	0.1 (0.1)	0.1 (0.1)
	Total	0.2 (0.2)	0.2 (0.2)	0.1 (0.1)

Note: Differences that are statistically significant are given matching superscripts.

linguistic and discursive choices, the lawyers constructed opposing views of the roles of the victims in the events being discussed.

3.1.1 The Crime Narrative

The main difference between the two sides with regard to the victims was how frequently they referred to them in the crime narratives. Table 4.9 shows that the victims were the agents of processes during the crime significantly more frequently in the prosecution main arguments (20.0 times per 1,000 words) than in the defense arguments (15.1 times per 1,000 words). As shown in Table 4.10, the victims were also the recipients of processes during the crime more frequently in the prosecution main arguments (9.0 times per 1,000 words) than in the defense arguments (6.4 times per 1,000 words).[8,9] Additionally, because the prosecution arguments were longer on average, these results mean that the prosecution referred to the victim as either an agent or recipient more total times than the defense did. Thus, the prosecutors emphasized the victims by including more information about them, and, in some cases, repeating the same information.

As should be clear from the previous discussions, usually this did not mean that the defense simply denied the prosecution's story. Instead, they often presented alternative narratives for the victims and what they experienced/did during the time of the alleged crime, but they generally included different and less information about these stories, spent less of their arguments focused on them, and used different linguistic structures and terms than the prosecution did. They silenced or nearly silenced the information included in the prosecutions' stories.

In some of the cases, the defense went as far as silencing the victim's role in the crime narrative or at least significantly de-emphasizing it. For instance, in the defense argument in case #10, the victims (there were two) were the agents of two processes and the recipients of two processes during the crime, none of which was related at all to the sexual abuse the defendant was charged with. Instead, the processes represented the victims' reactions to the violence that the defendant had inflicted on them (but for which he was not charged at that time), as in the following example:

(20) [The defendant's violent acts] caused people to turn against him.

As discussed earlier, the lawyer also silenced the sexual nature of these acts by referring to them with generalizations (e.g., *the incidents* and *the events*) when he referred to them at all. As can be seen in example (21), the defense lawyer not only silenced the sexual nature of the events and the defendant's role in them, but also erased the victims' roles as well by not including them as the recipients of sexual material processes:

(21) If this were really going on, all these things happening over this long period of time in this household, in this small household, wouldn't the mother know it was going on?

In contrast, the prosecution emphasized the victims in the crime narrative, focusing much of their attention on the alleged sexual acts, and the victims' roles in them. In fact, one or both of the victims were the agent of a process that had occurred during the crime 21.9 times per 1,000 words (165 tokens) and the recipient of one 14.6 times per 1,000 words (110 tokens) in the prosecution argument. These high frequencies are the direct result of the prosecution consistently emphasizing what the defendant had allegedly done to the victims and how the two young women had responded. While this was partly accomplished by the lawyer referring to the same topics more than once, it was more the result of the prosecution spending much of their arguments providing explicit descriptions of the defendant's sexual acts with the victims or their body parts as the recipients, as in this example:

(22) And the third incident she described, how in the living room at the ____ residence, on the couch, the Defendant wanted to tell her about the different anatomical parts to the female anatomy, and pulling her down, of touching her over her pants in her vaginal area.

Thus, the two sides created opposing arguments by the prosecution emphasizing the sexual acts involving the victims, while the defense silenced the sexual nature of the events and the victims' roles in them.

Another case in which the defense silenced or severely de-emphasized the victims in the crime narratives was #11. In this particular case, there were six victims, and in total, they were the agents of six processes during the crime narrative and the recipient of nine more in the defense argument. In comparison, they were the agent of 224 processes and the recipient of ninety-seven in the prosecution's crime narrative. Additionally, as mentioned above, victims #1 and #2, who had experienced the most serious crimes (sexual assault, kidnapping, assault), were completely silenced in the defense's crime story. What had allegedly happened to them was not mentioned at all, even in the form of a denial. This made their stories irrelevant to what had happened to the other women for the purposes of the defense argument, even though the prosecution had made all of the crimes a series of interconnected events. When victims #3 through #6 were the agent or recipient of a process, the perpetrator was either silenced through the use of passive constructions (e.g., *was struck with a gun*) or referred to as *the man*. Thus, any link between the defendant and the victims in the context of the crime was erased.

While these particular defense lawyers represented what reportedly happened to the victims during the crime as unnecessary and unrelated to their arguments, most of the defense lawyers did include at least some references to the victims in their crime narratives. In these cases, more subtle patterns of silencing, de-emphasizing, and emphasizing were used in that the differences were not necessarily seen in how frequently the victims were referred to, but rather in terms of the process types, the specific processes, and the linguistic forms that were included during the lawyers' discursive reconstructions of the crime. These differences are particularly seen in the material, verbal, behavioral, and possessive processes involving the victim.

For both sides, when the victim was the agent or the recipient of a process, it was most often a material process, just as it had been for the defendants. However, in the prosecution arguments, the victims were more often the recipients of such processes than the agents of them (while the defendants had rarely been the recipients of them). This is, of course, not surprising given the fact the prosecution lawyers were focused on what the defendants did to the victims. What is perhaps more noteworthy is that the difference in the frequencies was actually quite small, as the prosecution also included the victims as the agents of processes quite often. Additionally, while the defense did include the victim as an agent more often than as a recipient, the difference was again minimal. Thus, the prosecution's additional focus on what was done to the victim during the crime was only a small part of how the two sides created opposing representations of reality. More important differences are the actual material processes the two sides included and how they referred to them.

The prosecution usually represented the victims as the agents of three different sets of material processes. The first group included the everyday, normal processes the victims were doing right before or as the crime was taking place (if it occurred over a period of time). For instance, in case #11, the defendant approached the victims when their cars were stopped at stoplights or in parking lots, so the prosecution included details of what the victims were doing in or around their cars (e.g., *got in her car out in the parking lot*, *was driving back from [the pharmacy]*) and/or where they were driving to when the crime occurred. In the cases involving sexual assault or abuse, the prosecution often included what the victims were doing when the sexual processes began, for example, watching a movie, changing clothes, or partying. Another set of material process included in the prosecution crime narratives represented what the victims did to resist the criminal acts. For instance, in case #17, the defendant had stabbed two men, one of whom died. The prosecution admitted that the victims fought back to defend themselves, as in the following example, which describes the murder victim's actions:

(23) He pushed the defendant, having asked him repeatedly to leave. He eventually did hit the defendant.

The final class of material processes the prosecution lawyers included for some of the victims during the crime narratives described the ways in which the victims tried to escape from the defendants. An example of this can be seen in (24) from case #11. In this excerpt the prosecution describes how the victim escaped her kidnapper after he drove her into a river.

(24) She was in the back seat, was able to get herself out of the car, as she said, swim through the icy water, out of the car and climb up the bank to safety.

Thus, while on the surface it is perhaps surprising that the prosecution lawyers included the victims as the agents of many processes during the crime, this is not because they represented the victims as willing or even active participants in it. Instead, the prosecution lawyers were simply providing the background details necessary for understanding how the crime occurred and describing the victim's reactions to the defendants' criminal behaviors.

When the prosecution lawyers described the actual criminal acts, the victims were often the recipients of processes rather than the agents of them. Two examples, one from case #2 and one from case #11, can be seen here.

(25) He started hitting Mr. Harrison, and then he had put the knife back on his belt and started hitting Mr. Harrison.

(26) . . . while he raped her, placed her in the trunk and led her to believe, as she indicated to you many times, that she thought she was going to be killed throughout that evening. That the defendant picked her up, demanded her property, took the property from her.

The one exception to this pattern was actually in the sexual assault/abuse cases in which the victim's body parts were the recipients instead of the victims' themselves. Thus, the victims were the agents of possessive processes, while their bodies were the recipients of the defendants' sexual material processes.

The defense lawyers in these cases silenced or de-emphasized the processes that the prosecution included, even though they also referred to the victims as the agents and the recipients of material processes at a relatively high frequency. The specific material processes they included varied, depending on whether or not the defense admitted that the basic events in question occurred or if they argued that the victim invented the entire story.

In seven of the seventeen cases in the corpus, the defense agreed with the prosecution that something had occurred, but they explained it in such ways that the defendant was not legally responsible. Obviously, the specific strategy the lawyers used in these cases affected how frequently the victim was referred to as an agent or recipient of different processes and process types and the linguistic forms the lawyers selected.

In case #6, for example, both sides agreed that the victim had been shaken, but in the defense argument, the shaking had only occurred after she had fallen, an event that the prosecution both de-emphasized and negated. Also, the defense said that the shaking was not done in anger as the prosecution had claimed but to try to help the victim. Importantly, though, because both sides agreed that the shaking had occurred, the victim was the recipient of material actions frequently in both cases. In case #7, the defense admitted that the defendant had done the sexual acts described by the prosecution, but they claimed that the victim was an active and willing participant, so they included her as the agent rather than the recipient of many of the processes. In case #17, the defense argued that the defendant was acting in self-defense because the victims were attacking him. Thus, the defense included the victims as the agent of more material processes during the crime than the prosecution did (12.2 per 1,000 words in the defense's argument, compared to 8.4 for the prosecution's). In fact, the defense lawyer frequently included the victims as the agents of violent material processes with the defendant as the recipient, as in the following excerpt:

(27) He starts that fight by shoving Beardsley over and over all the way to the ground and beating him. . . . This case is about Jim Mound leaving that home enraged and going out to confront and to beat Beardsley.

Interestingly, the defense used the verb *beat* with the victim as the agent fifteen times in their argument. The prosecution never used this term in their original argument, used it twice with the victim as the agent in their rebuttal (although they negated it), and used it once with the victim as the recipient. Thus, the defense emphasized this term while the prosecution mostly silenced it.

In four cases, the defense agreed with the prosecution that a crime was committed, but they argued that someone other than the defendant was the perpetrator. As a result, the prosecution and the defense both included the victims as the recipients of many violent or otherwise illegal processes, but the agents in each argument were different. For example, in case #13, both sides included the victim as the recipient of such verbs as *punch*, *shove*, and *throw*. The prosecution simply emphasized the punch by referring to it repeatedly, as that was what they said killed him, but the defense de-emphasized that particular process, which they argued was not the fatal blow.

A related but different pattern occurred in two other cases in that the defense also admitted that the victim had been injured, but they claimed that a completely different event caused this to happen. First, when the prosecution in case #5 had claimed that the defendant had attacked the victim after a soccer game, the defense denied there was a physical altercation and argued that the victim had suffered the injuries during the game itself. The victim was therefore the recipient of fewer processes in their argument because they de-emphasized the fight. Second, the prosecution in case #4 said the defendant caused the victim's injuries by beating her. The defense said that she got the injuries by falling from a roof. They described how she got to the roof and what she did there in the example.

(28) She got the extension ladder and leaned the extension ladder up against the shed. . . . She leaned the ladder against that, the extension ladder stuck up above the roof of the shed. She crawled up there, got off of the ladder, flipped the lid off of the stovepipe and then went back to get onto the ladder.

Because the victim in this case was responsible for her own injuries, according to the defense, she was the agent of significantly more material processes in their argument than in the prosecution's (19.1 times per 1,000 words in the defense argument, 2.1 times per 1,000 words in the prosecution argument). To put it another way, the defense emphasized her agency while the prosecution de-emphasized it.

Because the lawyers in the nine cases just discussed presented a crime narrative that shared many similarities with the prosecutions', both the defense and the prosecution in these cases included the victims as the agents and recipients of many material processes. The contrasting representations of reality were in the details of the described events (e.g., the identity of the agent of the processes, the amount of agency given to the victim). However, in the other eight cases in the corpus, the defense did not admit that the events in question had occurred. There were three patterns that the defense arguments in these cases fell into. The first was that the attorney de-emphasized the crime narrative and therefore denied it through omission. This was discussed earlier for cases #10 and #11, and the result for the victim was that their related material processes were silenced as well. The second pattern was that the defense negated the prosecution's crime narrative, repeating some of the victim's processes from the prosecution's story but with a negative marker in the clause. However, this was a rare strategy, as it only occurred twice in the seventeen-case corpus. The final strategy, which was slightly more common, was for the defense lawyers to present an alternative story about what occurred during the time when the crime had supposedly taken place. In these arguments, the defense still referenced the victims as agents and recipients of some material processes, just fewer and different ones than the prosecution did.

The two cases in which the defense negated the prosecution's narrative, both of which involved the sexual abuse of a child, followed a very different pattern than any of the other cases in the corpus in that the defense included some of the prosecution's details of the alleged crime. In one of the cases, #16, the defense was able to deny the charges because in some interviews, the victim had stated that it did not occur. The defense emphasized these interviews while the prosecution emphasized the ones in which he said it did. As a result, in their crime story, the defense included the victim as the recipient of material processes and the defendant as the agent at roughly the same rate as the prosecution did (7.1 times per 1,000 words for the defense, compared to 6.4 times per 1,000 words for the prosecution), although mostly these constructions had negated verbs. However, the defense silenced the expert testimony about why the victim, a four-year-old, may have said that the events did not happen when they actually did. As a result of this pattern, not only did the defense in that case emphasize their negation by emphasizing the words *not* and *no*, but they used silencing to ignore contradictory evidence.

In the other case involving significant negation, case #8, the defense attorney used his crime narrative to argue that the victim had not done a certain material process she had testified about and therefore was not a credible witness. Specifically, the victim had claimed that the sexual assault had occurred after she and the defendant had returned from a late night bike ride. The defense attorney spent a significant portion of his argument arguing that that it was impossible that the bike ride had occurred, and then he used this conclusion as evidence that all of the subsequent events had also not happened.

> (29) Eight-year-old girls do not go bike riding at one o'clock in the morning in the rain in a cemetery in the dead of winter. . . . If [they] didn't go bike riding in the rain at one o'clock in the morning in the middle of winter, then they didn't get wet, and if they didn't get wet, they didn't come home and change their clothes, and if they didn't come home to change their clothes, Mr. Hoff didn't start rubbing her back as Stephanie tried to sleep downstairs on the couch, and if that didn't happen, then none of it happened.

The presumption was that if the victim did not tell the truth about one event, she must have created the entire story. Because of this increased focus on the victim's crime story, the defense lawyer included the victim as the agent of a process more than was average (but still less than the prosecution did). More important, he emphasized his negation of the events she included in her version of the crime.

Additionally, when compared to the prosecution, the defense attorney also emphasized his personal negative evaluation of the victim's claims by repeatedly referring to them as *unbelievable*, *ludicrous*, and *impossible*, as in this excerpt, which occurred at the start of the defense argument (after only ten clauses):

> (30) I feel compelled to change that statement from unbelievable to impossible. It is impossible for the State's case to be true. I'm going to repeat that: It is impossible. It is not possible for the story that you have heard from Stephanie Bogosian to be true.

As can be seen in this example, the lawyer even mentioned in his metadiscourse that he was being repetitive, and he ultimately used the word *impossible* twelve times, *not possible* twice, *unbelievable* seven times, and *silly* and *ludicrous* once each. By doing so, he emphasized his own thoughts about the crime story. The prosecution attorney silenced the concept of possibility/impossibility in her main argument and de-emphasized it in her rebuttal, as she only referred to these types of adjectives (*not unbelievable*, *not silly*, *not impossible*, *believable*) four times. Therefore, even though the patterns of silencing, de-emphasizing, and emphasizing when it came to the victim in this case were different from those in most of the other cases in the corpus, they still played a significant role in the construction of the two side's contrasting crime narratives.

There were four cases that utilized the third strategy in that the defense presented an alternative story about non-criminal events that they claimed occurred when the crime was supposed to have taken place. This strategy was used in cases where there was no physical evidence and the prosecution had to rely on the testimony of the victims and the witnesses who supported them. The pattern across these cases is that because the defense lawyers denied that the crime occurred, they included the victim as either a recipient or an agent of a process much less frequently than in the prosecution did and so de-emphasized him/her.

The alternative crime stories tended to center around the victim, the defendant, and others participating in alternative events that would have made the illegal acts impossible or unlikely. In some stories, the victim and/or defendant had been with people who had testified that they had not seen anything criminal occur. The inference was that since those people had said that the crime did not occur, then it did not happen, despite the victim's claims otherwise. Such an argument relied on whose testimony the jurors believed.

In other cases, the additional material processes that the defense included for the victims were actions that the lawyers presumed and implied were not typical behaviors of victims. For instance, these included events in which the victim possibly could have reported the crime but did not.

Case #12 is an example of this type. This case, which was discussed in detail in Felton Rosulek (2008), involved a stepdaughter who claimed that the defendant sexually abused her over a twelve-month period. During the closing arguments, the defense, compared to the prosecution, de-emphasized the victim's material processes during the time of the alleged crime. Specifically, in the prosecution's argument, the victim was the agent of material processes 8.9 times per 1,000 words, while in the defense argument, she was only in this role 2.2 times per 1,000 words. As was expected, the prosecution included many sexual acts that the defendant forced the victim to do, what she was doing when he would approach her for sex, and how she tried to make him stop. In order to cast doubt on the victim, the defense silenced details of the abuse and instead referenced the victim as the agent of material processes that they presumed are typical of non-abused children. Some of these processes can be seen in the following list:

(31) acted like a normal child, was getting passing grades, was maintaining good relationships, was going to movies, was associating with boys, went out with boys in groups, showed no negative behaviors

They also included her as the agent of negated processes to discuss what the victim didn't do, which she, according to them, would have done if she had truly been a victim. For example, she *wasn't flunking any classes*. The prosecution did not include any of these processes.

A linguistic choice used to accomplish this same function was to state what the victim did or did not do in the form of a question as in the following excerpt:

(32) Why did she stay in the store for ten minutes? Why didn't she back off and run away right at the beginning?

The lawyers created a "fictive dialogue" (Pascual 2006) with the jurors, inferring that this is question that they were supposed to respond to. The either implied or stated answer to the questions was that the victim was not a victim because she did not do certain actions.[10]

Differing patterns for topics involving the victim in relation to material processes does not explain all the differences between the prosecution and defense crime narratives, although it does account for a great deal of them. A more nuanced understanding requires an examination of how the lawyers' linguistic choices to refer to the material processes also contributed to the creation of opposing representations. Specifically, when the lawyers happened to refer to the victim being involved in the same material process during the crime, they silenced, de-emphasized, or emphasized different aspects of it through their lexical selections.

When, as discussed in the previous chapter, the prosecution included the defendant as the agent of specific illegal processes but the defense used generalizations, this meant that the victims were the recipients of these different sets of verbs. For example, in case #12, the prosecution went into extreme detail about the sexual nature of the defendant's actions. The following is the most detailed the defense got:

(33) She testified a few days ago that my client sexually touched her.

This silenced the details of what occurred and the exact nature of the sexual touching, including what body parts were involved, how much penetration occurred, how each reacted to it, and what other actions were involved, all topics the prosecution emphasized.

Another pattern was for the two sides to simply select words with different semantic features. For example, in case #13, the prosecution de-emphasized the violence of Boy #2 who was not charged by saying that the he *shoved* or *pushed* the victim. The defense, on the other hand, as part of their strategy of blaming Boy #2 for the actual fatal act, emphasized the idea that he caused the victim to leave the ground, using the verb *throw* fifteen times with the victim as the recipient and also using the verb phrase *pick* [the victim] *up like a rag doll*. The prosecution silenced this aspect of the event. Then, during the rebuttal, the prosecution used the verb *pound on* with the defendant as the agent and the victim as the recipient (instead of *hit* or *assault*, which both sides had been previously using) to foreground the violence the victim suffered. While these are just a few examples from one case, they demonstrate how a larger pattern of opposing lexical choices were used for the purposes of silencing, emphasizing, and de-emphasizing certain pieces of information.

The fact that the lawyers for the opposing sides use different verbs is not a new finding (e.g., Drew 1985; Eades 2006), although it had not been analyzed in detail in closing arguments. What is new here is that the quantitative results show that the opposing lawyers tended to never or only rarely use the terms the other side used. By doing so, they silenced properties of the events that the other side included and sometimes even emphasized. Thus, lexical selection helped dictate how reality was constructed by determining what features of events were excluded and what level of importance was given to included information.

Syntax was also used for these same purposes. When the defense used nominalizations and de-activations (e.g., *the abuse*, *the incident*) to refer to the illegal event, this silenced the victim as the recipient of the defendant's act as well as the defendant's responsibility. The same things were also accomplished through the defense lawyers' use of intransitive constructions when the defendant was the agent. For instance, in case #17, the defense de-emphasized the fact the victim was stabbed by the defendant by repeatedly not including him as the recipient of the defendant's material processes, as in the following example:

(34) He starts lashing out with that knife.

The victims were injured by this act of the defendant, but this detail was ignored. While these linguistic patterns were not as frequent as the two sides simply discussing completely different events, the important finding is that when the lawyers agreed on the basic series of events that took place, they still differed in what information about them they silenced, de-emphasized, and emphasized. This is directly in line with what others such as Ehrlich (2001) have found when studying other genres that occur during court proceedings.

In addition to these differences in reference to material processes involving the victims, other significant differences between the two sides in the crime narrative were the result of the prosecution including the victim as the agent of more verbal behavioral and possessive processes than the defense did. The victims' verbal processes in the prosecution's crime narratives included what they said to the assailant to try to stop him or her or how the victim asked others for help during the crime. For example, in case #10, the victim told the defendant that she was stopping the abuse:

(35) She told him that this relationship, that she was going to stop the abusive elements in this relationship.

The defense lawyers would have had to admit the crime took place for them to include what the victim said during the crime in their narratives, so they silenced these verbal actions. The behavioral processes the prosecution included were such processes as such as *crying* and *hurting* as a result of the crime. Again, as the defense usually denied the crime occurred, they ignored these processes that the victim experienced as a result of it. Finally, examples of things possessed by the victims in the prosecution crime stories included body parts, lives, injuries, stories, friends, and family members. One explanation for the prosecution presenting the victim as the agent of more possessive processes is that during the cases involving sexual abuse, the lawyers often described the abuse as happening to the victim's body parts rather than to the victim as a whole. An example of this is:

(36) The defendant put his finger in her vagina after applying a clear gel.

This distanced the victim from the abuse, but it also allowed more details to be included. As child sexual abuse is a difficult subject, perhaps the lawyers were making it easier for the jurors to think about it by distancing the child from the sexual acts. Regardless of the reason that the prosecution lawyers used such terms, it is the reason that they included the victim as the agent of possessive processes during the crime more frequently.

The final significant difference between the prosecution and the defense with regard to the crime narrative is in the frequency at which the victim was the recipient of a behavioral process. The defense included the victims in this role significantly more frequently than the prosecution did. Often the construction in the defense case was *see [the victim]* where the defense was claiming that the event could not have happened because a witness could see the victim but did not see the crime. For example, in the following excerpt from case #9, one of the sexual abuse cases, the defendant's mother claimed that she could see the victim when camping with her and the defendant. She claimed that she did not see any abuse:

(37) She can see Nicole when the curtain is pulled. She's there, and she says that his arm never comes down, never touches Nicki.

The prosecution silenced this incident and the defendant's mother's testimony so they did not have this example of the victim as a recipient of a behavioral process. Similar patterns to this occurred frequently enough across the cases that this became a significant way for the two sides to create opposing narratives through the inclusion of very different information.

Overall, these results show that the prosecution's crime narratives, because they were discussing the effects of the crime on the victims, included more of the victim's material, verbal, behavioral, and possessive processes. The defense, by silencing the alleged criminal acts, did not include the related processes of the victims in their crime narratives and thus referred to the victims in the context of the crime less frequently and silenced much of the prosecution attorneys' narratives.

3.1.2 The Investigation and Trial Narratives

When both the prosecution and the defense lawyers referenced the victims in their arguments, it was most often in the context of the crime. However, their participation in the investigation and the trial was also discussed as well. Interestingly, the lawyers tended to emphasize the victims' roles in the trial more than in the investigation, despite doing the opposite for the defendants. There are two reasons for this. One is that the investigations mostly involved the police observing the defendant and examining him or her. The victim only had to give a statement or two and then his or her job was done. Therefore, the investigations actually had less to do with the victims than the defendants. The other explanation is that most of the victims testified during the trials while the defendants did not. Their active role in this context provided content, particularly verbal processes, to include in the lawyers' narratives. The prosecutions then tended to use the victims' behaviors and statements during their testimony as evidence for their believability and as support for the lawyers' claims about what happened during the crime. The defense lawyers, on the other hand, highlighted the statements that the victims made that changed between the investigation and the trial and the statements they made that agreed with the defense's claims. This was especially relevant in cases #3 and #4, since in both cases, the victims recanted their stories while on the stand. As could be expected, this was something the defense emphasized and the prosecution silenced or de-emphasized. These differences between the opposing sides are not seen in the quantitative data but were revealed through a close qualitative analysis.

In many cases, the defense ignored the victim's testimony, but if the defense could attack the victim and his or her testimony, they did. As a result, in these cases, the two sides focused on different statements the victim made. The prosecution silenced controversial or contradictory testimony while the defense focused on it. Case #17 provides an interesting example of this. As was discussed previously, in this case, one victim was killed and the other injured. However, the assault victim, as a drug addict and convicted felon, was not particularly believable. Additionally, the prosecution de-emphasized him to counter the defense claim that the defendant had been defending himself against two men working together. These factors conspired together to mean that the defense referred to the verbal processes of the victim during the investigation and the trial significantly more frequently than the prosecution did. In fact, the prosecution silenced the victim's verbal processes in the investigation, while the defense included them 1.8 times per 1,000 words. The defense also constructed the victim as the agent of verbal processes during the trial 5.1 times per 1,000 words, while the prosecution de-emphasized him in this role, almost to the point of silencing him as (0.2 reference per 1,000 words). Specifically, the defense included his verbal processes to emphasize that he lied during both the investigation and the trial, as in the following example:

(38) So what that he lied to you, the most important witness in this case, who saw what happened, and so what that he lied to you? So what that he lied to the police about what happened? He sat before you and he claimed that he did not smoke any crack cocaine that day and that he didn't know if anybody else smoked it.

The prosecution silenced his verbal processes and thus his lies in their investigation narrative. They did admit that he lied during the trial, but they ignored what he had specifically said. They simply redefined it as unimportant:

(39) Nothing that Jonathan Hill testified about with respect to the incident itself relies on Jonathan Hill's testimony.

Thus, they silenced his untrue testimony that the defense had emphasized. As a result of these differences, the prosecution and the defense created distinctly different versions of the investigation and trial narratives.

In other cases, both sides discussed the same testimony, and this resulted in contrasting linguistic patterns to describe the same verbal actions. For example, in case #8, the defense claimed that the victim fabricated her allegations of abuse against the defense. They referred to her claims and testimony as a *story* twenty times and as her *testimony* only twice. They described what she said happened as *unbelievable*, as discussed earlier and as seen in this example:

(40) I told you that after you heard Stephanie Bogosian's story, you were going to be left with no choice but to find it unbelievable. . . . It is not possible for the story that you have heard from Stephanie Bogosion to be true.

The prosecution never once referred to it as a *story* or anything similar and labeled it her *testimony* six times. While *story* is not necessarily a negative term, their emphasis of it by repeating it so often, as well as their frequent use of negative adjectives, makes it appear to be a condemnation of what she said as being fictional. The prosecution silenced this possibility by using positive adjectives, not using the word *story*, and not addressing the defense's doubts, except for once in a quick sentence in their rebuttal.

Another noteworthy pattern in this case is that while both sides used verbs such as *say* or *testify* with the victim as the agent, the prosecution also used mental verbs such as *know* when discussing what she had claimed on the stand. This can be seen here:

(41) She knew two things: She knew it happened when she was in third grade, which would have started in _____ of ____, and she knew it happened in her house.

The defense never used this verb, though they did cast her as the agent of the verb *thought* when discussing what she had said to an investigator. These contrasting verbs again allowed the two sides to both discuss verbal processes, but the prosecution emphasized the victim's high level of conviction in her accuracy.

Returning to the corpus as a whole, another important difference between the prosecution and the defense in the investigation and trial narratives is that the prosecution included the victims' material actions significantly more frequently than the defense did (1.9 times per 1,000 words for the prosecution and 0.4 times per 1,000 words for the defense). This often was the result of the prosecution referring to the victims' actions that could be used as evidence that they were being honest. An example is in (42) from case #1. The lawyer assumed that looking people in the eye is proof that someone is telling the truth, so he included that the victim did this in his narrative.

(42) She looked you in the eye.

The defense in this case, as they did in most cases, silenced these acts unless the victim had behaved in an attackable manner. Thus, silencing, de-emphasizing, and emphasizing were again significant means for the two sides to use to create opposing representations of the same events.

3.1.3 Narratives from Other Contexts

A final result revealed in Tables 4.9 and 4.10 is that the defense included the victim as the agent of processes in narratives from outside the context of the case at hand significantly more frequently than the prosecution did. However, compared to the other narratives, these were rare. Interestingly, the prosecution constructed the defendant as the agent of significantly more outside processes than the defense did, and here the pattern was reversed. This means that both sides included more stories not directly related to the crime and trial for the person they did not want the jurors to believe. They did this in order to give the jurors more reasons to not trust him or her or why another explanation for the evidence was possible. For instance, in case #4, the defense claimed that the victim got her injuries from an accident she had while she was drunk, instead of from being beaten by her boyfriend, as the prosecution claimed. The defense included in their closing arguments stories about other previous times in which the victim had injured herself while intoxicated. They discussed these so that they could make parallels to their version of the crime narrative. Since this story was irrelevant to the prosecution's case, they silenced it.

3.1.4 Summary

To conclude, the differences in how the prosecution and the defense referred to the victims' processes allowed them to create very different representations of reality. Through their choices of what types of processes to include, the specific processes they referred to, and the linguistic means through which they depicted them, the lawyers systematically silenced, de-emphasized, and emphasized different information and events. This happened in every single case, just as it had for the defendants.

3.2 THREE CASES IN DETAIL

The previous discussion demonstrated the importance of silencing, de-emphasizing, and emphasizing in the corpus as a whole. The following analysis of three cases demonstrates how these processes were realized in individual cases.

3.2.1 Case #3

In case #3, according to the prosecution, the victim was beaten by her boyfriend after he caught her in bed with another man. The defense presented an alternative narrative that she was really beaten by this other man. The linguistic analysis reveals that each side generally included the victim as the agent and the recipient of the same types of processes. However, they silenced the specific processes included by the other side and replaced them with others to create opposing arguments.

Table 4.11 shows that the prosecution referred to the victim as the agent of processes during crime more frequently than the defense did, but the difference was not statistically significant.[11] Additionally, as is shown in Table 4.12, although the prosecution referenced processes with the victim as the recipient in the crime narrative more frequently than the defense did (7.0 times per 1,000 words for the prosecution, 5.0 times per 1,000 words for the defense), the difference was not significant. Table 4.11 also shows that the defense, unlike in the corpus as a whole, included more of the victim's processes that occurred during the investigation, while the prosecution focused more on those that occurred during the trial.

As mentioned above, the prosecution discussed the victim's processes during the crime more than the defense did. The first reason for this was that the prosecution constructed the victim as the agent of verbal processes in this context significantly more frequently (3.4 times per 1,000 words compared to 0.8 times per 1,000 words). One major difference was that the prosecution repeated nine times that the victim called for her son and her friend for help (instead of the defendant) while the defense only mentioned this twice. For the prosecution, the fact that she did this was evidence that it was the defendant who was attacking her. The defense, however, redefined it to argue that because she had called for those people, they had concluded the defendant was guilty (which made them biased). Thus, the prosecution emphasizing this verbal action more than the defense did and the two sides redefining the meaning of this action allowed them to create opposing representations of this event.

TABLE 4.11

Distribution of Processes with the Victim in Case #3 as the Agent

		Prosecution	Defense	Rebuttal
Crime	Material	4.8	4.4	1.1
	Verbal	3.4[1]	0.8[1]	—
	Behavioral	1.0	0.8	—
	Mental	1.0	1.7	—
	Quality	2.2	2.3	2.2
	Location	0.3	1.7	—
	Possessive	3.9	2.5	—
	Total	16.7[2]	14.1[3]	3.3[2, 3]
Investigation	Material	0.7	—[4]	2.2[4]
	Verbal	1.5	1.5	—
	Mental	—[5]	1.7[5]	—
	Quality	—[6]	1.7[6]	—
	Possessive	—	0.8	—
	Total	2.2[7]	6.0[7]	2.2
Trial	Material	1.4[8]	—[8]	—
	Verbal	0.5	1.0	—
	Behavioral	0.3	—	—
	Mental	0.7	0.6	—
	Quality	—	0.2	—
	Possessive	0.3	1.2	—
	Total	3.2	3.3	—

Note: Differences that are statistically significant are given matching superscripts.

While the prosecution generally emphasized the victim's roles in the crime more than the defense did, the defense did refer to her as the agent of locative processes significantly more frequently. The prosecution had argued that the victim's son had seen his mother before she went in the bedroom with the defendant. The son had testified that she did not appear to have been beaten at that time, thus negating the defense's argument that another man had attacked her before the defendant had arrived. The defense emphasized the victim's specific location during this event to claim that she was too far away and in a shadowed area so the son did not have a clear view. She could have been beaten already, and he would not have known. Thus, her location was an important issue to them. The prosecution de-emphasized her location, only saying that the son pointed to a location on a diagram of the house and said that that was where his mother was. This is just more evidence that the two sides' crime narratives differed with respect to the victim because the two sides emphasized different issues and redefined them to fit their case.

The two sides created significantly different investigation narratives because the defense emphasized the victim's role in it more, and the two sides

TABLE 4.12

Distribution of Processes with the Victim in Case #3 as the Recipient

		Prosecution	Defense	Rebuttal
Crime	Material	6.8[1]	5.0	—[1]
	Verbal	0.7	—	—
	Behavioral	—	0.6	—
	Mental	0.2	—	—
	Relational	1.2	0.6	—
	Total	8.8[2]	6.2	—[2]
Other	Material	0.5	—	—
	Total	0.5	—	—
Investigation	Material	0.2	0.8	—
	Behavioral	—	0.2	—
	Total	0.2	1.0	—
Trial	Material	0.3	—	—
	Verbal	0.2	—	—
	Total	0.5	—	—
Future	Mental	—	0.2	—
	Relational	0.2	—	—
	Total	0.2	0.2	—

Note: Differences that are statistically significant are given matching superscripts.

included different topics. The prosecution discussed how she went to the hospital and how she and the defendant did not help look for the other man who had allegedly attacked her. The prosecution also included two incidents in which the victim *confided* in two different friends that the defendant had beaten her. The defense silenced all of these topics. Instead, they argued that she *gave numerous conflicting statements* during the investigation. Because of this focus, they emphasized her mental processes and her qualities in this context. For instance, the defense said the victim was *extremely intoxicated* and *was incoherent* during the first part of the investigation. Then, they said that when she *was not intoxicated*, she denied the defendant beat her in a letter she wrote to the judge. These changing states were important to the defense because they were claiming that they caused her to make the different statements. The prosecution ignored these topics because they silenced her sober statements entirely. They never included the fact that she changed her story in their argument and this led to them referring to her less often in the investigation story. Finally, the prosecution referred to the victim as the agent of material actions during the trial, but the defense silenced them. The prosecution included how she behaved on the witness stand and how this indicated that she was scared of the defendant:

(43) I asked her to identify the defendant. She wouldn't look. I had to say is he the man that's sitting on my left? And she nodded. She wouldn't even look at him.

The prosecution used these material processes as evidence of her fear, and they argued that it caused her to lie on the stand. The defense silenced these material processes and focused on her testimony that the defendant had not assaulted her.

In conclusion, in this case, both sides silenced the topics discussed by the other side as a means of creating opposing arguments. The two sides created arguments that were about entirely different events. While redefinition was used as a discursive strategy to represent reality differently, silencing was the consistent pattern across the different narratives and the victim's processes included in them.

3.2.2 Case #6

Case #6 was the shaken baby case in which the victim died. This had a significant impact on the closing arguments in that for both the prosecution and the defense, their references to the victim were almost completely limited to the crime narrative. They could talk about her parents and what the victim couldn't do during the trial, the present, and the future (because she was no longer alive), but this was an insignificant portion of the argument quantitatively (though not necessarily emotionally). Since both sides admitted that the defendant shook the victim, the differences between the two sides really was caused by what the defense said the victim was doing right before the shaking occurred and how frequently the prosecution referred to the effects of the shaking on the victim.

The quantitative effects of these differences can be seen in the frequencies presented in Tables 4.13 and 4.14. In the crime narratives, there was a significant difference between the prosecution and the defense in how frequently the victim was an agent (16.8 times/1,000 words in the prosecution main argument, 9.1 times/1,000 words in the defense argument) and as a recipient (6.7 times/1,000 words in the prosecution main argument, 4.4 times/1,000 words in the defense argument). In other words, the prosecution emphasized the victim, both what happened to her and how she reacted, more than the defense did. Unlike in the corpus as a whole, the prosecution referenced the victim, as either an agent or a recipient, more in the crime narrative than they referenced the defendant. Also, the defense referred to the defendant more than the victim in this narrative, but in the corpus, the frequencies were roughly equal for the two social actors. In other words, in this particular case, the prosecution emphasized the victim and the violence she experienced more than the defendant and what she did, and the defense attorney focused on how the defendant reacted to the situation. To put it yet another way, the prosecution put a toddler, a very sympathetic victim, in the foreground more in this case than in many of the others and more than the defense did.

The first significant difference between the prosecution and the defense is that the prosecution included the victim as the agent of significantly more

TABLE 4.13

Distribution of Processes with the Victim in Case #6 as the Agent

		Prosecution	Defense	Rebuttal
Crime	Material	1.3	1.5	2.7
	Behavioral	7.8[1]	4.7[1]	1.8
	Mental	0.5	0.1	—
	Quality	0.9	0.6	—
	Location	—	0.5	—
	Possessive	6.3[2, 2]	1.6[2]	—[3]
	Total	16.8[4, 5]	9.1[4]	4.5[5]
Other	Material	0.3	0.7	—
	Total	0.3	0.7	—
Investigation	Possessive	0.5	0.2	—
	Total	0.5	0.2	—
Trial	Verbal	0.1	—	—
	Possessive	0.2	—	—
	Total	0.3	—	—
Present	Possessive	0.1	0.1	—
	Total	0.1	0.1	—
Future	Possessive	0.1	—	—
	Total	0.1	—	—

Note: Differences that are statistically significant are given matching superscripts.

behavioral processes during the crime than the defense did (7.8 times/1,000 words compared to 4.7 times/1,000 words). Despite the high frequency at which these types of processes were referred to, the actual verbs used were relatively small and mostly overlapped between the two sides (e.g., *fall*, *cry*, *die*, *suffer*, etc.). The key difference between the two sides was that the prosecution emphasized two verbs that the defense de-emphasized: *suffer* (using it as the verb thirteen times, while the defense used it only once) and *die* (using

TABLE 4.14

Distribution of Processes with the Victim in Case #6 as the Recipient

		Prosecution	Defense	Rebuttal
Crime	Material	5.0	4.2	4.5
	Relational	1.8[1]	0.1[1]	0.9
	Total	6.7	4.4	5.4
Investigation	Material	0.6	—	—
	Behavioral	0.2	0.1	—
	Total	0.8	0.1	—
Future	Material	0.2	—	—
	Total	0.2	—	—

Note: Differences that are statistically significant are given matching superscripts.

it eleven times, while the defense again used it once). By repeating these two particular processes, the prosecution emphasized the catastrophic impact the events had on the victim, while the defense de-emphasized and almost silenced them.

Interestingly, in this case, the prosecution directly attacked the defense argument that the victim had fallen and that the fall had caused her death. Even though both sides referred to this same topic, the difference was that over half of the prosecution references to her falling included the adverb *backwards*, a word the defense silenced. The reason for this was that in the victim's original statements she had said *backwards*, but this was not the version the defense brought to the trial. The prosecution used her quotations as objects and evidence of her changing story, and thus included the verb *fall*. In contrast, the defense re-created her story about the child falling as their own crime narrative. The frequency at which each side used the term *backwards* is quantitative evidence of how the two sides differed with respect to the defendant's statements about the victim.

Another difference between the two sides that the quantitative results revealed is that the prosecution included the victim as the agent of possessive processes much more frequently (6.3 times/1,000 words compared to 1.9 times/1,000 words). One reason for this was the prosecution's repetition of the phrase *Serena Hu's death* twenty times. Through this repetition, they emphasized the outcome of the criminal events and what had ultimately happened to the victim. The defense only referred to this event, *her death*, once, and in doing so, they de-emphasized it, just as they had done by not including the victim as the agent of the verb *die*. Furthermore, the prosecution continued to emphasize the victim's injuries, referring to *her head*, *her brain*, *her neck* more frequently than the defense did.

Additionally, the prosecution included the victim as the recipient of more processes, specifically material and relational ones. In terms of material processes, the prosecution included her as the recipient of the verb *kill* six times, while the defense did not. Again, this was a means through which the prosecution emphasized the fact the child had died at the hands of the victim. The prosecution also included the victim as the agent of *shake* more often than the defense did, although both included it, and as discussed in the previous chapter, the prosecution included more adverbs and prepositional phrases stressing the violence with which the shaking was done. As a reminder of that analysis, the defense did address the prosecution's claim that the shaking was violent, although they de-emphasized it by discussing it for only a few clauses, and they silenced the length of time the shaking lasted.

The final numerical difference between the two sides occurs in the frequencies for the victim's relational processes. This is a result of two patterns. First, the prosecution included the fact that the defendant was *alone with* the victim, but the defense silenced this. The second pattern is that the prosecution repeatedly quoted the law that the charges required the defendant *to have intentionally inflicted bodily harm upon* the victim. Because of the way the legalese is structured, the victim was the recipient of a relational process rather than a material process for these statements. However, the importance of this finding is still that the prosecution emphasized how the defendant herself caused the victim to be injured, while the defense de-emphasized this and focused on how a fall had caused the injuries. Neither side denied that she was injured, they just differed in terms of who/what caused it, and this was reflected in their linguistic and discursive patterns.

As in the other cases, the quantitative results do not tell the whole story of how the two sides constructed opposing representations of the same events. For example, there was only an insignificant difference in the frequencies for the two sides' material processes with the victim as the agent. However, they included very different terms. The defense described the victim as the agent of *climb*, *pull herself up*, *stand*, and *get out* because they were claiming that she, as a precocious toddler, climbed into her chair and fell. The prosecution silenced these terms and instead had the victim as the agent of *struggle*, *try*, and *get away* as they described how the victim was scared of the defendant and made the defendant upset by not wanting to be held by her. Thus, what the numbers do not reveal is that while both sides included the victim as the agent of material processes, they described very different events and silenced those discussed by the other side's.

Overall, the differences between the prosecution and the defense case when it came to the inclusion of the victim were relatively subtle. The prosecution emphasized her more, while also emphasizing the violence that occurred and her ultimate death from it. The defense acknowledged that she was injured and died, but they de-emphasized it. They also set up a backstory for how it occurred. What was also interesting about this case is that both sides acknowledged the other's claims, although they de-emphasized them overall by spending only a very small percentage of their arguments discussing them. This is a perfect example of how a majority of the lawyers' strategies for creating an opposing view of reality were silencing, de-emphasizing, and emphasizing topics in a contrasting pattern to the other side.

3.2.3 Case #7

Case #7 was the "he said–she said" sexual assault case. The prosecution claimed that the victim was asleep during the sexual encounter. The defense argued that she was awake and an active participant. The differences resulted in significant contrasts in the frequencies of reference during the crime narrative.

As can be seen in Tables 4.15 and 4.16, the victim was the agent of processes during the crime and during the trial much more frequently in the

TABLE 4.15

Distribution of Processes with the Victim in Case #7 as the Agent

		Prosecution	Defense	Rebuttal
Crime	Material	5.2[1]	20.3[1, 2]	3.4[2]
	Verbal	2.6	5.2	3.4
	Behavioral	3.9	4.4	—
	Mental	3.2	6.3	3.4
	Quality	3.9	4.7	—
	Location	0.9	0.8	—
	Possessive	11.4	12.1	5.0
	Existential	—	0.3	—
	Total	30.9[3]	54.0[3, 4]	15.1[4]
Investigation	Material	1.7	1.4	1.7
	Verbal	30	1.4	3.4
	Mental	1.7	0.8[5]	5.0[5]
	Quality	0.2	—[6]	1.7[6]
	Possessive	1.3	1.4	—
	Total	7.9	4.9	11.7
Trial	Material	2.1	0.5	—
	Verbal	5.4	9.6	1.7
	Behavioral	—	—	—
	Mental	0.9[7]	3.3[7]	—
	Quality	0.9	—	—
	Possessive	0.6	1.4	—
	Total	9.7[8]	14.8[8, 9]	1.7[9]

Note: Differences that are statistically significant are given matching superscripts.

defense argument than in the prosecution argument. The defense emphasized the victim's agency during the crime even more than the prosecution did because they constructed her as an active participant rather than a victim. They also emphasized her actions that had occurred in the courtroom more. Additionally, the defense constructed her as the recipient of processes during the crime significantly more frequently than the prosecution did.

Though the difference is not significant, the prosecution constructed the victim as the agent of processes during the investigation more frequently than the defense did (7.9 times per 1,000 words, compared to 4.9 times per 1,000 words). While this cannot be seen in this particular table, these frequencies meant that the defense emphasized the defendant more than the victim in the investigation narrative, and the prosecution did the opposite.

The crime narratives presented by the prosecution and the defense differed mainly because the defense included additional events that the prosecution silenced, included the victim as the agent of sexual processes, and falsified the prosecution's claims. In the defense argument, the victim was the agent of material, verbal, and mental processes during the crime significantly

TABLE 4.16

Distribution of Processes with Victim in Case #7 as the Recipient

		Prosecution	Defense	Rebuttal
Crime	Material	1.7	3.3	1.7
	Verbal	0.6	1.6	—
	Relational	2.4	2.7	—
	Total	4.7	7.7	1.7
Investigation	Material	0.2	—	—
	Verbal	—	0.3	—
	Behavioral	0.2	—	—
	Relational	0.4	—	—
	Total	0.9	0.3	—
Trial	Material	0.6	—	—
	Verbal	0.2	—	—
	Behavioral	0.4	—	—
	Relational	0.9	—	—
	Possessive	—	0.5	—
	Total	2.1	0.5	—
Present	Relational	0.2	—	—
	Total	0.2	—	—
Future	Mental	0.4	—	—
	Total	0.4	—	—

Note: Differences that are statistically significant are given matching superscripts.

more frequently than she was in the prosecution argument. Also, the defense included the victim as the recipient of material processes more frequently than the prosecution did.

More specifically, the prosecution and the defense presented mostly the same narratives about what happened leading up to the sexual encounter. The differences between the two sides were in what the victim's role was in the sexual activities and what she did afterward. In the prosecution argument, the victim was not the agent of any sexual processes or of any processes to prepare for the sexual encounter. This was because the prosecution claimed she was asleep at this time, so she did not have any agency. However, the defense constructed her as the agent of processes that were not sexual in nature but were involved in the sexual event, as in (44), and processes that were explicitly sexual, as in (45) and (46):

(44) And she laid down on the right side, on the right side of the bed.
(45) Still on the bed, they were kissing.
(46) She proceeded to squeeze him.

In the sexual process in (45), the defendant and the victim were co-agents, but in (46), the defense cast her as the sole agent of the sexual action. Also, the defense included the victim's verbal acts during the sexual encounter when she told the defendant about her current mental state. The prosecution was silent about the defendant's claims that the victim was the agent of any of the processes during the sexual encounter.

The two sides also differed in the material processes that they referred to the victim doing in response to the sexual event. The prosecution claimed that she acted upset so she *jumped up*, *pulled up her pants*, and *ran out of the room*. The defense explicitly denied that she was the agent of such processes, and the evidence they offered was the victim's sister's observations of the events. They said that she *did not jump up*. Instead, she *moved her pants up slowly* and *laid there for a while*.

In summary, the two side's opposing representations of the victim's role in the criminal events were constructed in two ways. First, the defense included the victim as the agent of processes during the sexual encounter that the prosecution silenced. Also, the defense falsified several of the elements that the prosecution included in their narrative, specifically that the victim was asleep and that she quickly removed herself from the room after the sexual events. However, they did not emphasize these issues and focused more on what they believed she had done. Thus, both silencing and de-emphasis were strategies through which opposing arguments were created.

The next set of differences between the prosecution and the defense occurred in the investigation narratives. The victim was the agent of both material processes and verbal processes more frequently in the prosecution's argument than in the defense's, although the differences were not significant. Both sides included how she waited to tell the police but eventually called them. The prosecution also included her as the agent of processes that they claimed were typical of a victim, specifically that she stayed in her house for a month after the incident and that she acted upset with the police. The defense silenced these rather than falsifying them.

Another difference between the investigation narratives of the two sides was that each side emphasized a different social actor. The defense referenced the defendant's actions and statements during the investigation more than the victim's (9.5 times per 1,000 words for the defendant compared to 4.9 times per 1,000 words for the victim). The prosecution focused more on the victim's processes than the defendant's (7.9 times per 1,000 words for the victim compared to 5.2 times per 1,000 words for the defendant). Thus, each side represented a different actor as the more central figure in the investigation, and each side included more of the material and verbal processes of that actor that the other side silenced.

Both sides emphasized the victim more than the defendant in their trial narratives. However, the victim was the agent of processes in this context significantly more in the defense argument than in the prosecution argument.

This was partially the result of the defense including her as the agent of verbal processes significantly more frequently (9.6 times per 1,000 words in the defense argument, compared to 5.4 times per 1,000 words in the prosecution argument). This was also due to the defense referencing the victim's mental processes significantly more frequently than the prosecution did (3.3 times per 1,000 words in the defense argument, compared to 0.9 times per 1,000 words in the prosecution argument). In some cases, the defense included her testimony because it was in agreement with their argument. In other instances, they included what she had said in order to attack her credibility as an authority, as in the following example:

(47) First she said that Ernie Ayres wasn't there to help get [her sister] back in and then she said he was.

The prosecution only once acknowledged that her story had changed, and they claimed only one unimportant detail was different—if her pants were around her ankles or all the way off when she woke up. They silenced the rest of her contradictory statements. Because the defense emphasized them, they referenced her as the agent of verbal processes more frequently.

The defense also emphasized the fact that the victim did not remember much of the evening and was often guessing, as in (48). They argued that her lack of recall was a reason for the jurors to believe she was lying.

(48) "I guess maybe," "I could guess," "I don't remember." These are phrases that we heard quite often during Bridget O'Day's testimony.

The prosecution acknowledged that the victim did not remember all of the details of that night, but they dismissed the importance of her lack of memory with this statement:

(49) Was she sincere when she told you she didn't remember every detail of that night? Of course.

The prosecution silenced specific things she did not know with one exception, that she did not remember bumping into things (the defense's explanation for her bruises), and they referred to the missing information using a generalization, *details*, just as had occurred in case #12, which was discussed earlier and in which the victim had included more information in her testimony than her previous statements. Through the use of this term, the prosecution erased the importance of the forgotten information, something the defense had emphasized.

Overall, the prosecution and the defense constructed contrastive representations of the victim's roles in the narrative by silencing, emphasizing, and de-emphasizing different processes and the defense employing falsification as a strategy.

3.3 SUMMARY

To summarize, the prosecution always included the victim's role in the crime story, but the defense varied from case to case. In some cases the defense silenced the victim's role in the alleged crime story. In others, the defense emphasized processes that she or he was the agent of even more than the defendant's processes. Even when the two sides each presented their own version of the crime, they silenced much of what the other side claimed happened. Instead of denying it, they simply erased it from their argument.

The prosecution tended to focus more than the defense did on what the victim said during the investigation and trial. The majority of verbal processes that the defense included from the victims were when the defense was claiming what the victim had said was false or contradicted a previous statement.

Finally, when one side emphasized the victim's behavior that made him or her look like she or he was telling the truth or a lie, depending on which side it was, the other side tended to simply silence this topic in their argument.

4 Discussion

This analysis showed three main things. First, silencing, de-emphasizing, and emphasizing information were again important tools for the lawyers to create representations of reality that were shaped by their own mental models. Throughout the corpus, both sides would include the victim in the same narratives, but either the types of processes each lawyer focused on for that actor or the specific processes within each category that they included would be different. By the lawyers doing this, the actor was not silenced or even de-emphasized in the narrative. Instead, certain processes they may have been a part of were not included and were replaced by others that were ignored by the opposing side. Thus, in the arguments, the lawyers did not need to deny that certain events took place. They simply ignored them and instead included other events that were not even necessarily contradictory to those included in the opposing side's argument.

Second, silencing occurred within certain narratives within a discourse, even when the actor or topic was not silenced in the discourse as a whole. In some of the cases discussed here, a social actor would be referenced relatively frequently overall, but he or she would be ignored, for instance, in the crime narrative or in the investigation narrative. Thus, a true analysis of silencing includes which portions of a discourse someone was silenced in, not just if he or she were excluded from the discourse in general.

Finally, syntactic and lexical choices were also means for de-emphasizing and silencing. For instance, the defense lawyers would refer to the victims as recipients of criminal processes, but they would silence their client as the agent.

To summarize, the results of this analysis show that there were three layers of silencing that both the prosecution and the defense lawyers used to create opposing discourses. They did not necessarily deny that people did, said, felt, and so on, certain things. They instead silenced the events, the actor's participation in them, or the more negative details of them.

The beginning of this chapter raised the issue of defense lawyers' arguments that the term *victim* should be avoided. While this is an opportunity for the defense to claim a bit of control over the prosecution, it misses the bigger picture. Most things the prosecution says tend to use the assumption that the crime occurred, so limiting the use of *victim* as a term of reference does little to nothing to correct the issue for the defense. In fact, many prosecution lawyers in this corpus did not use this term anyway, choosing instead to use the person's name or a pronoun.

5

The Jurors

The defendant and the victims impacted by the crime are obviously central figures in the closing arguments, but the jurors are an important group of social actors as well. After all, they are the addressees for the closing arguments, and in many ways, each part of the trial itself has been conducted for their benefit, as they are the ones whom the lawyers are trying to persuade. In this chapter, I present an analysis of how the jurors' roles and identities were discursively constructed for them through the lawyers' silencing, de-emphasizing, and including or even emphasizing different aspects of the jurors' identities, experiences, and internal states.

To date, there has been very little work on how the jurors are discursively managed in the closing arguments (although Walter 1988, Fuller 1993, Stygall 1994, Hobbs 2005, and Pascual 2006 are exceptions to a limited degree) with regards to both their roles as hearers and as characters in the proceedings. Therefore, it is necessary to expand our discussion of the relevant literature to include studies on persuasion more generally in order to better flesh out our understanding of the issues.

Most of the research on the hearers in persuasive genres has tended to focus on the convincingness of different linguistic (e.g., Carpenter and Henningsen 2011) or argumentative/logical structures (e.g., Millar and Millar 1990; Payan and McFarland 2005; Sycara 1990) or on the lawyers' rhetorical strategies that are used to covertly manage the engagement of the audience: (1) speech acts such as apologies, invitations, requests, and questions (e.g., Blankenship and Craig 2006; Guerini and Castelfranchi 2007; Pascual 2006; Petty et al. 1981; Stygall 1994; Walter 1988); (2) narratives (e.g., Adaval and Wyer 1998; Amsterdam and Hertz 1992; Escalas 2007; Green and Brock 2000, 2002; Payan and McFarland 2005); and (3) speech styles (e.g., Erickson et al. 1978; Fuller 1993; Hobbs 2005; Koslow et al. 1994). This work has consistently shown that speakers attempt to turn their audience members into active participants rather than simply presenting information in front of them for their benefit, and speakers frequently manipulate and alter the social distance between themselves and their hearers. In this chapter, these previous analyses are confirmed and taken a step further by showing how lawyers silence the jurors' passive role in the proceedings as hearers, while portraying them as co-creators of the discourses.

One limitation of the studies that were just mentioned was that they only examined how the interpersonal relationships of the hearers are managed. They did not explore how the hearers' roles and identities are presented to them discursively (the ideational content about the hearers). Only a very small amount of work has been done on this particular issue. One article, Burnkrant and Unnava (1995), showed that making a discourse self-referencing to the audience by addressing them directly can increase persuasion. Two previous studies on courtroom discourse have suggested that lawyers do in fact do this. Stygall (1994) reported that the second-person pronoun *you* (referring to the jurors) was the most common pronoun used in closing arguments, and Tiersma (1999) found that in the OJ Simpson case, the lawyers used the inclusive *we* to create a sense of unity among the lawyer and the jurors. Additionally, Amsterdam and Hertz (1992) found that the defense argument in the case they analyzed was structured around a narrative about the jurors and the lawyers, and so in their case, the jurors were at least overtly referred to in the argument. However, these studies each only studied the arguments in a single trial, and they mostly focused on the presence of forms rather than the functions of them. This chapter shows that explicit references to the jurors in the closing arguments emphasize the characteristics the lawyers want the jurors to have, while also silencing any differences in opinion and experience the jurors may have.

A related study by Bülow-Møller (2005) found that building a common ground through assumed agreement occurs during negotiations. In this chapter, the data will show that this occurs in closing arguments as well, especially through the use of *we* as the agent of mental processes such as *know*, when the lawyer cannot actually be sure of the jurors' cognitive states.

1 The Theoretical Framework

Before turning to the methodology used in this chapter and the analysis itself, it is necessary to introduce the theoretical assumptions being made. The previous chapters demonstrated the importance of terms of reference and the syntactic roles they play for different processes and process types. The focus in this chapter is the same, except that personal pronouns, particularly *you* and *we*, are now key to the analysis. As deictics or shifters (Jakobson 1957; Silverstein 1995 [1976]), these terms have no meaning in isolation but instead point to the person(s) or the entity(s) that the speaker wants the hearer(s) to focus on in a certain context (c.f., Benveniste 1971 [1958]; Biber et al. 1999; Brown and Yule 1983; Morford 1997). These pronouns can refer to an aspect of the context that is already known (e.g., the speaker referring to himself or herself as *I*), or due to their nature, they can "establish an interactional group" (c.f., Morford 1997; Silverstein 1981; Wortham 1996: 332). For example, in the context of the trial, the first-person plural pronoun can label many disparate people as being members of a single unit such as one that consists of the lawyer speaking and the jurors, the lawyer and his or her client, or the lawyer and the attorney for the other side. These pronouns, by giving disparate individuals a common identity, silence the differences present among them. Thus, when lawyers use *we* to refer to themselves, the jurors, and others, they erase the social distance between the referents and themselves and set themselves up as a representative member of this particular group.

Whether pronouns are simply pointing to a pre-existing entity/group or creating a group, they are also marking the "participation framework" (Goffman 1981), labeling and defining the roles of the participants in the discourse. As discussed earlier, discourses are not just distributing representations of the world, they are also interactions among the speaker, the hearer(s), the context, and the content. Pronouns, vocatives, and other related linguistic structures allow a speaker to organize the relationships among the participants (Wortham 1996). For instance, by using second-person pronouns to refer to a set of people, the speaker defines who the addressees are. In closing arguments, lawyers, by using *you* to refer to the jurors, construct them as the intended or ratified recipients (Goffman 1981). Additionally, by using first person pronouns, the speaker anchors himself or herself (and sometimes others) as a character in the discourse and can mark his or her level of responsibility for the message being conveyed. This will prove to be important in the ensuing discussion, as the lawyers use first-person plural pronouns to silence the passive role of the jurors in the creation of the present discourse.

2 Methodology

In order to systematically analyze the discursive construction of the jurors, the same basic steps were taken that were used to analyze the inclusion/exclusion of the defendants and victims. First, the arguments were analyzed for any time the jurors were mentioned explicitly as an agent or a recipient of a process, any time they were the implicit reference in one of these roles (e.g., the unstated subject in a command or a conjoined clause), and any time they were referenced with a vocative. Second, all of the explicit references, whether the jurors were agents, recipients, or vocatives, were analyzed to determine the type of term of reference used: a second-person pronoun, a first-person plural pronoun, or a noun phrase. Third, all of the implicit and explicit references were divided based on the narrative in which each occurred (trial, present, future, outside the courtroom). There was an additional distinction made between clauses describing the forthcoming speeches by the lawyers and judge (the rest of the arguments and the judge's instructions) and the events beyond that. Once the clauses were divided in this way, each set was analyzed for the types of processes for which the jurors served as agents and the types of processes for which they were the recipients. Once again, two-sided Z-tests for the Comparison of Proportions were calculated to allow for comparisons of the results for the prosecution and the defense.

3 Results

3.1 FREQUENCY OF REFERENCE

Table 5.1 shows the frequency of references to the jurors, both as a complete group and as part of a larger group that also included others (e.g., the lawyer presenting the argument), compared to the references to the defendants and victims.[1] The important generalization is that the jurors were more emphasized in the defense arguments than in the prosecution arguments and, in fact, were mentioned as often or more often than the defendants in the defense arguments.

The first key difference shown in the table is in the distribution of the frequencies of references to the jurors in the different arguments. Compared to the prosecution main argument, the defense referred to the jurors as a

TABLE 5.1

Explicit References to the Jurors Compared to References to the Defendants and the Victims

		Prosecution	Defense	Rebuttal
Jurors alone	Explicit reference	19.9[1]	23.5[1]	22.6
	Agent or recipient	22.1[2, 3]	26.2[2]	25.7[3]
	Vocative	0.4[4, 5]	0.9[4]	0.9[5]
Jurors alone and with others	Explicit reference	24.7[6, 7]	30.9[6]	28.1[7]
	Agent or recipient	27.7[8, 9]	34.8[8]	31.7[9]
	Vocative	0.4[10, 11]	0.9[10]	0.9[11]
Defendants	Explicit reference	38.6[12, 13]	27.5[12, 14]	34.1[13, 14]
	Agent or recipient	42.7[15, 16]	28.8[15, 17]	34.6[16, 17]
	Vocative	—	—	—
Victims	Explicit reference	35.0	30.1	26.5
	Agent or recipient	43.8	34.3	29.9
	Vocative	—	—	—

Note: All numbers indicate the frequency per 1,000 words. Differences that are statistically significant are given matching superscripts.

complete unit an extra four times in every 1,000 words, and in that same span, also included an additional reference to them as part of a larger group. Since the prosecution arguments were an average of 5,314 words and the defense arguments were an average of 4,792 words, this resulted in the defense referring to the jurors almost twenty times more in each argument than the prosecution did. To put it another way, the defense defined the jurors as more central to their argument and were more focused on their knowledge, beliefs, experiences, and future tasks. The defense spent more time actively addressing the jurors and constructing their identity within the trial context. That being said, the jurors were definitely not backgrounded in the prosecution arguments; they were simply emphasized more in the defense arguments.

Another difference seen in the table is in the order of prominence given to the different social actors. In the prosecution's main arguments, they emphasized the victims and defendants the most, and the jurors were referenced much less frequently in comparison. In fact, the victims and the defendants were each referred to almost twice as often as the jurors were. As a result, significantly more focus was placed on the defendants and victims, which made them the central figures of the arguments rather than the jurors. On the other hand, the defense lawyers placed more emphasis on the victims and on the jurors and slightly less attention was given to the defendants. The explanation for this finding is that the prosecutors were more focused on the crime narratives, while the defense lawyers paid more attention to the "here-and-now" and to the future. These larger patterns resulted in different levels of emphasis being given to these social actors.

An example will help make the differences clearer. The following excerpts are the first hundred words from the closing arguments in case #1. They were selected to illustrate the patterns being described because the case came first in the list, but they perfectly exemplify the differences between the prosecution and the defense attorneys that were found throughout the corpus.

(1) Prosecution: The last thing on Ashlee Gutteridge's mind as she walked into the Bushra Market on June 1st of last year, was that she was going to have to fight off the sexual advances of the 65-year-old owner. But that's exactly what happened. You heard her testify. She walks into the market, planning on getting some doughnuts or other treats for the day. She walks in. The defendant grabs her and kisses her on the cheek. He then follows her over to the doughnuts, where Ashlee has gone to try to avoid the situation. She's looking at the doughnuts, picks up . . .

(2) Defense: Ladies and gentlemen of the jury, may it please the Court, counsel, ladies, and gentlemen of the jury: First of all, we all want to thank you for your patience and being here and going through this process. It's inconvenient for everyone, I know, and some more than others, but this is the way the jury, the American justice system,

> works, where people like you come here and help out with these matters. You are governed by the law that the judge has read to you, and you are required to follow that law, and I'd just like to first . . .

First of all, the prosecution's introduction silenced the jurors by not mentioning them at all. Instead, this section only discussed the defendant and the victim. At the same time, the defense ignored the crime, the defendant, and the victim and only referenced the jurors, the lawyers, and the judge. As a result, the jurors were given more emphasis in the defense argument than anyone else was. These introductions set the scene for the arguments to come. The prosecution's summation was mostly a crime narrative, while the defense's tended to be a discussion of who the jurors were and what they should do in this case.

The final important difference seen in Table 5.1 is the contrasting patterns between the prosecution's main arguments and their rebuttals. In the rebuttals, the prosecution lawyers emphasized the jurors slightly more than they had originally. For example, in the main arguments, the jurors were mentioned explicitly 24.0 times per 1,000 words, but in the rebuttals, they were referenced 26.3 times per 1,000 words. Specifically, the jurors served as agents and recipients more often in the rebuttals and were referred to in more vocative constructions. Unlike the defense lawyers, the prosecution lawyers still emphasized the defendants more than any other social actor in both the main arguments and the rebuttals, but the difference was just not quite as extreme in the rebuttals.

Overall, these results are more evidence that the lawyers for the two sides spent their arguments mainly focused on different topics, rather than arguing over the same ones. In some ways, the prosecution arguments, the defense arguments, and the rebuttals were simply three different monologues presented in succession, rather than dialogues in which the input of one speaker is addressed or at least responded to in the next speaker's contribution.

3.2 TERMS OF REFERENCE

In the previous chapters, the terms of reference that the prosecution and the defense used were quite different. While an analysis of the terms used to refer to the jurors is less revealing, it still demonstrates the importance of the processes of silencing, de-emphasizing, and emphasizing.

3.2.1 Pronouns

Most of the references to the victims were pronouns, either second-person[2] or first-person plural pronouns. In fact, 85.1% of the prosecution arguments' references to the jurors, 81.0% of the defense arguments' references, and 81.7% of the rebuttals' references were pronouns.

Often the pronoun was *you* because this is the standard formal second-person plural pronoun in the region in which the trials occurred. When Stygall (1994) observed the use of this pronoun in closing argument, she mentioned that referring to the jurors with a single pronoun for all of them emphasizes that they are a group instead of individuals. This is true, but it is simply an effect of the rules of the genre. The state's *General Rules of Practice for the District Courts* disallows the jurors from addressing any of the jurors individually or by name.[3] The lawyers in the corpus thus had two options, to refer to them as a group or to not refer to the jurors directly at all. They often made the former choice.

What is more interesting is the lawyers' use of first-person plural pronouns, *we*, *our*, and *ours*. The defense lawyers, as could be expected from the results discussed earlier, referred to the jurors with these terms more frequently than the prosecution did (4.0/1,000 in the prosecution arguments, 5.6/1,000 in the defense arguments, and 3.6/1,000 in the rebuttals). At least to a limited degree, this meant that the defense emphasized the jurors and their membership in certain groups more often. Specifically, most of these (prosecution arguments: 80.3%; defense arguments: 78.7%; and rebuttals: 65.7%) referred to the jurors and the lawyer speaking as a single unit,[4] as in the following example:

(3) Not the situation here, and that's what I'm trying to illustrate for you, that we haven't even gotten close yet when we're down here at preponderance of the evidence to what the [State] must prove or the burden that they bear in a criminal case.

In other instances, the first-person plural pronouns included even more people in addition to the jurors and the lawyers. For example, some included all of the people involved in the trial:

(4) This is a very special thing that we're doing here. A very special thing. Participating in the jury system.

Other times, the first-person plural pronouns included all people in an even more broadly defined and highly populated social group, such as all people who live in the United States or even all people:

(5) Our entire history of freedom has been written in criminal courtrooms starting in England, and our forefathers brought it to America and incorporated it into the Constitution.

(6) We don't read minds as humans, obviously.

The first reason that the use of these pronouns was significant is that they permitted the lawyers to create groups that either did not necessarily exist previously or did not otherwise have easily defined boundaries. This was especially true for the use of a first-person plural pronoun to refer to the jurors and the lawyer, because they were not necessarily a natural or uniform group. They were playing very different roles in the trial, especially during the closing arguments. By law, the lawyer only played the role of speaker, and the jurors only inhabited the role of hearers. They were not allowed to change roles, except metaphorically. Second, the lawyer had significantly more power and status than the jurors did in this context, and perhaps more than the jurors had in other parts of their lives as well. Third, the lawyers had made a decision about which side of the case they were in agreement with, but the jurors had not necessarily done so. If they had, the lawyer had no way of knowing this, and they may actually have decided that they disagreed with the lawyer. Fourth, and finally, the jurors were going to make the final decision in the case, but the lawyer would not have any active role in that particular process. For all of these reasons, and perhaps for others, the jurors may not have considered themselves to be members of social group with the lawyer, but the use of the first-person plural pronoun forced them to be. It silenced all of these the differences and focused only on the jurors' and the lawyer's similarities (both those that were real and those that the lawyer wanted to exist). As Tiersma (1999) stated with regard to these pronouns in the OJ Simpson defense arguments, they created a sense of "group solidarity, a feeling of us versus them" (191).

In addition to creating groups and erasing differences, the use of first-person plural pronouns to refer to the jurors and others also permitted the lawyers to reference certain features of the jurors' identities and to highlight them as relevant for the current discourse. For example, when the lawyers referred to all Americans as *we*, this included the jurors. By referencing the jurors' membership in this group, it created a certain identity for them that was useful for the lawyer's case at that instant. Since each jury was a monolithic entity that did nothing but sit and listen during most of the trial, they started the closing arguments with very few salient characteristics as a social group. When the lawyers referred to them as members of other groups that were socially understood as having certain features, this was the lawyers' means of assigning characteristics to the jurors and defining them as fitting the identities that suited the lawyers' case.

3.2.2 Noun Phrases

In addition to using pronouns, the lawyers used noun phrases to refer to the jurors as well. Two classifications, one formal and one informal, were used more frequently than the others. The most common term was *ladies and gentlemen (of the jury)*, which was almost always used in vocatives and in the standard opening *May it please the court, counsel, and ladies and gentlemen of the jury*. Its function in this formulaic expression and its frequent use demonstrated that it is entrenched as the default term in this particular context and register. The term *folks* was also used as a vocative, but this was much rarer, as it was produced by only four attorneys, three of the prosecutors and one defense lawyer. The obvious difference between these two terms is the level of formality. *Folks* is quite casual and perhaps unexpected in this context, and because of that, it provided the lawyers with an opportunity to decrease the social distance between themselves and the jurors. Additionally, it is more neutral than alternatives such as *guys*, which was never used in the corpus, and the selection of this particular term helped the lawyer to develop a different aspect of his or her identity than just being an educated lawyer.

Another set of terms that were used to refer to the jurors were functionalizations that focused on their role in the context. For instance, the lawyers called them *minds*, *judges/triers of fact*, *jurors*, and *ones/people who …* An example can be seen here:

> (7) As the triers of fact, you are the ones who hear the facts and determine what the facts are and what is proven.

Basically, these terms were used to remind the jurors of why they were there and what their job entailed. These features became the relevant parts of these people's identities, at least at that point in the discourses.

Overall, the actual terms used for the jurors were limited mostly to pronouns, simply because they were a group whose individual members had to remain anonymous. Despite this, the terms that were selected by the lawyers allowed them to reference features of the jurors' identities that were not necessarily obvious otherwise and to silence differences between the jurors and others, including the lawyers speaking.

3.3 THE ROLES OF THE JURORS IN CLAUSES

As with the defendants and victims, the terms used for the jurors did not tell the whole story. A complete analysis of the roles these individuals played also includes their distribution across different narratives and a discussion of the types of roles they played in clauses.

Unsurprisingly, the prosecution and the defense referenced the jurors in the contexts of the trial, the present, the near future (within the closing arguments), the distant future (after the closing arguments), and outside the courtroom. However, as Table 5.2 shows, for both sides, most of the references occurred in the contexts of the trial, the present, and the distant future.

The largest differences between the two sides were that the defense and the prosecution in their rebuttals emphasized the role of the jurors in the present, in the distant future, and in outside or generic contexts more than the prosecution did in their main argument. When the lawyers were discussing the "here-and-now," this difference occurred for both second-person pronouns to just refer to the jurors and first-person plural pronouns to refer to the jurors as part of a larger group that also included the lawyer. The real-world

TABLE 5.2
Distribution of the Jurors' Roles across Narratives

		Prosecution	Defense	Rebuttal
Trial	Jurors	7.1	6.5	6.0
	Jurors + Others	0.7	1.0	0.6
	Total	7.8	7.5	6.6
Present	Jurors	6.2[1, 2]	7.5[1]	8.2[2]
	Jurors + Others	3.1[3]	4.2[3, 4]	2.3[4]
	Total	9.3[5]	11.7[5]	10.5
Near future	Jurors	0.4	0.5	0.2
	Jurors + Others	0.1	0.04	—
	Total	0.5	0.5	0.2
Distant future	Jurors	7.5[6, 7]	11.3[6]	11.1[7]
	Jurors + Others	—	—	—
	Total	7.5[8, 9]	11.3[8]	11.1[9]
Outside/generic	Jurors	2.2[10]	3.2[10]	3.1
	Jurors + Others	0.8[11]	1.4[11]	1.0
	Total	3.0[12, 13]	4.6[12]	4.1[13]

Note: Differences that are statistically significant are given matching superscripts.

meaning of these differences is that the defense emphasized the jurors as active participants in the discourse creation more than the prosecution did in their main arguments, and the defense also comparatively emphasized what they thought the jurors would and should do when reaching a verdict. The prosecution did this more often in the rebuttals, but as will be discussed later, they told the jurors to do a very different set of actions.

3.3.1 The Trial Narrative

While the differences between the prosecution and defense frequencies were small, the prosecution in their main argument did reference the jurors in the context of the trial slightly more often than the defense did. There was a slight tendency for the defense lawyers to use *we* more and thus to include themselves with the jurors in this context, but again, the difference was quite negligible. Instead, the use of silencing, de-emphasizing, and emphasizing can be seen through a more qualitative analysis of the roles the jurors were said to play for different types of processes in each case.

The lawyers for both sides frequently included the jurors in the trial narrative to remind the jurors of what they had experienced or done earlier in the trial. In some instances, the lawyers referred to previous statements made by a lawyer, a witness, or the judge in order to link back to those previous discourses and recontextualize them. An example can be seen here:

(8) And I told you that in jury selection when we talked about that. It's reasonable doubt. It's what makes common sense.

The prosecution and the defense both did this, but they linked back to different discourses (Felton Rosulek 2010a, b). For instance, in case #1, the prosecutor referred back to the judge's description of how to decide on someone's credibility. The defense silenced this and instead included the judge's definitions of the presumption of innocence and reasonable doubt. The prosecution lawyer completely silenced the first topic, and while he did address the second in his rebuttal, he ignored the judge's definition. Thus, the lawyers were still able to create different representations through silencing different earlier events.

At other times, the references to the jurors at earlier points in the trial were made to silence or de-emphasize the presence of the lawyers while increasing the role of the jurors in the earlier proceedings. This occurred when the lawyers represented the jurors as the intended recipients of previous discourses (e.g., a witness's response to the lawyer's questions, the judge's legal ruling) rather than just overhearers, which was the role it probably appeared they were playing. One way in which the lawyers accomplished this was through the use of constructions where the jurors were the recipients of past verbal, material, and relational processes that had the witnesses, the lawyers, and the judge as the agents. Examples of this phenomenon are as follows:

(9) Ms. Kinnison was candid with you yesterday, ladies and gentlemen, and she was looking you right in the eye and telling you these things.

(10) The defendant lied to you here today.

(11) Detective Goodman showed you a shirt, pointed out some stains on this shirt, but no testing was done on that shirt.

In each example, the witnesses had originally made these comments and actions in response to questions posed by the lawyer. However, the lawyers silenced their own role and only included the jurors as the hearers. While some witnesses may have looked at the jurors rather than the lawyers, in many ways their testimony had been a conversation between them and the lawyers. The jurors just happened to be ratified overhearers.[5] By the lawyers silencing their own role and only including the jurors', this made the testimony more personal to the jurors. They were entrusted with information, were insulted by being lied to (it was their face being threatened), and so on, rather than it being the case that they had only observed people talking and lying.

The lawyers also frequently included the jurors as agents of a behavioral process, often by themselves but sometimes with the lawyer and/or others, when discussing quotations and descriptions of the witnesses' testimony. This can be seen in these examples:

(12) You heard him explain what happened. You heard how he went to that house asking for help, how he went up onto the steps, and how Mr. Mound came out in a rage, drunk, drugged.

(13) Well, when she's sober those defenses go right back up and you saw them, you saw them in court.
(14) You saw him. You saw how credible he was. How candid he was.
(15) And what we heard from the doctors is no, that's not, that's not the case.

These references to the jurors were unnecessary/optional, but the fact that the lawyers included them anyway is very important discursively. For example, in (14), the lawyer could have said, "He was credible. He was candid." In (15), "The doctors said, 'No that's not—that's not the case,'" would have been equally sufficient. However, by repeatedly referring to the jurors as having experienced these events, the lawyers did two things. First, the lawyers reminded the jurors that they were present when this information was revealed and that they were the recipients of the utterances/actions. This gave the lawyers an opportunity to recontextualize the original events and made the presence of the jurors in the earlier times relevant. Second, and more interestingly, the lawyers silenced the fact that the jurors may not have experienced these same things or reached the same conclusions about them. In reality, the jurors may not have had the same sensory experiences or interpreted the witnesses' testimony in these ways, but in the discursive representation of the jurors that the lawyer created, they did. For instance, the jurors may not have interpreted the witness in (13) as having her defenses up, and they may not have found the witnesses in (14) to be credible. However, the lawyers silenced these possibilities and represented the jurors as accepting those statements. If the jurors were to take the lawyers' representations of them as true, then they would be one step closer to accepting the lawyers' full arguments. Since the two sides almost always included different quotations from the witnesses for the jurors to accept and they silenced those included by the opposition (Felton Rosulek 2010a, b), these were key to the creation of the divergent arguments.

To summarize, the prosecution and the defense both made references to the jurors and what they had experienced during the trial. These references made it possible for the lawyers to silence, de-emphasize, and emphasize different information. Through these processes, the lawyers' own roles in events were silenced or de-emphasized and a representation of the jurors was discursively created that depicted them as having had more important roles in past events than they actually had had and that portrayed them as having experienced and interpreted events in ways that they might not have done. Thus, these references to the jurors increased the hearer-focused nature of the arguments, and they gave the lawyers a chance to portray the jurors as the lawyers wanted them to be, not as they necessarily were.

3.3.2 The Present Context

While the difference between the prosecution's and the defense's rate of reference to the jurors in the trial narrative was small, it was a bit larger in the present, the "here-and-now." The defense referred to the jurors in this context more frequently than the prosecution did (11.7 times per 1,000 words for the defense, 9.3 times per 1,000 words for the prosecution in their main argument, and 10.5 times per 1,000 words for the defense in their rebuttal). As a result, the defense emphasized the jurors and their current role in the proceedings more. The data also show that, once again, the defense made even more references to the jurors using *we* in this context, and thus, they emphasized their shared identity of interlocutors.

There were several reasons that the prosecution and the defense mentioned the jurors in this context, each of which shows the importance of silencing, de-emphasizing, and emphasizing. The first was to complete interpersonal speech acts such as greetings, statements of gratitude, and apologies, as in the following examples:

(16) And at the outset we both would like to thank all of you for your time, your effort, your patience in this matter.
(17) I almost want to apologize to you for the amount of time I'm taking but, you know, his statement is important.

Such statements served an interactional purpose, as the lawyers used politeness strategies to manage and perhaps improve their relationship with the jurors while addressing their face needs/wants (Goffman 1967; Brown and Levinson 1987) of the jurors. Additionally, thank-yous, apologies, greetings, and the like are hearer supportive (Edmondson 1981) and, by extension, make the discourses more hearer-oriented, which, as discussed above, may have made them more persuasive. Basically, the lawyers, by completing these acts—which were not necessarily essential or relevant to the logical argument being made—found another way to manage the interpersonal goals of the discourses and to include and even emphasize the jurors and their role as the intended recipients of the discourses. By using politeness formulae to accomplish this, the lawyers potentially made the jurors feel more positive about themselves, the lawyers, and their arguments.

Another reason that the lawyers referenced the jurors was to define their roles, rights, and responsibilities so that everyone was aware of them. Of course, the prosecution and the defense differed slightly regarding what they were (e.g., the defense in several cases said the jurors were the defendant's *protection against the government*, something the prosecution obviously never said). Often, the lawyers used hyperbole and references to the jurors as part of a bigger process to capture the importance of their role, as in this example:

(18) And that's where you the citizens, the truly neutral parties, come in here to place yourselves between the State and a person who's been accused. And there's no higher thing that a person can be asked to do.

Through these references, the lawyers constructed the identity of the jurors as fit the lawyer's argument. Each side included and often emphasized the aspects they wanted the jurors to consider important features the other side silenced.

The lawyers also referenced the jurors in vocative constructions, as in:

(19) I don't necessarily disagree with that, folks.

As shown in Table, vocatives occurred in the defense arguments and the prosecution rebuttals more than twice as often as in the prosecution main arguments. According to Leech (1999), vocatives have three main functions: (1) to get the addressee's attention, (2) to limit the intended addressees, and (3) to maintain a social relationship with the addressees (108). Presumably, in the closing arguments, all three functions were in play with each use of the vocatives. The jurors had to sit and listen silently to the lawyers talk for a significant amount of time. Their attention might have waned, and so the lawyers could use vocatives to recapture their interest. Perhaps this is one reason that they occurred more frequently in the defense and rebuttal arguments, as the jurors had been listening for longer. In addition to regaining the jurors' attention, vocatives reminded the jurors that despite the larger audience present for the arguments, they were the intended recipients of the message. Finally, vocatives also may have helped negotiate the social distance between the jurors and the lawyer. The frequent use of *ladies and gentlemen* kept the context of the discourse formal, but since it was used in a vocative, it made the discourse more personal. It was all part of the lawyer's balancing act.

The next function of references in the jurors in the "here-and-now" was to silence the jurors' lack of power in the creation of the arguments. Quite frequently throughout the summations, the lawyers produced a meta-discourse that accompanied their narratives. In other words, they provided a commentary for what they had said, what they were saying, and what they were going to say. What was interesting about this is that they often included the jurors in it. Sometimes they were the hearers/recipients:

(20) I would suggest to you none.
(21) I'd remind you that . . .

By including the jurors in this meta-discourse, the lawyers were able to focus on the jurors' presence and to maintain the personal nature of the arguments, just as they had with the vocatives. This was another way in which the lawyers could reference the fact that the jurors were the intended recipients of the arguments.

What was even more interesting, though, was when the lawyers used first-person plural pronouns in this commentary, as in the following examples:

(22) So we're talking about the same type of offense.

(23) What we are using to evaluate the testimony of witnesses here.
(24) So let's deal with that aspect right up front.

By using the first-person plural pronouns here, the lawyers kept open the possibility that the jurors would include themselves in the reference (consider it an inclusive rather than an exclusive pronoun). If they did so, the jurors would be constructed as being active participants in the creation of the discourse and the related activities (e.g., thinking, dealing, evaluating). This silenced the fact that the jurors were silent and passive recipients and depicted them as having an active role that they did not have. It also constructed the jurors as more equal to the lawyers and thus lessened some of the social distance between them.

Finally, lawyers referenced the jurors in the present as the agents of mental processes, as in the following:

(25) You know that [the witness is] telling you the truth.
(26) You know that they didn't do it.
(27) Everything that she told you fits with everything else that we know to be true in this case.
(28) We know it took place over a period of time because we can see the photographs of the room.

The jurors did not necessarily know or believe these things, but the lawyers were representing it as a given that they did. This is the same as when the lawyers said the jurors had *seen* or *heard* something that they might not have seen or heard. Once again, if the jurors agreed with the representations of their mental states or at least did not question the truth-value of the second halves of the utterances, then they had accepted one tenet in the lawyer's argument. These statements silenced any doubts the jurors may have had with these assertions. Also, when the lawyers used first-person plural pronouns rather than second-person pronouns, they included themselves as accepting the claims. By doing so, they placed even more social pressure on the jurors to accept these statements as true. As is probably now expected, each side simply included different conclusions that the jurors supposedly *knew*, and silenced or de-emphasized those included by the other side.

In conclusion, this analysis, just as with the ones before it, showed that silencing, de-emphasizing, and emphasizing were once again important means through which the lawyers created opposing representations of the same reality. Both sides silenced doubt and social differences between the jurors and the lawyers while including only the information that helped their side's case. The defense simply did this even more than the prosecution did.

3.3.3 The Near Future Narrative

Both sides referred to the jurors in the near future sparingly (0.5 times per 1,000 words). Since this time period included the rest of the current lawyer's argument, the other lawyer's argument, and the judge's instructions, this was partly due to the short time span being covered. The two reasons that the lawyers did talk about this time were to provide an overview of what was to come (and they often included the jurors in this meta-discourse, as discussed previously) and to instruct the jurors on how to respond to what they would hear. However, the infrequency of references to the jurors in that time is more evidence that neither side was very interested in discussing the other side's argument; mostly they silenced or at least de-emphasized it and focused on their own.

3.3.4 The Distant Future Narrative

When lawyers referenced the jurors as a group, they were most often pointing to them in the more distant future, which included the jurors' deliberations and the rest of their lives. Though both sides made references to this context frequently, the defense lawyers made them significantly more often than the prosecution did. However, the prosecution made them in their rebuttal arguments just as frequently as the defense did in their main arguments.

In this context, lawyers told the jurors what their side wanted them to do as they decided the outcome of the case. This can be seen in this example from a defense lawyer:

> (29) Put evidence on a pedestal and look at it 360 degrees. Better yet, put it on a pedestal and get a microscope of reasonable doubt and look at it 360 degrees. I'm using sort of a metaphor, but I'm suggesting to you that you need to look at the facts in this case closely, especially the ones that I'm highlighting.

The defense lawyers in general referred to and therefore emphasized their instructions to the jurors much more than the prosecution lawyers did. They were much more focused on the jurors not assuming the defendant was guilty but instead applying the legal concepts of the presumption of innocence and reasonable doubt.

While the defense lawyers tended to spend more of their arguments telling the jurors what to do rather than focusing on the crime and investigation narratives, both sides told the jurors how to judge certain witnesses, what specific evidence or testimony to look at, and what conclusions they should make. However, the specific details for these instructions were very different for each side. Either they told the jurors to do contradictory things or they ignored the topics the other side included and instead included something different. For example, the lawyers often silenced the witnesses who were helpful to the opposing side's argument. If the lawyers did mention the person's testimony, they de-emphasized the witness by spending only a few clauses attacking their statements or their credibility. They almost always silenced what they had said (Felton Rosulek 2010a, b).

3.3.5 Outside Contexts

Finally, references to the jurors were used to relate the trial experience to other parts of their lives. The following two examples demonstrate this function, the first using second-person pronouns and the second using first-person plural pronouns:

(30) One way of viewing what is proof beyond a reason able doubt is to look at this as what type of evidence would you rely upon in deciding your most important daily affairs. One of the most important decisions that a person makes is the decision to undergo surgery or have one's child undergo surgery, particularly major surgery

(31) We make these decisions every day. It's not an unusual thing for us to do, and we base those decisions on the best evidence we can get. And when we're comfortable with the evidence, that the evidence is such that we can make a decision that we believe to be beyond a reasonable doubt, we buy the house, we get married, we decide that our parents or our children will have surgery.

In these excerpts, the lawyers used references to the world outside the courtroom to discursively link the jurors' previous experiences with their current ones.[6] The defense tended to do this more often. While it is likely that some lawyers do make references to the opposition's stories of this type, such tales were always silenced in the other side's argument in this corpus.

4 Conclusions

In summary, lawyers referenced the jurors for several purposes. The first was to remind the jurors that the events of the trial had all been done for their benefit. This silenced the lawyers' role in the proceedings and made the discourses more hearer-oriented. Second, the lawyers told the jurors what they had experienced and what they knew. The lawyers did not actually know what the participants were thinking, but they represented the jurors as accepting the tenets of the lawyers' own arguments. This silenced the jurors' doubts, the differences between them and the lawyers, and the opposing claims the other side was making. Next, these references occurred as part of a metadiscourse in which the jurors' role as the recipients or even as co-creators of the discourse was emphasized, and their lack of power and the differences between them and the lawyers were silenced. Finally, references to the jurors were used to instruct the jurors on how they should act in the future. The two sides included different actions and silenced those encouraged by the opposition. The defense tended to spend more of their arguments doing these things, which de-emphasized the crime and the investigation narratives—topics that the prosecution emphasized.

These results are key for understanding how the lawyers, or even how speakers in general, make their arguments relate to the hearer. As we know, in the real world, closing arguments and other persuasive discourses are much more, more than just their ideational meta-function, more than the communication of the speakers' representation of the world. They are also communicative interactions in which speakers manage their relationships with the hearers. Lawyers use silencing, de-emphasizing, and emphasizing for both. They are linguistically able to silence the difference between themselves and the jurors by using first-person plural pronouns. At the same time, they overtly construct an identity for the jurors that gives them more power and status in the context than they actually have/had, which is based on features that suit the lawyers' goals, and which ignores both real and potential differences between the lawyers and the jurors. Finally, they make the arguments hearer-oriented by overtly including the jurors in various events, by being polite to them, and by comparing the current events to those the jurors are more familiar with.

6

The Lawyers

In the previous chapters, we have examined the linguistic construction of the defendants, victims, and jurors. In this chapter, we turn to another significant group, the lawyers themselves. Lawyers have many extra-linguistic and even non-linguistic ways in which to create identities for themselves and for each other: their physical appearance and body language; their presentation style and other forms of non-verbal communication (c.f., Barge et al. 1989; Hahn and Clayton 1996; LeVan 1984; Sigal et al. 1985; Spiecker and Worthington 2003), and their control of linguistic varieties and style (c.f., Fuller 1993; Hobbs 2003). However, here the focus is on how lawyers linguistically mark or fail to mark their presence as speakers/interlocutors (the interpersonal meta-function) and how they discursively construct their own and the other side's roles and identities in the narratives (the ideational meta-function).

Attorneys for the prosecution and for the defense are in many ways battling against each other as individuals. Both sides have the same goal: to have their argument accepted by the jurors. In every case, one side will achieve this while the other will fail. Thus, lawyers must make themselves seem more believable and trustworthy than the opposition. They can do this in three ways: they can impugn the character and credibility of the other side, they can build up a positive image of themselves, or they can do a combination of both.

Within the courtroom setting, certain standards apply for how lawyers are to behave and how much they can attack each other personally in that lawyers are expected to act with a great deal of civility and respect toward each other (Aaronson 1995; Cary 1998; Dickson and Bunton Jackson 1994; Jenkins 1993). However, not everyone follows this behavioral code. For instance, during proceedings that took place in a courtroom in Ohio in 1998, two lawyers became so enraged with each other that the one called the other "a piece of shit" and the other responded that he was "a total asshole" (*Cuyahoga County Bar Association v. Gonzalez*, 89 Ohio St.3d 470). While the corpus used for this analysis[1] did not contain any attacks that were this marked or inherently negative, the fact is that they occur in some cases. When they do, because they go against social norms for this particular context, they definitely emphasize a lawyer's negative evaluation of the opposition.

In most cases, though, the de-construction of the other side's positive image was much rarer and much less marked. Often, the two sides simply ignored each other. When they did discuss the other side, they did so neutrally or to point out features of the opposition's identity or group memberships that might be seen as negatives. Otherwise, the lawyers instead spend more of their arguments building up their own identities either by referring to their own actions and mental states or by marking their membership in groups that carry more positive characteristics. By using such references, the lawyers tried to create a relatable identity for themselves while still pointing to their own knowledge and status.

1 The Representation of the Opposition

1.1 FREQUENCY OF REFERENCE

As can be seen in Table 6.1, compared to the defendants, victims, and jurors, the opposing side was rarely mentioned in the closing arguments. This simply reflects the fact that the lawyers silenced or at least de-emphasized the other side's argument.

Table 6.2 presents the breakdown of the data based on whether the reference was to the other side alone or to them as part of a larger group. It also includes data for implicit references to the other side as the agent or recipient of a process.

TABLE 6.1
Frequency of Reference to the Opposing Side

	Prosecution	Defense	Rebuttal
Opposing side	2.3 (207)[1, 2]	7.2 (590)[1]	8.2 (155)[2]
Lawyer who was speaking	15.1 (1366)[3, 4]	18.0 (1469)[3]	20.3 (382)[4]
Defendants	38.6 (3490)[5, 6]	27.5 (2239)[5, 7]	34.5 (634)[6, 8]
Victims (excluding cases with more than one victim)	35.0 (2179)	30.9 (1993)	27.3 (397)
Jurors	24.7 (2230)[11, 12]	30.9 (2518)[11]	28.1 (528)[12]

Note: Number per 1,000 words and total number of tokens. Differences that are statistically significant are given matching superscripts.

TABLE 6.2

Frequency of Reference to the Opposing Side

		Prosecution	Defense	Rebuttal
Other side alone	Explicit reference	0.9[1, 2]	5.5[1]	6.5[2]
	Agent or recipient	1.0[3, 4]	6.3[3]	7.2[4]
Other side as part of a group	Explicit reference	1.4	1.8	1.8
	Agent or recipient	1.6[5]	2.4[6]	2.1
Total	Explicit reference	2.3[7, 8]	7.2[7]	8.2[8]
	Agent or recipient	2.5[9, 10]	8.8[9]	9.2[10]

Note: Number per 1,000 words. Differences that are statistically significant are given matching superscripts.

The most striking result from these tables is that the prosecution lawyers in their main arguments almost completely silenced the defense. To take this a step further, a closer analysis reveals that every single prosecution lawyer de-emphasized the opposition in his or her main argument. In fact, if we examine the references that were only to the defense (as opposed to the defense and others), three prosecutors completely silenced the defense, one referred to them only once, and eight referred to them between two and four times. In the other five arguments, there were between nine and seventeen references to the defense, and so even in these cases, they were de-emphasized. The importance of these quantitative results is that the prosecution lawyers were mostly ignoring the defense lawyers, their role in the trial, the questions they had asked, and the arguments they had made or were about to make. The prosecutors focused their arguments on their own understanding of the crime and how the jurors should apply the law to it, and they de-emphasized or silenced the fact that the defense was making contrasting claims. While this finding may in part have been a result of the prosecution presenting their arguments before the defense did, the truth is that defense had been an active part of each trial. As a result, the prosecution was fully capable of including them and countering the arguments they were likely to make. They simply did not do this.

In comparison, the defense referred to the prosecution significantly more frequently. However, this did not mean that the defense generally emphasized the prosecution and by extension their argument. They, too, de-emphasized the opposing side while instead focusing on the defendants, victims, jurors, and themselves. The defense just did not do this as completely and thoroughly as the prosecution did. To put the numbers in perspective, the defense explicitly referred to the prosecution 6.6 times per 1,000 words, but they referred to the jurors 29.2 times per 1,000 words, the defendants 27.5 times per 1,000 words, and the victims 30.1 times per 1,000 words. Also, as will be discussed later in this chapter, the defense lawyers referred to themselves 18.0 times per 1,000 words. Each of these numbers is significantly larger than the frequency for their references to the opposition. The effect of these differences is that the defense arguments, like the prosecution arguments, emphasized their own claims and conclusions and de-emphasized what the other side had said or done.

The final result that is evident from Table 6.1 is that the prosecution, when they gave a rebuttal, did refer to the defense, both alone and as part of various groups, at a higher rate. In the state in which these trials took place, as is common across the United States, the prosecution rebuttals are limited to claims actually raised by the defense in their arguments. Thus, these arguments are in theory focused on the opposing side's argument. However, even then, the defense lawyers were mentioned infrequently compared to the other relevant social actors, and their specific claims were mostly ignored. The prosecutors still emphasized their own claims and argument, and simply referred to the other side a few times to make some connections between what the defense had said and what the prosecution believed instead. The jurors, the defendants, and the victims were still the main focus, and the other side was mostly irrelevant to the discussion.

1.2 TERMS OF REFERENCE

Not only did the prosecution and defense lawyers tend to ignore each other, but when they did mention the other side, they tended to ignore the individual identity of the person/people.

As can be seen in Table 6.3, in the prosecution main argument and in the defense argument, they both used pronouns and nominations less than they used other terms—specifically, functionalizations and impersonalizations.[2] The distribution for the types of terms was mostly consistent between the two sides, although the prosecution was slightly more likely to use a name than a pronoun, while the defense was slightly more likely to use a pronoun than a name.

TABLE 6.3

Terms of Reference for the Opposing Side (Alone)

		Prosecution	Defense	Rebuttal
Pronouns	Percent of references	*20.3%*	*24.6%*	*18.0%*
	Number per 1,000 words	0.2[1, 2]	1.4[1]	1.2[2]
	Total number	16	110	22
Nomination	Percent of references	*20.3%*[3]	*16.3%*[4]	*68.0%*[3, 4]
	Number per 1,000 words	0.2[5, 6]	0.9[5, 7]	4.4[6, 7]
	Total number	16	73	83
Other	Percent of references	*59.5%*[8]	*59.1%*[9]	*13.9%*[8, 9]
	Number per 1,000 words	0.5[10]	3.2[10, 11]	0.9[11]
	Total number	47	264	17

Note: Differences that are statistically significant are given matching superscripts.

However, the pattern changed significantly in the prosecution rebuttals. In these, they used the defense lawyer's name rather than a functionalization or impersonalization. This was such a strong tendency among the prosecution lawyers that it was true not only in the corpus as a whole but also in each case as well. Fourteen of the cases had a rebuttal, and in every case, the prosecution referred to the defense counsel by name more times in their rebuttal than in their main argument (despite the rebuttals being much shorter). In thirteen of those cases, the prosecution referred to the defense lawyer by name only two times or less (six times they never did) in their main argument but used it in their rebuttals. Table 6.4 provides some clues as to why this occurred. A majority of the nominations in the prosecution rebuttals occurred when they were discussing the argument the defense lawyer had just presented. In their other narratives, they tended to use less personal terms. Since most of the prosecution references to the defense in their rebuttals were about their closing arguments (85.9%), this accounts for the high frequency of nominations. By inferring and then emphasizing that a single person was responsible for the other side's closing arguments and the claims contained within them (which may or may not have been true), the prosecution challenged the jurors to make their decision based on whether or not they believed that particular individual.

1.2.1 Pronouns

Other than in the rebuttals, the true differences between the prosecution and the defense were not in the types of terms of reference they used but in the specific forms they selected within each category. To start with, the two sides tended to use different pronouns for each other. The prosecution almost always used a third person singular pronoun (*she* or *he*). In fact, they only used a third-person plural pronoun *they* or *them* four times in total (in either their main arguments or rebuttals, and this occurred twice in one argument) (10.5% of pronouns referring to just the defense). In comparison, the defense used a third-person plural pronoun fifty-one times, or 52.0% of the times they used a pronoun to refer to just the prosecution. Additionally, they used a third person gender-neutral pronoun *it(s)* twelve times (12.2%). These forms can be seen in the following examples:

(1) The State referred to that in their closing argument.
(2) The State with its Power Point presentation has pulled out a few quotes.

This difference highlights a pattern that was mentioned earlier for the rebuttals, which is that the prosecution painted the defense as a single person making all of the claims and doing all of the work. In comparison, the defense suggested that the prosecution was a large entity working against their client, and the use of the third person plural and singular gender-neutral pronouns followed from this.[3]

1.2.2 Functionalizations and Impersonalizations

These contrasting strategies are again seen in the other terms the two sides used. The prosecutors mainly used functionalizations such as *the defense counsel*, *counsel*, *the/his attorney/lawyer*, although once in a while they did use a closely related impersonalization, *the defense*. In doing so, the prosecutor de-emphasized the individual identity of the defense lawyers, except for their professional role in the courtroom context, and by using these particularly terms, they indexed all associations the jurors may have had with the concept of a defense lawyer.

Although the defense attorneys also used a functionalization, *the prosecutor(s)*, to refer to the opposition, this was rare. Instead, they used an impersonalization, *the State*, for most references, although they did also use the related term *the government*. Two examples can be seen here:

(3) The State has presented its case to you.
(4) Don't listen to the conclusion that the State has come to because they obviously came to this conclusion a long time ago.

The frequent use of these impersonalizations did three things. First, by using these forms significantly more frequently than they used the prosecutor's name, the defense de-emphasized the humanity and the individual identity of the person or people who had presented the case. Only one or two lawyers had actually been involved in the trial for the prosecution in each case, but they were erased and made part of a larger collective. Second, and more important, these terms combined all people involved in the prosecution's case (e.g., the police who conducted the investigation, everyone working in the prosecutor's office, the actual lawyer who gave the argument, the entire government, all citizens of the state) into a single unit. By doing this, the defense created the impression that all of these people were working together against the defendant. This was particularly important in examples like (2) because the defense could then argue that because one sub-set of people made a mistake or a flawed decision, then all of the conclusions that the group made following it were also erroneous. Finally, by using the term *the State*, the defense indexed all of the associations the jurors might have with large powerful institutions, the government, bureaucracy, and authority. Of course, legally the State was the entity bringing charges against the defendant, and this was part of the formal documents. However, the defense did not have to use this term. By doing so, they made the power of the State a relevant issue. This is clearly seen in this example:

(5) Now when you think about reasonable doubt, this case has a title and the title is "State of ______ vs. Carolyn Joan Jakobson." And if you think about it, that's kind of a heavy thing. The State of ______ versus this woman sitting over here. Okay. The State versus

> an individual person. And you think, well, gee, that's pretty unfair, the State versus an individual person . . . if you think about the scariness of that title, and what does she have against the State of ______? Well, folks, she has you. You stand between her and the State of ______. That's a pretty awesome thing.

The defense lawyers, by referring to the prosecution as *the State*, emphasized the supposed hegemonic power of the prosecution in this context.

There was one category of term of reference that the prosecution and the defense agreed on: nominations. They always used a formal version of the opposing lawyer's name, either *Mr.* ______ or *Ms.* _______. There were no exceptions to this pattern, and it suggests that the formality of the context constrained the names that the lawyers used. What is noteworthy, though, is that this pattern did not extend to the defendants, victims, or the witnesses. As discussed in the previous chapters, lawyers for both sides frequently used the defendants' and victims' first names, although they often included their last name as well. The same pattern held for the witnesses in the trials. Even some of the medical doctors who testified as experts had their first name included (although always preceded by their title and followed by their surname). Also, except for one exception in which the male prosecutor referred to the female defense lawyer as *Miss* ____, the female lawyers were referred to as *Ms.* ______ despite the fact the female defendant, victims, and witnesses were often referred to as *Miss* ______ or *Mrs.* ________. While part of this may have been a factor of age and marital status (which is unknown for most of the participants in the trial), it also is another level of professional courtesy shown to the opposing lawyers that was not shown to the other people who were referred to. It also indexed or maybe even emphasized the status differences between the lawyers and the others involved in the case.

In addition to referring to the opposing side as a single unit, the lawyers also referred to them as part of larger group including the jurors, themselves, and others. Because of the broad nature of the references being made, it wasn't as if the speakers were explicitly pointing to the opposition but rather that they could not exclude them from such conglomerates. As was discussed in the previous chapter, many of the lawyers referred to macro-level groups such as *all people* or *citizens of the United States* to discuss basic commonalities that everyone, including the lawyers and the jurors, shared. These actually accounted for most of the additional references to the opposing side beyond those that referred to them alone. Another set of terms that was also discussed previously was references to everyone *here/in this room/who participated in the trial.* Once again, these did not specifically highlight the opposition but instead linked all of the lawyers, the jurors, the judge, and the other courtroom workers into a single unit, pointed to their common experiences, rights, and responsibilities, and de-emphasized their differences.

A more interesting phenomenon is that in some instances, the lawyers referred to themselves and the other side as a single unit, through either a functionalization (*the attorneys/lawyers/those of us who are in this business* [eleven times total]) or a second-person plural pronoun (however, another group that was constructed contained all the lawyers involved in the case):

(6) What the attorneys say in our statements is not evidence.

By using such terms, the lawyers momentarily silenced the differences between themselves and the opposition.

Overall, despite there being few quantitative differences between the prosecution and the defense in terms of the types of terms they used (except in the rebuttals), they did refer to each other in significantly different ways. The prosecution focused on the idea that a single person was responsible for the other side's argument, while the defense emphasized that the prosecution was part of a much larger government entity. By doing so, the defense silenced or at least de-emphasized the individual identities of the prosecutors and diminished the importance of the jurors perhaps liking/accepting the prosecutors as people.

1.3 THE ROLES OF THE OPPOSITION IN CLAUSES

Table 6.4 shows the distribution of references, divided by type, across the narratives and voices.[4] The first number in each category represents just references to the opposition alone. The number that follows in parenthesis is all references to the other side, including those when the lawyer speaking and others are included.

1.3.1 The Trial Narratives

One important finding from this table is that a majority of the references to the opposition alone came when the lawyer was discussing the past. In the prosecutions' main arguments, they discussed what the opposition had done during the trial. While the defense and rebuttal arguments also included this topic, most of their references to the opposition were in the discussion of the argument they had just given. Interestingly, the prosecution did not try to assume what the defense was going to say and so they rarely discussed their opponents' argument until the rebuttal. Specifically, they made 0.2 references to the defense argument per 1,000 words in their main argument, compared to 3.3 such references/1,000 words in the defense arguments and 6.2/1,000 words in the rebuttals.

1.3.2 The Present and Future Narratives

Another result that Table 6.4 shows is that the prosecution silenced the topics of the general role of the defense in the proceedings and what the

TABLE 6.4

Distribution of References by Type and Narrative

		Prosecution	Defense	Rebuttal
Pronoun	Past	0.1[1,2] (0.2)[3,4]	1.0[1] (1.0)[3]	1.1[2] (1.2)[4]
	Present	0.0 (0.6)	0.1 (0.6)	0.1 (0.4)
	Future	0.0 (0.0)	0.1 (0.1)	—
	Abstract/Generic	—(0.7)[5]	0.2 (1.3)[5]	—(0.9)
Nomination	Past	0.2[6,7]	0.8[6,8]	4.1[7,8]
	Present	0.0[9]	0.1	0.3[9]
	Future	0.0	0.0	—
	General	—	0.0	—
Other	Past	0.3[10,11] (0.3)[13,14]	2.0[10,12] (2.0)[13,15]	0.9[11,12] (1.1)[14,15]
	Present	0.2[16] (0.3)[18,19]	0.7[16,17] (0.7)[18]	0.1[17] (0.9)[19]
	Future	0.0[20] (0.0)[21]	0.2[20] (0.2)[21]	—
	General	—[22] (0.0)[24]	0.4[22,23] (0.6)[24,25]	—[22] (0.0)[25]
Implicit	Past	0.1[26,27] (0.1)[28,29]	0.6[26] (0.6)[28]	0.7[27] (0.7)[29]
	Present	—(0.1)	0.0 (0.1)	—(0.3)
	Future	0.0 (0.0)	0.0 (0.0)	—
	General	—(0.0)[30]	0.1 (1.1)[30,31]	—(0.1)[31]
Total	Past	0.7[32,33] (0.7)[35,36]	4.3[32,34] (4.8)[35,37]	6.7[33,34] (7.0)[36,37]
	Present	0.2[38] (1.0)[39]	0.9[38] (1.4)[39]	0.4 (1.3)
	Future	0.1[40] (0.1)[42]	0.3[40,41] (0.4)[42,43]	—[41,43]
	General	—[44] (0.8)[46]	0.8[44,45] (2.2)[46,47]	—[45] (1.0)[47]

Note: Number per 1,000 words. Differences that are statistically significant are given matching superscripts.

law tells them they can and cannot do. The defense did include these issues in most arguments. They also tended to include what the prosecution had to prove/what their burden was, why they were allowed to go first and last, and so on. In other words, when the two sides are compared to each other, the defense emphasized procedure and the level of proof the prosecution must reach, while the prosecution silenced the rules the defense was working under.

Finally, the defense included the prosecution in the present and in the future more often than the prosecution referenced the defense in these contexts but still did not do it frequently. Some of these occurred in interactive greetings that both used:

(7) May it please the Court, counsel, members of the jury . . .

In other instances, one side evaluated the other's case, as in:

(8) The State's case is all speculation. Their case is all circumstantial.
(9) The State's case is lacking.

The final tokens were when the lawyers expressed the similarities or differences in opinion between the two sides:

(10) I agree with Mr. Roades.
(11) I have a difference of opinion with Mr. Roosevelt.

While neither side emphasized these topics, the defense did refer to them slightly more than the prosecution did. The defense was simply more likely to indicate that the other side had an alternative argument, although as these examples show, they often remained vague rather than discussing the specific details they disagreed with, so they were still able to de-emphasize or even silence the prosecution's claims.

1.4 SUMMARY

Silencing, de-emphasizing, and emphasizing again played important roles in the ways the prosecution and the defense constructed the opposition. Both sides, but especially the prosecution in their main argument, included only a few references to their opponents and thus de-emphasized them compared to the other issues they discussed. The defense lawyers emphasized the fact that the prosecution was part of the government through the terms they chose in order to construct the idea that the prosecution was a monolithic giant entity working against an individual. This contrasted with the prosecution attorneys, who created the sense that the defense's case was the opinion of a single person by using the lawyer's name to refer to him or her. Thus, across the choices the lawyers made, they systematically silenced, de-emphasized, and emphasized different aspects of who the other side was. They tended to not overtly attack the other side, and when they did, it was often very restrained. While this may not be true in all trials, these results show that mostly ignoring the other side, except to point out whether they should be viewed as an individual or as part of a large group, was a common strategy in this corpus.

2 Lawyers' Constructions of Themselves

2.1 FREQUENCY OF REFERENCE

In addition to creating discursive representations of the attorneys for the other side, the lawyers also had to construct identities for themselves in the arguments. Like any speaker, they had to negotiate their roles both as speakers and as characters in the events being described, as well as their relationships with the different participants, the context, and the content of the discourses themselves.

Importantly, the lawyers mentioned themselves significantly more frequently than they mentioned the other side—more proof that each side was emphasizing its own argument and de-emphasizing or silencing the other's. As Table 6.5 shows, a majority of each side's self-references were to themselves

TABLE 6.5

Frequency of Reference to Lawyer Speaking

		Prosecution	Defense	Rebuttal
Speaker alone	Explicit reference	8.7^{1,2}	10.9^{1,3}	14.2^{2,3}
	Agent or recipient	10.0^{4,5}	12.8^{4,6}	17.4^{5,6}
Speaker as part of a group	Explicit reference	6.5	7.0	6.1
	Agent or recipient	7.4	8.1^{7}	6.4^{7}
Total self-references	Explicit reference	15.1^{8,9}	18.0^{8}	20.3^{9}
	Agent or recipient	17.4^{10,11}	20.9^{10,12}	23.8^{11,12}

Note: Number per 1,000 words. Differences that are statistically significant are given matching superscripts.

alone, while the rest are references to them as part of a group including people such as the jurors, other lawyers, or all Americans.

A comparison of the prosecution and the defense main arguments reveals that the defense made more references to themselves, both alone and as part of groups. Specifically, the defense referred to themselves explicitly 2.9 more times per 1,000 words than the prosecution did and as an agent or recipient of a process 3.5 more times per 1,000 words. In fact, this pattern held true in twelve of the seventeen trials where, despite the defense arguments generally being shorter in terms of total words, they still contained more references to the lawyer speaking. Although there were five exceptions to this pattern and although the actual difference per 1,000 words was relatively small, the fact is that in general the defense lawyers tended to talk more about themselves and thus emphasized their own role in the events more than the prosecution lawyers did.

What is more remarkable is the difference between the prosecution's main argument and their rebuttal. Despite making fewer references to themselves as part of a group in their rebuttals, the prosecutors significantly increased their references to themselves as individuals. In fact, they even referred to themselves more often per 1,000 words than the defense lawyers did. In other words, the rebuttals were when the prosecutors emphasized what they had said during the trial and in their main argument, what they thought, and what they wanted done. This is particularly interesting because the rebuttals were the lawyers' opportunity to refer to their opponent's argument, but once again, they were emphasizing themselves and their own understanding of the case.

2.2 TERMS OF SELF-REFERENCE

As mentioned, there were two types of references used for the lawyer who was speaking: first person singular terms and first person plural terms. Each will be discussed separately, with Table 6.6 showing the distribution of the singular references, and Table 6.7 displaying the breakdown of the plural references.

TABLE 6.6

Terms of Reference for the Speaker

		Prosecution	Defense	Rebuttal
Pronouns	Percent of references	*98.2%*	*98.9%*	*99.6%*
	Number per 1,000 words	8.5[1, 2]	10.9[1, 3]	14.1[2, 3]
	Total number	769	888	266
Other	Percent of references	*1.8%*	*1.1%*	*0.4%*
	Number per 1,000 words	0.2	0.1	0.1
	Total number	14	10	1

Note: Differences that are statistically significant are given matching superscripts.

TABLE 6.7

Terms of Reference for the Speaker with Others

		Prosecution	Defense	Rebuttal
Pronouns	Percent of references	*82.2%*[1]	*96.7%*[1, 2]	*80.9%*[2]
	Number per 1,000 words	5.3[3]	6.8[3, 4]	4.9[4]
	Total number	479	552	93
Other	Percent of references	*17.8%*[5]	*3.3%*[5, 6]	*19.1%*[6]
	Number per 1,000 words	1.2[7]	0.2[7, 8]	1.2[8]
	Total number	104	19	22

Note: Differences that are statistically significant are given matching superscripts.

As would be expected, almost all first person singular references (over 98% in every type of argument) were pronouns (*I, me, my*, and *myself*).

The non-pronoun references occurred in the introductions, when the lawyers gave their names and/or job titles. As can be seen from the total number of each, not every lawyer did this, and in fact, the defense lawyers were less likely to introduce themselves by name.

As can be seen in Table 6.7, the first person plural references were much more interesting than the singular terms.

The most obvious difference is that prosecutors used fewer pronouns (*we, our*, etc.) than the defense did and a much higher percentage of their first person plural references were noun phrases to specifically name which group they were referring to (e.g., *the State*,[5] *attorneys*, *all the citizens of this country*). The defense was more prone to using an undefined *we* for which the context had to be used to determine the referents. An example can be seen here, where *we* refers to the defense team:

(12) The presumption of innocence also means that we don't have to prove anything. In the instructions that you read, that was one of the sentences under the definition. We can just sit back and let the State prove their case.

In some instances, the exact group was not determinable from the surrounding discourse, and thus every hearer was forced to decide if they were being included and who else might also have been included in the reference. Given Biber et al.'s (1999) finding that it is common that hearers are forced to make assumptions about who is being referred to by a first-person plural pronoun, it is not surprising this is true in the closing arguments as well.

Table 6.8 further breaks down the first person plural references to show who was minimally included in the reference.[6]

While both sides used plural references to include themselves in a group with the jurors (as was discussed in the previous chapter), the defense lawyers used more of their self-references for this purpose. At the same time, the prosecution lawyers referenced their entire side as being responsible for the argument more often than the defense lawyers did. This is important because the defense had also emphasized this idea that the prosecution was a larger entity than just the lawyer presenting the argument. The only other difference is that the defense lawyers referred to all people as having certain traits or tendencies more often, but the difference was relatively minor.

The first-person plural pronouns that included at least the lawyer and the jurors (and in some cases all participants in the trial or all people) were discussed in the previous chapter, so they will not be discussed in detail here. However, the important finding is that the lawyers were creating a group that silenced the differences between themselves and the jurors. In doing so, they constructed the jurors and sometimes others as being in agreement with the lawyer's argument, which was what the lawyer ultimately wanted. To put it another way, the lawyers emphasized the similarities they had with the other referents and silenced their differences.

When the lawyers used pronouns to refer to their entire side as acting as a single group, they were including the idea that each of the speakers was simply the presenter of the argument but that the entire side (be it the government, all of the lawyers on the team, the defendant and the lawyer, etc.) was responsible for the message. In some instances, this was used when multiple lawyers had been in charge of different portions of the trial:

TABLE 6.8

Distribution of First Person Plural References

	Prosecution	Defense	Rebuttal
Lawyer and jurors	49.6%[1] (3.7)[3, 4]	63.4%[1, 2] (5.1)[3, 5]	38.3%[2] (2.4)[4, 5]
Lawyer and side	28.4%[6] (2.1)[8]	11.7%[6, 7] (0.9)[8, 9]	29.2%[7] (1.9)[9]
Lawyer and a witness	0.3% (0.0)	0.2% (0.0)	0.0% (—)
All lawyers	8.0% (0.6)	5.6% (0.5)	9.2% (0.6)
All participants	3.5% (0.3)	1.7%[10] (0.1)[11]	7.5%[10] (0.5)[11]
All people	10.2%[12] (0.8)[13]	17.5%[12] (1.4)[13]	15.8% (1.0)

Note: Differences that are statistically significant are given matching superscripts.

(13) We told you this was going to be a simple case, straightforward. We put on just a handful of witnesses, and their testimony wasn't very long.

The division of labor among the different attorneys was erased, and their actions were constructed as being those of the group rather than those of individual actors. At other times, the use of these pronouns simply created a united voice among all members of the team to show that a claim or situation was bigger than just one person's opinion or request, as in the following example:

(14) And this is the dilemma we're in. How do we prove it didn't happen? We prove it by showing the circumstances, possible motivations, evidence of innocence, and we ask that you view and interpret this under that, that prism of innocence.

In such instances, the jurors' reaction to the individual lawyer who was speaking was less relevant than how they felt about the team of people being represented. For example, if the jurors did not like the lawyer, they could still accept the request by seeing it coming from another person whom they did like.

The next group referenced with *we* was all lawyers, and on the surface, this is perhaps unexpected in that the lawyers were using their arguments to differentiate themselves from the other side. Yet with these pronouns, they were aligning themselves with their opposition. Importantly, this grouping tended to be used in two contexts: (1) when the speaker was emphasizing his or her status as a lawyer and (2) when politeness was maximized and face-threatening acts were being mitigated. An example of the second is when an attack on the opposition was mitigated by the use of a first-person plural pronoun, as in:

(15) What the attorneys say is not evidence.

The lawyer used this statement to discredit the other side while not explicitly saying that the other person as an individual had lied or was at least wrong. Thus, in these limited situations, the lawyers' larger goals overrode the need to separate themselves from the other side.

Overall, second-person plural references permitted the lawyers to create groups that did not necessarily exist in reality or that were not necessarily obvious to the listeners. In doing so, they emphasized the characteristics they shared with the other members of the group and silenced their differences.

2.3 THE ROLES OF THE SPEAKERS IN CLAUSES

References that the lawyers made to themselves served many purposes. Many, both singular and plural, were used to create a meta-discourse, a discussion of what the lawyer had said, was saying, and was going to say. In other words, they were used by the lawyers to create an explicit outline of the discourse for the jurors to follow. Other first person references were to the mental and physical properties of the lawyers: what they had heard/seen, what they knew and/or believed, and what they wanted or hoped for. Lawyers rarely, if ever, mitigated statements with *I think that*, which would have implied a lack of certainty. By not using such forms, lawyers silenced their own doubts and the holes in their knowledge. In many cases, they included other people such as the jurors, other lawyers, or all people in the reference to create a sense of shared understandings and experiences. Finally, they used self-references to create a polite persona. Some lawyers spent the opening of their arguments providing information about themselves (their name, role, etc.), thanking the jurors, and apologizing or at least acknowledging the time and effort they spent. All of these types of references allowed the lawyers to give themselves visible roles as characters in the discourse rather than just being the animator and author.

Table 6.9 presents the breakdown of the different types of references as well as the totals, depending on which narrative/voice they occurred in. For both sides, most of the references to the lawyers were in the present context, when they were interacting as the speaker rather than as a character in a narrative. References to what they had done, said, or thought in the past were the next most common. The least frequently used categories were references to

TABLE 6.9

Distribution of References by Type and Narrative

		Prosecution	Defense	Rebuttal
Pronoun	Past	2.5[1, 2] (1.5)[3, 4]	3.4[1] (2.3)[3]	4.1[2] (3.0)[4]
	Present	9.0[5, 6] (5.5)[7, 8]	11.7[5] (7.2)[7, 9]	11.8[6] (9.0)[8, 9]
	Future	1.5 (1.4)	1.3 (1.2)	1.3 (1.3)
	General	0.8[10, 11] (0.2)[12]	1.3[10] (0.2)[13]	1.8[11] (0.9)[12, 13]
Other	Past	0.4[14] (0.1)	0.0[14] (—)	0.1 (—)
	Present	0.9[15] (0.1)	0.2[15, 16] (0.1)	1.1[16] (0.1)
	Future	0.0 (0.0)	0.0 (0.0)	0.0 (—)
	General	0.0 (—)	0.1 (—)	0.1 (—)
Implicit	Past	0.2[17] (0.1)[19]	0.2[18] (0.1)[20]	0.6[17, 18] (0.4)[19, 20]
	Present	1.1 (0.4)	1.5 (0.6)	1.5 (0.4)
	Future	0.9[21] (0.9)[23]	1.0[22] (1.0)[24]	2.4[21, 22] (2.4)[23, 24]
	General	0.1[25] (0.0)	0.3[25] (0.1)	0.1 (0.1)
Total	Past	3.0[26] (1.6)[28, 29]	3.6[27] (2.4)[28, 30]	4.9[26, 27] (3.3)[29, 30]
	Present	11.0[31, 32] (5.9)[33, 34]	13.4[31] (7.9)[33]	13.2[32] (9.4)[34]
	Future	2.4[35] (2.3)[37]	2.3[36] (2.2)[38]	3.7[35, 36] (3.7)[37, 38]
	General	0.9[39, 40] (0.2)[41]	1.7[39] (0.3)[42]	2.0[40] (1.0)[41,42]

Note: Number per 1,000 words. Differences that are statistically significant are given matching superscripts.

the lawyers in the future and to them in general or abstract contexts. At least from a quantitative perspective, there were very few differences between the prosecution and the defense.

Two main differences are seen in this table. The defense emphasized themselves and their role in the present and past proceedings slightly more than the prosecution did in their main arguments. The defense focused more on their own actions, their evaluations of the people and data, and their role in the present events more than the defense did. The prosecution shifted to be more like the defense in their rebuttals, but in their main arguments, they did not include themselves as much.

On the other hand, the prosecution discussed the future[7] more, at least in their rebuttals. This was simply the result of a higher percentage of the references in the rebuttals being a meta-discourse, as in the following example:

(16) And I'll read the definition for that.

Interestingly, the rebuttals were shorter and fewer details were given about topics, so more of the clauses were spent introducing new topics and saying what was to come.

This table also does not reveal all of the differences between the two sides in terms of their first person references. For instance, it does not show that when discussing the past (the trial and the earlier parts of the closing arguments), almost half of the prosecution's first person plural references referred to their entire side (0.7 references per 1,000 words in the main argument, 0.8 references per 1,000 words in the rebuttals[8]), while the defense mainly silenced the other members of their team in this context (0.1 references per 1,000 words, difference significant for $p<0.000001$). This same pattern held in the present interactive voice as well. This meant that the prosecution was emphasizing what their team had done, said, and thought. In contrast, the defense lawyers used their past and present references mostly to refer to themselves and the jurors as a unit in order to foreground their shared experiences and interpretations of events, people, and evidence.

3 Conclusions

To conclude, although there were only a few differences between the prosecution and the defense, they did add to the creation of opposing arguments. Defense lawyers tended to emphasize themselves more and while doing so, focused on building a shared relationship with the jurors. On the other hand, the prosecution tended to refer to themselves slightly less often and to spend more of their references creating a meta-discourse to organize their argument. More important, however, each side emphasized themselves and their own claims while silencing or at least de-emphasizing the other's. By doing so, they created arguments about very different topics and sets of claims.

Silencing, de-emphasizing, and emphasizing were also seen in the patterns of self-reference that both sides used relatively equally: they emphasized themselves, their position in the context, their own interpretation of the events, and their commonalities with other people, particularly the jurors. They silenced or de-emphasized doubts, differences of opinion, and uncertainty.

Through these processes, the lawyers managed to create representations of themselves that included disparate characteristics. They made themselves seem similar to the jurors (through first-person plural pronouns) and likable (through polite forms), yet they also portrayed themselves as authoritative (the silencing of doubt and uncertainty). As discussed in Chapter 1, lawyers are constantly trying to manage these two sides of their courtroom identity, and they do it through a number of means: code-switching into a nonstandard dialect to seem likable (Fuller 1993; Hobbs 2003) or into legalese to seem knowledgeable (Felton Rosulek 2009). In this chapter, self-references, along with silence, de-emphasis, and emphasis, were shown to be another set of tools for them to use.

7

The Big Picture

When the results of this book are taken at their most general, they confirm what several researchers have found: that the prosecution and the defense focus on different topics in their closing arguments. Walter (1988) found this to be true, as did Amsterdam and Hertz (1992), Costanzo and Peterson (1994), and Hobbs (2005). How the analysis presented in this book differed from the earlier studies is that it examined a relatively large corpus, used both qualitative and quantitative methodologies, and examined how various linguistic and discursive choices all worked together to accomplish the lawyers' opposing goals. In the end, the finding that emerged was that the processes of silencing, de-emphasizing, and emphasizing, understood as parts of a continuum from exclusion to inclusion, are the key means through which lawyers create contrasting representations of the same people, events, and issues.

Although the quantitative results comparing the prosecution's and defense's references to the various key social actors involved in a trial have been presented throughout the book, they are shown here again in Tables 7.1 and 7.2, except that now the prosecution's main arguments and rebuttals have been combined into a single value. In many ways, their two arguments were simply parts of a larger whole, and this represents that finding. In Table 7.1, only explicit references of the relevant social actor are included; in Table 7.2, instances when the referent was the assumed (but elided) agent or recipient of a process are also included. The most important pattern to notice in these tables is that for every single actor, the two sides differed significantly in terms of how frequently they included them.

As these results show, the prosecution tended to emphasize the defendant and victim more than the defense did, while the defense gave comparatively more focus to the victims and the jurors. The defense also spent more of their argument discussing the opposition (the prosecution) and themselves.

TABLE 7.1

Frequency of Explicit References

	Prosecution	Defense
Defendants	37.8[1] (4,124)	27.5[1] (2,239)
Victims (with and without cases with more than one victim)	36.4[2] (3,720)/33.3[3] (2,576)	29.4 (2,185)/30.1[3] (1,993)
Jurors	24.4[4] (2,663)	28.3[4] (2,307)
Opposing side	3.3[5] (362)	6.6[5] (537)
Lawyer who was speaking	16.0[6] (1,748)	18.0[6] (1,469)

Note: Number per 1,000 words and total number of tokens. Differences that are statistically significant are given matching superscripts.

TABLE 7.2

Frequency of Explicit or Implicit References

	Prosecution	Defense
Defendants	40.8[1] (4,442)	28.1[1] (2,291)
Victims (with and without cases with more than one victim)	40.8[2] (4,173)/37.3[3] (2,890)	33.9[2] (2,522)/33.8[3] (2,237)
Jurors	27.8[4] (3,031)	33.8[4] (2,752)
Opposing side	3.7[5] (404)	8.8[5] (715)
Lawyer who was speaking	18.5[6] (2,018)	20.9[6] (1,701)

Note: Number per 1,000 words and total number of tokens. Differences that are statistically significant are given matching superscripts.

Although these quantitative results are important for understanding how the lawyers created opposing arguments, they were only a small part of the story. The lawyers for the two sides included different information about each of these social actors by portraying them as the agents and recipients of different processes. For instance, the prosecution tended to emphasize the crime narrative and to silence what the defendant may have been thinking or feeling during the trial and closing arguments. The defense did the opposite.

The lawyers also selected very different lexical and syntactic forms. For instance, some of the prosecution lawyers emphasized the youth of the victims in their cases by referring to them by their nicknames, while the defense de-emphasized this by using their full names. Additionally, the defense often de-emphasized or even silenced the negative (violent, sexual, criminal, etc.) aspects of the defendant's alleged or known actions by not mentioning them or using generalizations, nominations, and other similar forms to hide their true nature. All of these forms worked together to allow the lawyers to present different understandings of the same reality, and they are all examples of silencing, de-emphasizing, and emphasizing.

1 Generalizability of the Results

Perhaps the most important question that arises from the analysis presented in this book is whether or not the results are generalizable beyond this speech community. The basic answer is that they are if we are talking about the processes of silencing, de-emphasizing, and emphasizing. The specifics of how lawyers may employ these are likely to differ, as there was a great deal of variation within the corpus itself, but that is actually not important. What is key is that these larger processes can be used to explain and unite all lawyers' seemingly unrelated linguistic and discursive processes. As will be argued in this chapter, even when individual lawyers make difference choices, these processes are still being used.

While it is not necessary that the specific patterns described in this book are found in closing arguments in other locations, there is also no reason to think that summations presented elsewhere are drastically different. While certain preferences and tendencies are likely to differ, most of the general patterns are likely to stay the same. In order to demonstrate this, the same analyses performed on the corpus were also applied to the closing arguments from a trial whose features made it fundamentally different from the cases described in the previous chapters. While a comparison with one case can hardly prove generalizability, the similar patterns found in the arguments from this other trial and the larger corpus suggest that the findings presented in the book are not limited to the legal community studied here.

1.1 THE SANDUSKY CASE

The case chosen was the Jerry Sandusky trial, in which a Pennsylvania State University football coach was charged with sexually abusing and assaulting 10 children over a period of several years. There are several reasons that this case was so different from those in the corpus. First of all, this trial and the others took place in towns almost 1,000 miles apart. According to basically every classification system (cultural, political, social, geographical) (Gastil 1992), these two locations are in different regions of the United States. Second, the Sandusky trial was dissimilar to the other cases in that it involved a public figure who was somewhat famous, and several people involved in the case were also well known. Therefore, it received a great deal of attention in the national and international press. As the defense lawyer said during his closing argument:

(1) With all the publicity—this has gone international, folks. This isn't Centre County. This isn't Pennsylvania. This isn't eastern United States. This is international.

None of the cases in the original corpus had this feature. Finally, the procedure for presenting the closing arguments in this case differed from those in the corpus in that the defense presented their argument first and then the prosecution gave theirs (i.e., the prosecution argument was both their main argument and their rebuttal). Given all of these differences, this is an ideal case for a comparison with the corpus.[1]

1.2 FREQUENCY OF REFERENCE

Table 7.3 presents a summary of the results for the corpus (with the prosecution main and rebuttal arguments combined) and the Sandusky trial.[2] While there are several obvious differences (e.g., the frequencies of reference to the defendant, the prosecution attorney's self-references), the Sandusky case, particularly the defense argument, is very similar to many in the corpus. Additionally, and more important, different patterns of silencing, de-emphasizing, and emphasizing were key for the Sandusky prosecution's and defense's creation of opposing arguments.

1.2.1 References to the Defendant

The first difference between the corpus and the Sandusky case is how infrequently the prosecution referred to the defendant and how frequently the defense did. In fact, the quantitative results for the defendant were the reverse of those in the corpus. However, a closer analysis reveals that given the variation found in the corpus, these results do not make the Sandusky case fundamentally different. As the descriptions of the three cases discussed in detail in Chapter 3 showed, many of the cases did not conform exactly to the results for the corpus as a whole. The Sandusky case simply reflects this high level of variation among arguments.

The frequency at which the defendant was the agent or recipient of a process for the defense argument in the Sandusky case was quite high compared to a majority of the cases analyzed, but even higher frequencies were found (range: 8.2–79.2 times/1,000 words). Therefore, the defense in the Sandusky trial could have been part of the corpus without being an outlier.

The bigger issue is that the prosecution's frequency for references to the defendant, 22.7 times per 1,000 words, was significantly different from the

TABLE 7.3

Comparison to Sandusky for Frequency at Which the Referent Played a Role in a Process

	Corpus Prosecution	Sandusky Prosecution	Corpus Defense	Sandusky Defense
Defendants	40.7^{1} (4,442)	22.7^{1} (268)	28.1^{5} (2,291)	49.8^{5} (526)
Victims (with cases with more than one victim)	40.8 (4,173)	42.5 (501)	33.9^{6} (2,522)	45.7^{6} (483)
Jurors	27.8^{2} (3,031)	37.0^{2} (436)	3.8 (2,752)	31.6 (334)
Opposing side	3.7^{3} (404)	12.4^{3} (146)	8.8 (715)	6.8 (72)
Lawyer who was speaking	18.5^{4} (2,018)	46.9^{4} (553)	20.9^{7} (1,701)	26.8^{7} (283)

Note: Number per 1,000 words. Differences that are statistically significant are given matching superscripts.

finding for the corpus as a whole and in fact was slightly lower than even the prosecution argument, with the most infrequent references to the defendant (the minimum was 23.8 times per 1,000 words). However, the difference between this case and the case with the minimum is small. Also, the finding that the defendant played a smaller role in the prosecution's version of events was actually a common pattern in the sub-set of cases in the corpus dealing with child sexual abuse/assault. Five of those six cases had frequencies less than the rate for the entire corpus, and three of the six were in the mid-20 range (24.5, 25.0, and 26.2 instances/1,000 words). Since these numbers are so similar to the Sandusky case, it appears that the prosecution's infrequent references could have been the result of the type of case being tried, rather than it being representative of the different speech communities. While it is possible that in other cases, or perhaps in other court systems, the prosecution does not focus on the defendant quite as often as the lawyers did in this corpus, this is not a necessary conclusion to make. Also, if it is true that in many cases, prosecution lawyers do not emphasize the defendant quite as much as they did in this corpus, that does not change the finding that silencing, de-emphasizing, and emphasizing are essential processes in how the two sides discuss the defendants. In the Sandusky case, the defense referred to the defendant more than twice as many times as the prosecution did. Thus, there is no doubt that the defense emphasized him while the prosecution de-emphasized him.

The reason the two sides in the Sandusky case differed with regard to the frequency of reference to the defendant is that the defense discussed many topics that the prosecution silenced. For example, the defense discussed how the defendant was negatively affected by the charges and trial:

(2) On November 5th of last year, Sandusky's world came to an end. His wife's world came to an end. His children's world came to an end. Everything they ever fought for, everything they ever believed in was challenged

(3) I wish I could get forgiveness now speaking to the mother . . . I wish I were dead . . . I feel horrible.

They also included his personal characteristics:

(4) He's touchy. He's feely. He's sensitive. He loves kids.

And they discussed events he took part in which showed him to be a "good" person:

(5) Jerry should have been mad. He was apologizing to Jerry, and Jerry said something to the effect, "Don't worry about it. I'm not angry. These kids have problems. These kids have issues. We have to be there for them."

The mental and qualitative processes in these examples were not included in the prosecution's case. The defense also included additional, non-criminal processes (often material or location processes) that the defendant was involved in at the time a crime supposedly took place:

(6) During football season in the fall . . . they were 17-hour days, starting at 7:00 in the morning and finishing up at 10:00 or 11:00 at night . . . he was home at night to have dinner with his kids.

Importantly, these are the exact patterns seen in case #12, which was analyzed in Felton Rosulek (2008), and in the three cases analyzed in detail in Chapter 3. The defense focused on the defendant's qualities, feelings and thoughts, and non-criminal processes, while the prosecution silenced them. This directly led to distinctly different interpretations of reality being presented in the arguments both in the corpus and in the Sandusky trial.

1.2.2 References to the Victims

Unlike the findings for the defendants, the results for the victims in the Sandusky case were not very different from those in the corpus. In fact, the prosecution in the Sandusky case referred to the victims as agents or recipients at about the same rate as the prosecutors did in the corpus as a whole. While it may be noted that the prosecutor in the Sandusky case referred to the victims more than the defendant, which was the opposite of the pattern found in the corpus, this was true in all of the child sexual abuse/assault cases analyzed here. Therefore, the results from the Sandusky trial are once again simply part of a pattern seen within this sub-set of trials, and as such they are a confirmation of how similar the Sandusky case was to the other cases analyzed here.

As for the Sandusky defense, as they had for the defendant, they referred to the victims quite frequently, more than in the corpus as a whole. However, once again, there was a large amount of variation seen in the corpus, and the results from the Sandusky defense fit in the range seen in individual cases (13.1–105.4 tokens/1,000 words). Also, in the corpus, when the victims in the cases were not necessarily sympathetic or were at least assailable, the defense tended to refer to them more often. In the Sandusky case, the defense claimed that the victims were just after money and attention, and so they discussed them more frequently in order to attack them negatively in this way.

Another similarity for the corpus and the Sandusky case was the finding that when there were multiple victims in a case, the prosecution and the defense tended to focus on different individuals. For example, in the Sandusky prosecution's closing argument, the victim who had provided the most explicit testimony was referred to quite frequently. He was explicitly referenced thirty-one times as an individual and was the sole agent or recipient of a process, some of them sexual, thirty-four times. In the defense argument, he was mentioned as an individual only once and was the recipient of one non-sexual process. Thus, he was included in the prosecution argument but was de-emphasized and almost silenced in the defense argument. This is the exact same pattern as was seen in case #11, which was described in Chapter 4, where the victim who suffered more heinous acts was emphasized by the prosecution and silenced by the defense.

1.2.3 References to the Jurors

The frequencies for the references to the jurors as agents or recipients in the Sandusky prosecution were also higher than the value for the corpus, but individual cases within it did have values as large, so again this does not necessarily represent a difference in the speech communities. Also, the numbers for the Sandusky defense for this form were very similar to those in the corpus.

Additionally, the types of processes used by both the prosecution and the defense with the jury as the agent or the recipient were the same in both the corpus and in the Sandusky case. For instance, during the trial narrative, the jurors were often the recipients of speaking or material verbs that represented actions that are involved in someone showing or demonstrating something:

(7) Folks, what he told you . . .
(8) I showed you a picture . . .

They were also the agents of the related behavioral processes:

(9) That's what you saw, the perfect serial pedophile. You heard it from the testimony.

In the "here-and-now," other than when the jurors were referred to in vocatives, they were often the agents of mental processes that silenced doubt:

(10) You know that's what he's doing
(11) That's what she said . . . if you recall that

Or else they were the agents or recipients of verbal processes as part of the meta-discursive framework being created by the lawyers:

(12) Let's talk about Gus Costas.
(13) I would submit to you . . .

Finally, the jurors were the agents of mental, verbal, material, and even possessive properties when they were told what to do in their future deliberations:

(14) Acknowledge it. Give them justice and give him the justice he really deserves. Find him guilty of everything.
(15) You have to use your common sense, folks.

As was shown in Chapter 5, these were the exact same types of processes in which the jurors were included in the arguments in the corpus. By using these forms, the lawyers silenced or de-emphasized the jurors' doubts and differences of opinion/understanding, constructed identities for the jurors that included or even emphasized certain properties beneficial to the lawyers, acknowledged and even overstated the role of the jurors as hearers/co-interlocutors, and instructed them on their future behavior. While different lawyers may have referenced the jurors with differing frequency and may have focused on one of these issues more than another, the important part is that the same types of constructions occurred across a variety of cases and locations, and the lawyers consistently employed the power of silencing, de-emphasizing, and emphasizing.

1.2.4 References to the Opposition

Another difference seen in Table 7.3 is that the prosecution in the Sandusky case discussed the other side more often, but the defense discussed them less. This is likely the result of the order of the arguments. In the corpus, the prosecution went first, and they tended not to discuss the defense case at all. If they did mention it, it was in the rebuttal, but this tended to be short and centered around a few issues. The defense, because they went second, could address the prosecution's claims in slightly more detail. In the Sandusky case, the order of the arguments was switched, and so the pattern was also reversed. However, the general tendencies were the same. Lawyers for both sides tended to silence what the other side said or did during the trial, they tended not to speculate on what the other side might say in a future argument, and most important, they de-emphasized the other side's argument while emphasizing their own.

1.2.5 Self-References

The final difference seen in Table 7.3 that separates the Sandusky case from the corpus as a whole was that the prosecution lawyer referred to himself frequently, in fact, more than any other social actor involved in the case. This was not true of the defense lawyer in this case, and this did not happen in any case in the corpus. This result was mostly the result of the Sandusky prosecutor spending a significant portion of his argument telling stories about himself that were not directly related to this case: what he did as a child, as a soldier, and as a prosecutor of murder cases. Additionally, he defended himself against the defense's suggestion that this case was a conspiracy to bring down a famous person. By focusing on these topics, he made his argument personal to him in a way that other lawyers analyzed here did not. While some did tell similar types of stories, they were relatively rare in the corpus, and none of them told three or spent such time on them. However, none of them needed to defend themselves against such claims. Also, this result still shows the importance of emphasis in the creation of opposing arguments. The prosecution lawyer emphasized himself. The defense lawyer did not and thus had more time to focus on other topics such as the defendant's personal characteristics.

1.2.6 Summary

Overall, for most of the quantitative results shown in Table 7.3, the prosecution and the defense in the Sandusky case (which took place in very different circumstances from those in the corpus) were more similar to those in the corpus than it might first appear. Even when the Sandusky case differed from the values for the corpus as a whole, the results tended to be in the range seen in the other cases, especially those that were similar to it in terms of type. The other differences were explainable given the specific circumstances of the Sandusky case and trial.

1.3 OTHER FINDINGS

In addition to the discursive patterns just described, there were many important similarities and some minor differences in the linguistic (lexical and syntactic) selections made in the Sandusky trial and in the corpus. Instead of presenting another complete analysis of a case as was done throughout the book, a few examples will be discussed here to prove this point.

1.3.1 Terms of Reference for the Defendant

Table 7.4 presents the non-pronominal references to the defendant in the corpus and in the Sandusky trial.[3] The number of tokens per 1,000 words is not necessarily comparable because of the decreased frequency of reference in the Sandusky prosecution and the increased frequency in the Sandusky defense. However, the percents for each type of reference show just how similar the Sandusky case was to the corpus. For this feature, there were no real differences between them.

Once again, the prosecution de-emphasized (almost to the point of silencing) the defendant's name and unique personhood while the defense emphasized it. The prosecution instead relied on functionalizations, mainly *the defendant* (77.6% of the functionalizations), a term the defense, at least in the Sandusky case, never used. Neither side used categorizations very often but did use them strategically, especially to point out relevant personal relationships (e.g., *his coach*, *his mentor*).

The only difference between the corpus and the Sandusky trial was that the types of nominations used were different. The most frequently used form for both sides in the Sandusky case was just the surname of the defendant (60% of the prosecution's references, 39.5% of the defense's terms). This form was relatively rare in the corpus. While one might suspect that it was because the

TABLE 7.4

Non-Pronominal Terms of Reference for the Defendant

		Corpus Prosecution	Sandusky Prosecution	Corpus Defense	Sandusky Defense
Nominations	Percent of references	*6.4%*	*2.3%*	*27.8%*	*27.6%*
	Number per 1,000 words	2.4^{1}	0.4^{1}	7.6^{3}	11.7^{3}
	Total number	262	5	622	124
Functionalizations	Percent of references	*29.9%*	*31.5%*	*4.7%*	*2.7%*
	Number per 1,000 words	11.3^{2}	5.7^{2}	1.3	1.1
	Total number	1231	67	106	12
Categorizations	Percent of references	*3.6%*	*5.6%*	*3.2%*	*5.3%*
	Number per 1,000 words	1.4	1.0	0.9^{4}	2.3^{4}
	Total number	147	12	71	24

Note: Differences that are statistically significant are given matching superscripts.

defendant was a coach and this form is used in sports, it seems more likely that this is a tendency of the local speech community, as the lawyers also used each other's surnames to refer to each other (but in the corpus the lawyers always used a title and surname). The defense also used the defendant's first name frequently (41.1% of nominations), which some lawyers in the corpus did but most did not. This created a sense of a very informal and personal relationship between the lawyer and his client and between the defendant and the jurors.

1.3.2 Terms of Reference for the Victims

With regard to the victims, just as in the corpus as a whole, there were few differences between the terms used by the prosecution and by the defense. Both sides referred to the victims with just their first name or else their first and last name. The defense tended to use the semi-formal terms, while the prosecution mostly used the informal first name only. Other than that, the one small difference between the prosecution and the defense was that the defense sometimes referred to the victims as *accusers* and *alleged victims*, which the prosecution never did. Thus the prosecution silenced these properties of their identities.

A final note about the lawyers' references to the victims is that the prosecution in the Sandusky case put up pictures of each of the victims, so they had a visual presence. This made them distinct from the other witnesses being discussed. The defense did not do this, and thus comparatively de-emphasized them as people. This was not done in the corpus, but since most of those cases only involved one witness and since they took place at least seven years before the Sandusky trial, the circumstances and changes in the use of technology could explain the difference.

1.3.3 Terms of Reference for the Other Social Actors

The terms of reference used for the other relevant social actors were mostly the same in the Sandusky case, as in the corpus. The jurors were called *ladies and gentlemen* or *folks* when not referred to with a pronoun. The lawyers did not refer to themselves by name but used first person pronouns. However, there were two differences found for the references to the opposing lawyer. First, the prosecution in the Sandusky case was referred to as *the Commonwealth* rather than *the State* because that is what Pennsylvania is known as. This is a trivial difference. Second, as mentioned above, the Sandusky lawyers referred to each other using just their surnames and not a title and a surname. Given how consistent this was across social actors, it seems this is likely a feature either of these two lawyers' idiolects or of the local speech community.

1.3.4 Metaphors

Other than the patterns for the terms of reference, another linguistic property that was examined was the use of metaphors. As was mentioned in earlier chapters, Cotterill (2003) had reported that in the closing arguments of the OJ Simpson case, the lawyers used many metaphors to point out or, to use the terminology of this book, emphasize certain properties of the defendant and each lawyer's argument. However, this pattern was not found in the corpus. It was also not seen in the Sandusky case. While the lawyer did use a few metaphors incidentally (*laid at the feet of Penn State*), there were not any that were used frequently or systematically. This is despite the fact that the prosecution had labeled Sandusky a *predatory pedophile*, which is ripe for hunting or animal metaphors. With the evidence from the corpus and the Sandusky case, we must conclude that while some lawyers, such as those in the OJ Simpson case, may use metaphors and figurative or poetic language for strategic purposes, many do not.

1.3.5 Syntactic Patterns

The final major linguistic pattern seen in the corpus was the defense lawyers' tendency to silence the active role of their client and the sexual, violent, or criminal nature of the act, information the prosecution emphasized. To do so, they often used more generalizations, nominalizations, and passives. These same patterns and forms were found in the Sandusky case. While the defense in the case did, in quotations, negations, and hypotheticals, refer to the alleged criminal acts using verbs such as *have anal sex* and *fondle* (a term the prosecution never used), they mainly avoided the details of the stigmatized acts. At the same time, the prosecution included them as they referred to additional sexual events the defense silenced and broke each event down into a series of processes involving the defendant, a victim, and/or their body parts.

As in the corpus as a whole, the defense in the Sandusky case often used linguistic means to silence the more negative elements of the defendant and his or her alleged role in the crime. For instance, they used vague generalizations and de-activations frequently, such as *things would happen* and *activities going on*, and they used non-sexual terms like *horseplay*, *fool around*. This is not to say that the prosecution did not also use less explicit forms at times, as they did use phrases like *what the defendant did to* _____. However, they did this when providing other specific details of the crimes (e.g., location), they often did not minimize the defendant's and victims' involvement in the processes as the defense had, and they used neutral terms (e.g., *do)* rather than replacing verbs depicting criminal acts with verbs with positive connotations (*horseplay*). Even more important, the prosecution included the sexual, violent, and criminal information elsewhere.

What was especially interesting about the Sandusky case is that the prosecution explicitly stated that the defense, during their examination of witnesses, had silenced the details of the crimes:

> (16) Defense counsel never—almost never and maybe never asked a question about the specific instance of these crimes. That is, about the sexual events, the abuse, the anal intercourse, the oral intercourse, the indecent assaults, all the things the defendant did. He never asked specifically about that. He asked about dates and places and car colors.

As this quotation and the above discussion show, the lawyers in this case behaved linguistically very similarly to those in the corpus. They all used the processes of silencing, de-emphasizing, and emphasizing strategically through the linguistic forms they selected.

1.4 CONCLUSIONS TO BE DRAWN FROM THESE COMPARISONS

At this point then, we can return to the big question of whether or not the corpus analyzed in this book can be generalized. The comparison to the results from the Sandusky case demonstrated that there is no reason to think they cannot be. While the level of variation in the quantitative results both within the corpus cases and between the corpus and the Sandusky case mean that the exact frequencies at which a social actor will be referred to in different narratives and roles cannot be predicted, the strategies that lawyers have available to them and that they use remain the same. Silencing, de-emphasizing, and emphasizing are key processes, regardless of who presents the argument and what speech community they participate in.

2 Silencing, De-Emphasizing, and Emphasizing to Explain Previous Findings on Courtroom Discourse

The concepts of silencing, de-emphasizing, and emphasizing can also be easily extended to the results from other analyses of courtroom discourse. While those studies may have been focused on different aspects of trial language, these processes unite their findings. Two examples will demonstrate this.

Much of the literature on courtroom discourse has examined lawyers' lexical choices (e.g., Cotterill 2001, 2003; Danet 1980a, b; Drew 1992; Eades 2008). For instance, Danet's (1980a) study showed that the defense in an abortion trial referred to the victim with scientific or impersonal terms, for example, *fetus*, while the prosecution used more emotionally evocative words, such as *baby boy* and *loved one*. Cotterill (2001) examined the distribution of several words or phrases in the opening statements of the OJ Simpson trial. One finding was that the prosecution repeatedly used the word *control* while discussing Simpson's and Brown Simpson's interactions. This lexical pattern helped shape the image of their relationship that was constructed. Regardless of the specifics of the studies, the results that have emerged are that lawyers tried to have strict control of the lexical properties of the words they used. They often picked specific ones for the particular details of the trial and used them or close synonyms repeatedly. During the examination of witnesses, they tried to force the witnesses to adopt the same forms. The model of silencing, de-emphasizing, and emphasizing explains all of this. Lawyers are attempting to silence or at least de-emphasize certain information about the topic at hand, so they select terms that do not include the dispreferred features. By avoiding other words, they erased that information from their argument. The words they used frequently emphasized the properties of the reference that the lawyers viewed more favorably.

Another set of literature has examined lawyers' linguistic styles. Some examined the use of different speech styles: for example, legalese or formal styles versus the use of informal, poetic, theatrical, or otherwise marked speech patterns (e.g., Aronnson, Jönsson, and Linell 1987; Matoesian 2001; Meyer 1994, 1996; Tiersma 1999), while others have examined the use of code-switching between different styles, dialects, voices, or roles (e.g., Felton Rosulek 2010a, b; Fuller 1993; Hobbs 2003). Whether a lawyer used a single linguistic style or switched among different patterns or voices, with any style they used, they were sending the message, "I have this socially understood identity." For example, when African American lawyers used African American English (Fuller 1993; Hobbs 2003; Tiersma 1999), they were implicitly but effectively telling the jurors, "I am part of African American culture, and therefore have the properties associated with that identity." Similarly, when lawyers used legalese, they indexed the fact that they had legal training.

When lawyers quoted experts and thus adopted their voice (Felton Rosulek 2010a, b), they informed the jurors that the information being distributed came from a source other than the lawyer. Thus, the lawyers provided additional knowledge about themselves or their message that they could not or did not necessarily say directly. When the lawyers used such styles repeatedly or for a long period of time, they emphasized the information being indexed by the speech form. When lawyers did not use a particular style, they silenced from their argument any references to the features it encodes or at least de-emphasized them (if the knowledge can be gained elsewhere, e.g., the lawyer's physical appearance).

To conclude, a lawyer's job during a trial is to provide the jurors with information, including knowledge about the lawyers themselves, about the crime and investigation, about the witnesses, about the law, and about how the jurors should think, act, and process the narratives they have been given. Lawyers have been shown to use many strategies while managing the messages sent to the jurors, but importantly, they have always been shown as trying to control and constrain exactly what versions of reality are available to the jurors. Based on what topic was being transmitted, they used a large variety of linguistic and discursive means, but they were always trying to silence certain information, de-emphasize harmful information that they did not silence, and emphasize the topics that benefited their case.

3 Silencing, De-Emphasizing, and Emphasizing across Genres

There is every reason to believe that this continuum from silencing to emphasizing occurs in every genre, not just in closing arguments or in courtroom discourse more generally. Whenever a speaker represents or creates reality, then they will have to exclude some topics while including others. Some information will be included neutrally compared to other information, some will possibly be given more status and weight, and some will possibly be given less. This is just a logical outcome of the fact that speakers have to make choices and the fact that speakers are inherently biased on some level. Additionally, as was discussed in Chapter 2, discourse analysts working in a wide variety of genres have discussed the ideas of inclusion and exclusion and de-emphasis and emphasis before, although they have not looked at them as part of this continuum or necessarily used this terminology. While this seems like a very basic claim, it is important for two distinct reasons. First, it provides us with a clear place to start when understanding how speakers' biases affect their linguistic and discursive selections and patterns. Because closing arguments occur in such a controlled context and the difference is the speakers and their points of view, this book was able to clearly demonstrate the importance of these processes. However, even for instances and genres when there is not a pair of discourses to compare, we can still determine how the speaker's biases "filtered" (Fairclough 2003) the choices they made.

Second, these processes unite a wide variety of otherwise distinct linguistic and discursive phenomena. As was shown throughout the book, speakers' lexical, syntactic, thematic, and discursive choices all work together to achieve silencing, de-emphasizing, and emphasizing. A discourse's ideational and interpersonal meta-functions are both shaped by these processes. In this section, I argue that we can bring in even more communicative forms that also function in similar ways.

Additionally, while this book has focused mostly on repetition as a means of emphasis, there are many other ways of giving information a more or less prominent role in a discourse and of modifying the likelihood of the hearer noticing and focusing on it. For example, in newspapers, the selection of a topic to include in the headline is key for understanding what is being emphasized. In advertisements for medical products, examining what is included in fine print or stated very quickly is helpful for understanding what is being de-emphasized. Therefore, in this section, I also include these other means of achieving silence, de-emphasis, and emphasis so that the model is more complete.

Table 7.5 presents a wide variety of examples of the different types of forms, structures, and choices that can be used for the purposes of silencing, de-emphasizing, and emphasizing. While the list is formidable, it is not meant to be exhaustive, as more research into these processes is sure to reveal additional strategies. Additionally, while the listed forms are meant to apply to the English language and in particular to American culture, there are sure to be other equivalent processes in any language and culture.

As it is not practical to include examples of all of these forms and structures, a few examples from several different categories will suffice.

Many studies have examined how passive-voice sentences provide more emphasis to the object-subject and decrease the attention given to the agent-object than the equivalent active voice sentences (e.g., Anisfeld and Klenbort 1973; Johnson-Laird 1968). Others have then studied how passives are used in discourses in order to exploit these properties. For instance, Trew (1979b) showed that the use of passives in headlines to de-emphasize the responsibility of the police in a deadly riot was directly related to the political leanings of the newspaper. Another study, Henley et al. (1995), examined the distribution of active versus passive voice sentences in newspapers articles. They found that for the representation of criminal and/or violent acts (e.g., *rape*, *murder*) committed by men, passive sentences were more common than active constructions. However, for neutral or positive verbs, more than half were in the active voice. This suggests that journalists have a tendency to de-emphasize perpetrators who have committed a taboo act, particularly when it involves

TABLE 7.5

A Selection of Means for Achieving Silence, De-Emphasis, and Emphasis

	Non-verbal	Phonetic	Morphemic	Lexical	Syntactic	Thematic	Discursive
Silence	¤ In visual representations, objects or texts may be • Not included • Hidden	¤ There may be no phonetic output related to topic	¤ Plurals can silence specific numbers and the diversity within the group ¤ Gendered forms can silence diversity ¤ Verb tenses and aspects can silence the relationship between one event and another, the dynamic nature of an event, and the length of time for which an event occurred.	¤ Features of a referent can be omitted if the lexical items do not include certain information (Huckin 2010)	¤ Passives without by-phrases for agents silence the responsible party. ¤ Nominalizations hide the agent and the dynamic nature of the process.	¤ A topic not being included erases it from the representation of reality.	
De-emphasis	¤ Visually, objects or texts may be • Smaller • In background ¤ For oral discourses, the accompanying communication (gestures, facial expressions, proxemics, etc.) can be minimized	¤ A compressed pitch range (Grosz and Hirschberg 1992; Wennerstrom 2001) may be used. ¤ Utterances can be produced with • Lower volume • Higher speed	¤ Weakening morphology can weaken information (e.g., the addition of *-ish* on adjectives	¤ Features can be de-emphasized if they are generally not pointed to with the terms used. ¤ Generalizations ignore details.	¤ Other forms can minimize one topic by highlighting another • Passives with a by-phrase de-emphasize the agent • Word order • Clefts, fronting, and other forms of focus ¤ Hedging minimizes certainty. ¤ Ellipsis makes a referent recoverable but not explicit. ¤ Information in a dependent clause cannot be challenged as easily	¤ A topic that is included but infrequently or only included in certain parts of the discourse is given less focus. ¤ Details may not be given about the topic.	¤ Topics included in the middle of a discourse may receive less notice ¤ Another topic being emphasized more takes the focus off of other topics.

Emphasis	¤ (from Kress and van Leeuwen 1996) Visual objects or texts may be: • In the foreground • Larger • In sharp focus • Well lit or highlighted • In an unexpected color, image, font, etc. • Pointed to by arrows or lines • In a predictable order and placement of presentation: top to bottom and across (van Dijk 2005), • A noticeable distance from other objects/text ¤ Gestures and physical acts accompanying oral discourse can be maximized in space and time.	Key output may be: • Stressed • Higher pitched or accompanied by more changes in pitch • Louder ¤ Some sounds may have a longer duration ¤ An atypical pronunciation of phonemes can be used (Fahnestock 2011) ¤ An unexpected prosody draws attention (Degand and Simon 2009) ¤ Pausing can be used strategically. ¤ Patterns can be repeated.	¤ Marked morphological choices (e.g., diminutives for adults, reduplication) can peak attention.	¤ The repetition of a lexical item or a related set of lexical items emphasizes the semantic features included in them ¤ Metaphors, hyperboles, etc. can capture attention.	¤ Changing the given/ new order can place some information more prominent: • Passives emphasize the object (Johnson-Laird 1968; Anisfeld and Klenbort 1973) • Word order does as well. • Clefts, fronting, and other forms of focus achieve this grammatically.	¤ A topic can be referenced frequently in all or in one or more parts of a discourse ¤ More details can be included or the same ones can be repeated.	¤ A topic can be included at a key juncture of the discourse (first, last, etc.) ¤ Marked choices might be made: • Genre • Language, dialect or style • Code-switching • Shifts in footing/ voices • Figurative language • Intertextuality • Rhetorical devices ¤ There can be a repetition of topic, form, or structure ¤ Multi-modal texts are used that include the information in multiple ways.

violence. The researchers also found that for non-neutral acts (either positive or negative), when a passive construction was used, the *by*-phrase providing the agent was absent in a majority of the clauses (i.e., the responsible party was silenced). A final aspect of this study was that they then analyzed the effects of passive versus active sentences on people's interpretation of the events. When test subjects read narratives about male-on-female violence, if passives were used, the readers were more accepting of the behavior, and male participants judged the male agents as less responsible. Thus, this study was able to show not only how passives are used to de-emphasize an agent but also how this can affect the recipients of the discourse.

Gender is an area in which the role of morphology in studying silencing, de-emphasizing, and emphasizing is key. In the English language, at least traditionally, the "neutral" or "generic" form is often either the masculine form (e.g., *mankind*, *he*) or is unmarked for gender but must have a morpheme added to it to make it explicitly female (e.g., *lion/lioness*; Graddol and Swann 1989, *actor/actress*, *hero/heroine*). Similarly, for some terms referring to professions or social roles, the assumed gender is so strong that a gender term is often added for group members who go against that norm (e.g., *male nurse, lady doctor*). Importantly, these forms show us that there is a basic form and a more morphologically complex form for many words with relation to gender. While the basic form is supposed to be neutral, it can actually be quite biased toward one gender (e.g., *he* is often not a neutral pronoun; see, for instance, Gastil 1990; Hamilton 1988; MacKay 1980; Moulton et al. 1978). Therefore, when such neutral forms are used, they de-emphasize or silence the opposite gender, depending on how strong the bias is and how leading the surrounding content is. For example, when *mankind* is used, this de-emphasizes women. When *nurse* is used, this may de-emphasize men. When the more morphologically complex form is used, this means the referent's gender is overtly included. If the use of that form is particularly marked, then it may even emphasize the person's gender (e.g., a "lady doctor" most likely emphasizes the fact the doctor is female since either this is a marked term or a marked situation, depending on the sub-set of society in which the phrase is used).

This property has been seen repeatedly in the literature. For example, Thompson and Scheid (1996) analyzed what they call the "invisibility" of women in adult education in the mid-twentieth century. (In this book, we would use the term *silencing* for the same phenomenon.) By studying articles in the *Journal of Adult Education*, they find that this processes partially occurred because the authors of articles almost always assumed hypothetical or generic referents were male if they filled neural (e.g., student) or traditionally male roles (e.g., politician). This was especially true for professionals (e.g., scientist, administrator) unless the role was traditionally female (e.g., librarian, typist). As a result, most pronominal references in the articles pointed to males (in one the ratio was fifty to one). The authors' conclusion was that women were silenced in part because the use of generic terms, including generic pronouns, hid the role of women in the topics being discussed.

A final example of how silencing, de-emphasizing, and emphasizing can occur is in the non-verbal communication that accompanies a verbal discourse (oral or written). By maximizing or minimizing the impact of the accompanying means of communication, such as size, speed, and power of hand gestures, placement of the text or speaker in space, strength of additional sensory input (color, visual contrast, non-verbal sounds, etc.), a speaker can draw attention to a particular piece of information or away from it. A prime place to study this in action is advertisements. Martínez Lirola and Chovanec (2012) analyzed advertisements for plastic surgery and found that despite the fact that men also undergo cosmetic procedures, the ads tended to emphasize women as patients, as pictures of them were larger and in the left side or the center of the space. Additionally, some of the text was positioned across the body of the woman while more procedural information (e.g., phone numbers for the business) was placed in the margins. The result of all of these visual cues is that they all worked together to focus on the female body and thus directed the text of the advertisements toward this sub-set of society.

Hansen and Machin (2008) analyzed how Getty's stock images are being used in the discourse of climate change. They found that the backgrounds of pictures related to nature were often missing, out of focus, or generic, and thus the original context in which they were taken was silenced or de-emphasized. Also, the people and objects in the foreground of the pictures tended to be timeless and generic but beautiful, hopeful, and symbolic. According to these researchers, the lack of specificity in these pictures de-emphasized logical arguments and specific issues, ideas, and solutions about climate issues and their effect on nature. As these pictures both represent and are helping to shape and create the current verbal texts on global climate change, the lack of information in them means that empirical and contextual information is being silenced or de-emphasized in these discourses.

To conclude, as this discussion has shown, silence, de-emphasis, and emphasis can be accomplished through a variety of means. The important feature that ties them together is the weight given to the information: Is it excluded from the discourse (silenced)? Is it given little importance and only a small opportunity to be noticed and considered by the hearer (de-emphasized)? Or is it given additional importance and made more salient for the hearer (emphasized)? Whenever a discourse is being used to distribute information (about the world, possible worlds, the speaker, the hearer, their relationship, etc.), then these processes are at work and are shaped by the speaker's intentions, goals, and biases.

4 Final Thoughts

The closing arguments in criminal trials are fascinating. They have the ability to tell us so much about how lawyers speak; how people in general present arguments, knowledge, and messages; and how they try to persuade each other. This book is not the end of what can be said about the closing arguments as a genre or about silencing, de-emphasis, and emphasis. However, it has provided a starting point for further examination of these topics.

This book will not make lawyers' or other speakers' techniques and strategies ineffective or obsolete, but hopefully, those who have read it, including potential jurors, are now more aware of what people do with language. If the book has served its purpose, it should now be clear that language does not merely present a reflection of reality but is instead an incomplete and biased interpretation of it.

Our understandings of the world around us are created and/or shaped by discourses, and it is important that we all have a better understanding of how they function. During occasions such as jury deliberations, where the goal is uncovering some sort of truth, it is especially important that we are aware of how we may have been affected by the discourses we have heard and to be critical thinkers as we use them. While we may not always be able to recover silenced information, we can be aware of what we do not know. We can question why certain topics were emphasized while others were de-emphasized and can determine if the level of importance given to them needs to be reconsidered. Additionally, as speakers, while we cannot avoid silencing, de-emphasizing, and emphasizing certain information, we can be conscious of the choices we make and how they may affect others' understanding of the world. Being aware of others' biases and our own will not remove their impact on how reality is recontextualized and re-created, but it will help us be open to questioning and reconsidering it. The analysis presented in this book has provided a set of tools for accomplishing this.

NOTES

Chapter 1

1. This book examines only closing arguments from trials conducted in the US legal system. Presumably, the processes of silencing, de-emphasizing, and emphasizing occur in the discourses in other judicial systems worldwide, but that is not being investigated here.

2. The term *linguistic* refers to the phonetic, lexical, and syntactic elements that comprise a clause. The term *discursive* refers to issues that involve an entire clause or more than one clause, such as topic choice, quotations, narratives, rhetorical structures, etc. Also, a discourse is defined as a communicative event or a series of communicative events tied together by a common element such as a topic or point of view.

3. The phrase *social actors* is used in this book to refer to the roles that are played in social contexts as well as the people who inhabit them. In the trials, different individuals are the defendants, victims, etc., but they are all filling the same basic roles under the same constraints. Therefore, they are all referred to as social actors.

4. Every lawyer did in this corpus.

5. Clauses represent events, actions, relations, and states, and these are called processes. In the English language, processes are almost always represented by a verb, but in some cases, such as possessive pronouns, they appear in other linguistic forms (Halliday 1994).

6. Both women and men can be defendants, but most in this corpus were male, so male pronouns will often be used.

Chapter 2

1. Power is understood here in its most basic sense: the ability of a social actor to exert his or her will, even if another party resists (Weber 1978: 53). Within CDA, that power is generally understood as originating from the social system in which the interaction takes place (Wodak and Meyer 2009). American society has given lawyers their power within the judicial system.

2. This is not to say that lawyers are necessarily being purposefully malicious or conniving. Instead, they are doing their jobs and taking part in the legal system as it has been set up. As part of this institution, it is quite possible that they are often unaware of their patterns of language use, and my informal discussions with lawyers have confirmed that this is often the case.

3. Importantly, when we talk about the world, as will be discussed in more detail, we are not confined to the current real world or to solid states of matter. We are discussing the physical and metaphysical world external to the speaker and the speaker's internal or mental/emotional world, as well as all possible worlds.

4. Various lists of discourse acts have been created (e.g., Hymes 1962; Jakobson 1960; Sinclair and Coulthard 1992), but they generally include at least these two functions.

5. For the purposes of this book, *persuasion* is defined as "human communication designed to influence others by modifying their beliefs, values, or attitudes" (Simons 1976: 21). The lawyers are trying to affect the beliefs of the jurors about what happened in the crime, investigation, and trial and what that means legally. Then they are attempting to force the jurors to behave in a certain way during the deliberations and the selection of a verdict. One way that lawyers attempt to persuade is through *argumentation*, which is defined as a "verbal, social, and rational activity aimed at convincing a reasonable critic of the acceptability of a standpoint by putting forward a constellation of propositions justifying or refuting the proposition expressed in the standpoint" (van Eemeren and Grootendorst 2004: 1).

Lawyers argue by putting forth a series of narratives and claims for how the law should be applied to them and why the other side should be rejected. By presenting this information as if theirs is the only true interpretation of reality, they argue that it logically leads to only one conclusion and one action for the jurors. In this book, the term *persuasion* is used as the more general concept in that it can occur through appeals to emotion and personal relationships (Virtanen and Halmari 2005) while *argumentation* is used to describe persuasion that relies on rationality.

6. These choices also represent the textual meta-function, which is the linguistic ways in which a text is organized or how the ideational and interpersonal experiences are turned into discourses (Halliday 1994). Textual meta-functions are seen in such structures as the theme/rheme, focus, and the conjunction systems. This will be examined in this book but only indirectly, as it is not being used to create meaning but to facilitate it.

7. Observations necessarily occur within the limits of human abilities and are influenced by the forces of social patterns and institutions (Berger and Luckmann 1966).

8. As will be discussed later in the chapter, even if the jurors had observed it, they would all have different knowledge about and understandings of it. If there are video or audio recordings, they are still biased because they only come from one angle; events and entities outside their scope or that occurred before or after they were turned on are still missing; and they cannot reveal people's intentions, thoughts, and emotions.

9. All speakers are biased in that they all enter a discourse with their own unique knowledge base, set of ideologies, past experiences, emotions, etc. They also come to an interaction with different goals, and this is especially true of opposing lawyers. Bias has nothing to do with a speaker's distance from the truth or reality.

10. This book is not the place to argue about how much personal choice speakers have and how much is determined by social forces, patterns, and rules. When I use the word *choice*, I do not imply complete independence or consciousness.

11. *Footings* are "participant's alignment, or set, or stance, or posture, or projected self . . . a change in footing implies a change in the alignment we take up to ourselves and the others present as expressed in the way we manage the production or reception of an utterance" (Goffman 1981: 128).

12. *Voices* are speaker's "interactional positioning" (Wortham 2001: 62).

13. Narratives are simply "representation[s] of an event or a series of events" (Abbott 2002: 13).

14. See Holt 1996; Kuo 2001; Li 1986; Mayes 1990; White 2006 for additional discussions of speakers using character voices as sources of evidence for their claims.

15. *Genre* is defined here as "abstract, socially recognized ways of using language" (Hyland 2002: 114). For example, sermons, newspaper articles, lectures, and even closing arguments are all genres.

16. A similar idea was described in Blom and Gumperz (1972) and was called *metaphorical code-switching*. Each language in their data or each voice in this corpus can evoke another context, topic, genre, speaker, or set of relationships.

17. They may also suggest the speaker is acting with deference for the hearer(s) (Holmes 1984).

18. Since all the speakers in the corpus described in this book are speaking English, this is not a vital issue here, but it can be in other contexts.

19. Of course, genres are not static or self-contained, as speakers can shift among them or adopt features of one to add meaning to another (e.g., a lawyer using a preaching style in a closing argument brings in other aspects of the sermon genre as well, such as solemnity and a sense of authority about moral principles) (Briggs and Bauman 1992).

20. The patterns and rules of genres are likely to seem very natural, logical, and necessary for the members of the culture to which they belong. This is because genres are not just structures that reality is inserted into and shaped to fit. As Bakhtin (1981) discussed, they are also ideological vehicles. The culture of the society helps determine what is appropriate and shapes the values, relationships, and labels given to elements that can be included. Reality, by being transformed through the lens of a genre, will then both reflect and reconstruct the ideologies of the society.

21. To be even more accurate, the prosecution closing arguments and defense closing arguments each form a sub-genre that has certain features that distinguish it from the other (Walter 1988).

22. It is the goal of this book to describe the patterns that the lawyers are using in order to construct a version of reality and try to persuade others to accept it. While the conclusions reached here cannot necessarily be generalizable to the world outside the courtroom, because lawyers are part of a larger culture and closing arguments are part of a larger web of discourses, the findings described here should also apply to other genres and contexts.

23. Part of the reason a corpus of closing arguments is being used for this analysis is to mitigate to some degree the effects of the individual speakers and thus to lessen the impact of their idiosyncratic styles and choices.

24. As discussed earlier, the closing arguments are partially dialogic in that the lawyers for the opposing sides are responding to and anticipating the other side's remarks. This, too, has a great influence on the discourse.

25. Additionally, each juror affects how the discourse is interpreted, the meaning assigned to it, the model of reality he or she creates based on it, and its ultimate impact on the case. Despite this, we are not privy to the jurors' thought processes or their discussions. Therefore, we are focusing our attention here on the reality constructed by the lawyers.

26. We are not talking about silence in the literal sense when it means that no sound or linguistic forms are produced. Instead, this term describes the phenomenon where a discourse is created and certain information is not included/goes unsaid.

27. This is especially important in cases like the closing arguments because, as discussed earlier, the discursive representations are all the knowledge the hearers have of the

original events. Additionally, they are the forms that move forward and are re-created and re-used for later purposes such as the jury deliberations.

28. Presupposition in this book is understood to be pragmatic presupposition (Caffi 1994) rather than semantic presupposition.

29. The goal of this analysis is not to identify all excluded information but to describe many of the salient patterns. Due to the structured methodology and the definitions provided here, this book will do just that.

30. Tomlin (1985) actually adds an additional highest level of importance called *pivotal.*

Chapter 3

1. The prosecutor's actual job is to ensure justice and fairness, protect those who are innocent, and advocate for punishment of the guilty, but in the courtroom, prosecutors generally are driven to secure a verdict of guilty (King 1980).

2. The use of many similar terms has been banned either in individual cases or by appellate rulings that the use of such terms without evidence is a reversible error, but many have been used without consequence (Bishop 1977).

3. For this analysis, cases with more than one victim (cases #10, #11, and #17) were excluded from the totals for the victims because these numbers skewed the totals toward higher numbers.

4. The differences were only significant in nine of those cases (not in cases #1, #4, #6, #8, #10, and #16).

5. For example, in case #8, the prosecution's argument was 1,430 words compared to an average of 5,314.12 for all prosecution arguments.

6. One caveat is that in some contexts, the use of the last name, instead of the first name, is a marker of informality and social intimacy (Brown and Ford 1961). An example of such a context is an American sports team.

7. A quick anecdote from my ethnographic work for this project sheds light on when defense lawyers may use the term *defendant* to refer to the person on trial. I was talking to a public defender who was from the court system from which all of the cases in the corpus came but who was not represented in this corpus. I asked him how he liked to refer to his clients when speaking about them. He admitted to me that once he completely forgot his own client's name so had no choice but to refer to him as *the defendant* during his closing argument. While none of the defense lawyers in this corpus seemed to have had this problem because they all used their clients' names repeatedly, it does raise another reason why a functionalization might be used.

8. The lawyer did use several functionalizations for the defendant that referred to her role as a day care provider when stressing that she had broken the rules society expects for people in this role. This is a common pattern across the cases.

9. This pattern was not found in the prosecution rebuttals, as in these discourses the frequency of references to the defendant as an agent dropped to defense argument levels. The explanation for this is that the prosecution focused their original arguments more on the crime narratives and mostly de-emphasized or even silenced other topics such as the law and the role of the jurors, two topics the defense included and comparatively emphasized more. When the prosecution gave a rebuttal, they also included these additional topics as well and thus reduced the importance of the crime story.

10. This was also demonstrated in Felton Rosulek (2008), which examined a single case in detail.

11. See Ehrlich (2001) for a detailed discussion of nominalizations and other means of hiding the defendant's agency.

12. The prosecution included Boy #1 as the agent of more than twice as many processes during the crime as Boy #2 (207 to 92), but the defense had both boys as the agent of roughly the same number of processes (seventy-one to seventy-four). While the prosecution did refer to Boy #2 more times than the defense did, the references were less frequent as their argument was longer (prosecution: 10.7 references per 1,000 words; defense: 18.3 references per 1,000 words). Thus, in the prosecution's argument, the role of Boy #1 was much more integral to the events than Boy #2 was, while Boy #2 was equally as active as #1 in the defense argument.

13. These findings are especially significant given the results of Henley et al. (1995). In that study, the authors showed that after reading reports of violence against women, if the passive rather than the active voice was used to describe the violence, males were more likely to believe that less harm was done to the victim and that the abuser had less responsibility. Respondents of both genders had a higher level of acceptance for the violence when the passive was used. Lamb and Keon (1995) were not able to confirm those results, but they did find less harsh punishment was given when the passage implied shared responsibility. Thus, there is at least some evidence that the patterns of passivization and increased agency for victims affect how listeners/hearers interpret descriptions of events.

Chapter 4

1. As was discussed in Felton Rosulek (2009), this same pattern occurred in Case #10. Here, the defense silenced the older victim who was claimed to have suffered significantly more abuse at the hands of the defendant.

2. When a single term was used to refer to multiple victims, it was only counted once.

3. Since twelve of the twenty-three victims were children, this partially explains this result, as the lawyers, across the board, used more informal nominations for the young people. This follows the pattern of society in that more respectful terms such as the inclusion of the referents title are generally given to older individuals.

4. However, the defense lawyers used a formal nomination significantly less frequently for the victims than they had used them for the defendants, so they did not show the victims quite as much respect.

5. The results for the defense are skewed by one case, #16. Without this case, the defense still used classifications more than the prosecution did (1.9 times per 1,000 words, 5.3% of references).

6. The only exception is that the lawyer did refer to one of the witnesses with a title twice, but that was a man who had passed away between the time of his grand jury testimony and the trial, so using a respectful term to refer to him was explicable.

7. For the cases with more than one victim, when more than one victim was an agent or a recipient, this token was only counted once toward the final tally, instead of being counted for each victim separately.

8. These results were not found in the prosecution rebuttals as they referenced the victims even less often than the defense lawyers did, but this a result of the topics that were focused on in the rebuttals.

9. This is also more evidence that the prosecutions emphasized the crime narratives in their main arguments more than the defense attorneys did.

10. This idea that victims should act in certain ways both during and after sexual abuse is at least partially the result of the speakers (and perhaps the hearers) adopting an "utmost resistance standard" as the main ideological perspective through which they view, interpret, and judge a victim's response to sexual abuse and assault (Ehrlich 2001). "Utmost resistance" was once part of many legal statutes regarding rape and even today is replacement "reasonable resistance" is still used (Estrich 1986, 1987; Smith 2004). The assumption is that there is a necessary and appropriate set of responses individuals should have to unwanted sexual contact, and not doing such actions means that either the crime did not take place or that the sexual interaction was acceptable to the person. When the defense lawyers in this corpus included actions that the victims did not do or when they judge the victim's actions as unexpected for a person in that situation, they have adopted these resistance standards that are not necessarily true reflections of victim responses (Ehrlich 2001).

11. Both sides emphasized the processes of the defendant more than the processes of the victim during the crime.

Chapter 5

1. The columns in the table divide the references into three types. Explicit references are when a pronoun (*you*, *we*, etc.) or a noun phrase (*ladies and gentlemen*, *jurors*, *citizens*) was used. Any time the jurors were the agent or recipient of a process, whether it was an overt or assumed reference, is included in the next column. The final column presents the data for when the jurors did not serve a syntactic or thematic role but instead were named in a vocative construction, as in:

(32) Here in this courtroom, the stakes, ladies and gentlemen, are much higher.

In such constructions, the jurors were mentioned but only to label them as the intended recipients of the utterance, and they did not play a syntactic role in the clause.

2. The dialect of English used by the speakers in this study does not have a separate second-person plural pronoun, at least in formal settings such as a trial.

3. One lawyer in the corpus did directly address an individual juror, even using the person's name. The lawyer had repeated a cultural maxim in Spanish and apologized to a juror who presumably was fluent in the language. This went unchallenged by the opposing counsel or the judge.

4. With this use of *we*, it is not always clear if it is the lawyer and the jurors only or if other participants are also included. It does not matter, however. The jurors are the addressees and so their inclusion along with the speaker is a possible reading and is assumed even when the ratified overhearers (the judge, the other side, etc.) (Goffman 1981) could also be included.

5. This is not to say that the lawyers never had themselves as the recipients of the verbal and material processes of the witnesses. It is only that frequently, they silenced their own role linguistically.

6. A side note is that no lawyer in the corpus discussed how jury duty is different or new to most of the participants. It is an interesting part of this genre that lawyers are willing to acknowledge the jurors' effort and potential discomfort but seem to ignore any confusion they may be having in this rather esoteric context.

Chapter 6

1. The methodologies used to conduct this analysis were the same as those used in the previous chapter, except the focus was on both first person pronouns and third person self-references.

2. In this chapter, the impersonalizations being described were references to individuals and groups by the organization or institution they were associated with (e.g., *the State*, *the government*).

3. What is especially interesting about the distinction is that frequently, there were the same number of lawyers (one or two) for each side who were directly involved in the case. In fact, in some cases, there was only one prosecutor sitting at the table, while there were two defense attorneys present for their side. However, the pronoun usage remained the same.

4. "General" references include two categories. The first is present tense references that represent statements about the other side that are not specific to this particular trial, as in the following example:

(17) The State has a right to give a statement first.

The second number (the one in parenthesis) indicates when the lawyers included more than just the opponents in this type of reference.

5. The defense lawyers often emphasized the fact that the prosecution could be referred to as the *State*, and the constructed this as a negative. While the prosecution did not emphasize this term, they also did not silence or deny it. In fact, some referred to themselves this way repeatedly.

6. For the first person plural pronouns that are classified as referring to the lawyers and jurors, there was often no evidence that other people (e.g., all people present in the courtroom) were not also being referenced, but there was also no explicit evidence that they were being included. Thus, the jurors and the lawyers were just the lowest common denominator. Take the following example, which is classified as referring to the lawyers and jurors:

(18) We know that there were sex videotapes in the house that she had access to, and she admitted even looking at one.

In this case, any ratified recipient of this utterance could reasonably be included in *we*. This changes nothing. The important part is that the lawyer was saying that both the jurors as the primary recipients and the speaker, the lawyer himself, were in agreement.

7. The table reveals a pattern of lawyers' style that occurred regardless of what side they were on. If they were discussing the future (what they would be doing), they used first person singular references. If they were discussing general or abstract concepts, they used first person plural references. It was only in the other categories that they shifted back and forth.

8. The difference between the frequencies for the prosecution and defense remains significant, even when cases in which there was more than one lawyer for one of the sides are excluded.

Chapter 7

1. Importantly, this case was selected for the described reasons as well as the availability of its official transcripts. It was not analyzed at all prior to its selection.

2. While the superscript numbers in the table only mark statistically significant differences between the corpus and the Sandusky trial, the frequencies for the defendants, the opposing side, and the lawyer who was speaking also were significantly different between the Sandusky prosecution and the Sandusky defense.

3. While the superscript numbers in the table only mark statistically significant differences between the corpus and the Sandusky trial, the differences in the Sandusky prosecution's and defense's percentages of nominations and functionalizations, as well as the frequencies for these two categories, were also statistically significant.

BIBLIOGRAPHY

Aaronson, M. N. (1995). Be just to one another: Preliminary thoughts on civility, moral character and professionalism. *St. Thomas Law Review*, *8*, 113–155.

Abbott, H. P. (2002). *The Cambridge introduction to narrative*. Cambridge: Cambridge University Press.

Adaval, R., and Wyer, R. S. (1998). The role of narratives in consumer information processing. *Journal of Consumer Psychology*, *7*(3), 207–245.

Agha, A (2005). Voice, footing, enregisterment. *Journal of Linguistic Anthropology*, *15*(1), 38–59.

Aldridge, M., and Luchjenbroers, J. (2007). Linguistic manipulations in legal discourse: Framing questions and "smuggling" information. *International Journal of Speech, Language, and Law*, *14*(1), 83–105.

Amsterdam, A. G., and Hertz, R. (1992). An analysis of closing arguments to a jury. *New York Law School Law Review*, *37*, 55–122.

Anisfeld, M., and Klenbort, I. (1973). On the functions of structural paraphrase: The view from the passive voice. *Psychological Bulletin*, *79*(2), 117–126.

Aronsson, K, Jönsson, L., and Linell, P. 1987. The courtroom hearing as a middle ground: Speech accommodation by lawyers and defendants. *Journal of Language and Social Psychology*, *6*, 99–115.

Austin, J. L. (1962). *How to do things with words*. Cambridge, MA: Harvard University Press.

Babcock, B. (1977). The story in the story: Metanarration in folk narrative. In R. Bauman (Ed.), *Verbal art as performance* (pp. 61–79). Prospect Heights, IL: Waveland.

Bach, K. (1994). Conversational implicature. *Mind and Language*, *9*(2), 124–162.

Bach, K. (1999). The myth of conventional implicature. *Linguistics and Philosophy*, *22*(4), 327–66.

Bacigal, R. J. (2008). *Criminal law and procedure: An overview* (3rd ed.). Clifton Park, NY: Delmar Cengage Learning.

Baker, P. (2006). *Using corpora in discourse analysis*. London: Continuum.

Bakhtin, M. (1981). Discourse in the novel. In M. Holquist (Ed.), *The dialogic imagination: Four essays by M. M. Bakhtin* (pp. 259–422). Austin: University of Texas Press.

Bakhtin, M. M. (1986). *Speech genres and other late essays*. Austin: University of Texas Press.

Barge, J. K., Schlueter, D. W., and Pritchard, A. (1989). The effects of nonverbal communication and gender on impression formation in opening statements. *Southern Communication Journal*, *54*(4), 330–349.

Bauman, R. (1986). *Story, performance, and event: Contextual studies of oral narrative* (Vol. 10). Cambridge: Cambridge University Press.

Bauman, R., and Briggs, C. L. 1990. Poetics and performance as critical perspectives on language and social life. *Annual Review of Anthropology, 19*, 59–88.

Bekalu, M. A. (2006). Presupposition in news discourse. *Discourse & Society, 17*(2), 147–172.

Bennett, W. L. (1978). Storytelling in criminal trials: A model of social judgment. *Quarterly Journal of Speech, 64*(1), 1–22.

Bennett, W. L. (1979). Rhetorical transformation of evidence in criminal trials: Creating grounds for legal judgment. *Quarterly Journal of Speech, 65*(3), 311–323.

Bennett, W. L. and Feldman, M. S. (1981). *Reconstructing reality in the courtroom: justice and judgment in American culture*. New Brunswick, NJ: Rutgers University Press.

Benveniste, E. (1971 [1958]). Subjectivity in language. In *Problems in general linguistics* (pp. 223–230). Coral Gables, FL: University of Miami Press.

Berg, D. (2006). *The trial lawyer: What it takes to win*. Chicago: ABA Publishing.

Berger, P., and Luckmann, T. (1966). *The social construction of reality*. Harmondsworth: Penguin Books.

Besnier, N. (1992). Reported speech and affect on Nukulaelae atoll. In J. Hill and J.T. Irvine (Eds.), *Responsibility and evidence in oral discourse* (pp. 161–181). Cambridge: Cambridge University Press.

Biber, D., Johansson, S., Leech, G., Conrad, S., and Finegan, E. (1999). *Longman grammar of spoken and written English*. Essex, UK: Pearson Education.

Bishop, A. N. (1977). Name calling: Defendant nomenclature in criminal trials. *Ohio Northern University Law Review, 4*, 38–76.

Blankenship, K. L., and Craig, T. Y. (2006). Rhetorical question use and resistance to persuasion: An attitude strength analysis. *Journal of Language and Social Psychology, 25*(2), 111–128.

Blom, J. P., and Gumperz, J. J. (1972). Social meaning in linguistic structures: Code-switching in Norway. In J. J. Gumperz and D. Hymes (Eds.), *Directions in sociolinguistics* (pp. 407–434). New York: Holt, Rinehart, and Winston.

Bloome, D., Power Carter, S., Morton Christian, B., Otto, S., Shuart-Faris, N. (2005). Microethnographic discourse analysis and the exploration of social identity in classroom language and literacy events. In *Discourse analysis and the study of classroom language and literacy events: A microethnographic perspective* (pp. 84–136). Mahwah, NJ: Lawrence Erlbaum Associates.

Bogoch, B. (1999). Courtroom discourse and the gendered construction of professional identity. *Law and Society Inquiry, 24*(2), 329–375.

Bolinger, D. (1980). *Language: The loaded weapon*. New York: Longman Press.

Briggs, C. L., and Bauman, R. (1992). Genre, intertextuality, and social power. *Journal of linguistic anthropology, 2*(2), 131–172.

Brown, R., and Ford, M. (1961). Address in American English. *The Journal of Abnormal and Social Psychology, 62*(2), 375–385.

Brown, P., and Levinson, S. C. (1987). *Politeness: Some universals in language usage*. Cambridge: Cambridge University Press

Brown, G., and Yule, G. (1983). *Discourse analysis*. Cambridge: Cambridge University Press.

Bruner, J. (1991). The narrative construction of reality. *Critical Inquiry, 18*(1), 1–21.

Bruner, J. (2002). *Making stories: Law, literature, life.* New York: Farrar, Straus, and Giroux.

People v. Bryant, No. 03-CR-204, Dist. Ct., Eagle Cty., June 24, 2004.

Bülow-Møller, A. M. (2005). Persuasion in business negotiations. In H. Halmari and T. Virtanen (Eds.), *Persuasion across genres: A linguistic approach* (pp. 27–58). Amsterdam: John Benjamins.

Burnkrant, R. E., and Unnava, H. R. (1995). Effects of self-referencing on persuasion. *Journal of Consumer Research*, *26*, 17–26.

Caffarel, A., Martin, J. R., and Matthiessen, C. (2004). Introduction: Systemic functional typology. In *Language typology: A functional perspective* (pp. 1–76). Amsterdam, Philadelphia: John Benjamins.

Caffi, C. (1994). Pragmatic presupposition. In R. E. Asher and J. M. Y. Simpson (Eds.) *The Encyclopedia of Language and Linguistics*, *Volume 6*, (pp. 3320–3327). Oxford: Pergamon Press.

Caldwell, H.M., Perrin, L. T., Frost, C. L. (2002). The art and architecture of closing argument, *Tulane Law Review*, *76*, 963–1072.

Carpenter, C. J., and Henningsen, D. D. (2011). The effect of passive verb constructed arguments on persuasion. *Communication Research Reports*, *28*, 52–61.

Cary, J. M. (1998). Teaching ethics and professionalism in litigation: Some thoughts. *Stetson Law Re*view, *28*, 305–318.

Chafe, W. L. (1970) *Meaning and the structure of language.* Chicago: University of Chicago Press.

Chapman, S., and Routledge, C. (1999). The pragmatics of detection: Paul Auster's "City of glass." *Language and Literature*, *8*(3), 241–253.

Chilton, P. (2004). *Analysing political discourse: Theory and practice.* London: Routledge.

Chvany, C. V. (1990). Verbal aspect, discourse saliency, and the so-called "perfect of result" in modern Russian. In Nils Thelin (Ed.), *Verbal aspect in discourse.* Amsterdam: John Benjamins.

Clark, H. H. (1992). *Arenas of language use.* Chicago: University of Chicago Press.

Coe, K., Domke, D., Graham, E. S., John, S. L., and Pickard, V. W. (2004). No shades of gray: The binary discourse of George W. Bush and an echoing press. *Journal of Communication*, 54, 234–252.

Corcos, C. A. (2013). Magical images in law. In A. Wagner and L. Cheng (Eds.) *Exploring courtroom discourse: The language of power and control* (pp. 131–176). Surrey, UK: Ashgate Publishing.

State v. Cortes, 84 Conn. App. 70, 851 A.2d 1230 (2004).

Costanzo, M., and Peterson, J. (1994). Attorney persuasion in the capital penalty phase: A content analysis of closing arguments. *Journal of Social Issues*, *50*(2), 125–147.

Cotterill, J. (2001). Domestic discord, rocky relationships: Semantic prosodies in representation of marital violence in the O.J. Simpson trial. *Discourse & Society*, *12*(3), 291–312.

Cotterill, J. (2003). *Language and power in court: A linguistic analysis of the OJ Simpson trial.* New York: Palgrave MacMillan.

Cotterill, J. (2004). Collocation, connotation, and courtroom semantics: lawyers' control of witness testimony through lexical negotiation. *Applied Linguistics*, *25*(4), 513–537.

Coulson, S. (2001). *Semantic leaps: Frame-shifting and conceptual blending in meaning construction*. Cambridge: Cambridge University Press.

Coupland, N., and Coupland, J. (1997). Discourses of the unsayable: Death-implicative talk in geriatric medical consultations. In A. Jaworski (Ed.), *Silence: Interdisciplinary perspectives* (pp. 117–152). Berlin: Mouton de Gruyter.

Danet, B. (1980a). "Baby" or "fetus?" Language and the construction of reality in a manslaughter trial. *Semiotica*, *32*(3–4), 187–219.

Danet, B. (1980b). Language in the legal process. *Law and Society Review*, *15*, 445–565.

Degand, L., and Simon, A. C. (2009). Mapping prosody and syntax as discourse strategies: How basic discourse units vary across genres, In D. Barth-Weingarten, N. Dehé, and A. Wichmann (Eds.), *Where prosody meets pragmatics* (pp. 81–107). Bingley, UK: Emerald Group Publishing.

Dickson, B., and Bunton Jackson, J. (1994). Renewing lawyer civility. *Valparaiso University Law Review*, *28*(2), 531–541.

Dik, S. (1997). *The theory of functional grammar: Part 1, the structure of the clause* (2nd rev. ed.). Berlin: Mouton de Gruyter.

Dressen, D. (2002). Identifying textual silence in scientific research articles: Recontexualizations of the field account in Geology. *Hermes*, *28*, 81–107.

Drew, P. (1985). Analyzing the use of language in courtroom interaction. In T. A. van Dijk (ed.), *Handbook of discourse analysis*, Vol. 3 (pp. 133–147). London: Academic Press.

Drew, P. (1992). Contested evidence in courtroom cross-examination: The case of a trial for rape. In P. Drew and J. Heritage (Eds.), *Talk at work: Interaction in institutional settings* (pp. 470–520). Cambridge: Cambridge University Press.

Dunmire, P. L. (2011). *Projecting the future through political discourse: The case of the Bush Doctrine*. Amsterdam: John Benjamins.

Duranti, A. (1983). Somoan speechmaking across social events: One genre in and out of a Fono. *Language in Society*, *12*, 1–30.

Duranti, A. (1994). Introduction. In *From grammar to politics: Linguistic anthropology in a Western Samoan village* (pp. 1–13). Berkeley: University of California Press.

Eades, D. (2006). Lexical struggle in court: Aboriginal Australians versus the state. *Journal of Sociolinguistics*, *10*(2), 153–180.

Eades, D. (2008). *Courtroom talk and neocolonial control*. Berlin: Mouton de Gruyter.

Eckert, P., and McConnell-Ginet, S. (1992). Think practically and look locally: Language and gender as community-based practice. *Annual Review of Anthropology*, *21*, 461–490.

Edmondson, W. (1981). *Spoken discourse: A model for analysis*. London: Longman.

Ehrlich, S. (2001). *Representing rape: Language and sexual consent*. New York: Routledge.

Ehrlich, S. (2002). Legal institutions, nonspeaking recipiency and participants' orientations. *Discourse & Society*, *13*(6), 731–747.

Erickson, B., Lind, E. A., Johnson, B. C., and O'Barr, W. M. (1978). Speech style and impression formation in a court setting: The effects of powerful and powerless speech. *Journal of Experimental Social Psychology*, *14*(3), 266–279.

Escalas, J. E. (2007). Self-referencing and persuasion: Narrative transportation versus analytical elaboration. *Journal of Consumer Research*, *33*(4), 421–429.

Estrich, S. (1986). Rape. *The Yale Law Journal*, *95*(6), 1087–1184.

Estrich, S. (1987). *Real rape.* Cambridge, MA: Harvard University Press.

Faber, B. (2006). Popularizing nanoscience: The public rhetoric of nanotechnology, 1986–99. *Technical Communication Quarterly, 15*(2), 141–169.

Fahnestock, J. (2011). *Rhetorical style: The uses of language in persuasion.* Oxford: Oxford University Press.

Fairclough, N. (2003). *Analysing discourse: Textual analysis for social research.* London: Routledge.

Fairclough, N. (2010). Language and ideology. In *Critical discourse analysis: The critical study of language* (2nd ed., pp. 56–68). New York: Routledge.

Fairclough, N. L., and Wodak, R. (1997). Critical discourse analysis. In T. A. van Dijk (Ed.), *Discourse studies: A multidisciplinary introduction,* Vol. 2, *Discourse as social interaction* (pp. 258–284). London: Sage.

Felton Rosulek, L. (2008). Manipulative silence and social representation in the closing arguments of a child sexual abuse case. *Text and Talk, 28*(4), 529–550.

Felton Rosulek, L. (2009). The sociolinguistic creation of opposing representations of defendants and victims. *International Journal of Speech, Language, and Law, 16*(1), 1–30.

Felton Rosulek, L. (2010a). A close analysis of the functions of reanimated voices in the closing arguments of criminal trials. In A. Johnson and M. Coulthard (Eds.), *The Routledge handbook of forensic linguistics* (pp. 218–230). London: Routledge.

Felton Rosulek, L. (2010b). Legitimation and the heteroglossic nature of closing arguments. In D. Schiffrin, A. De Fina, and A. Nylund (Eds.), *Telling stories: Language, narrative, and social life* (Georgetown University Roundtable on Langauges and Linguistics) (pp. 181–194). Washington, DC: Georgetown University Press.

Flowerdew, J., and Leong, S. (2010). Presumed knowledge in the discursive construction of socio-political and cultural identity. *Journal of Pragmatics, 42*(8), 2240–2252.

Foley, W. A. (1997). *Anthropological linguistics.* Oxford: Blackwell Publishing.

Foucault, M. (1972). *The archaeology of knowledge.* New York: Harper and Row.

Fowler, R. (1991). *Language in the news: Discourse and ideology in the press.* London: Routledge and Kegan Paul.

Fowler, R., Hodge, B., Kress, G., and Trew, T. (1979). *Language and control.* London: Routledge and Kegan Paul.

Fox, A. (1983). Topic continuity in Biblical Hebrew narrative. In T. Givón (Ed.), *Topic continuity in discourse: A quantitative cross-language study* (pp. 215–254). Philadelphia: John Benjamins.

Fuller, J. (1993). Hearing between the lines: Style switching in a courtroom setting. *Pragmatics, 3*, 29–43.

Garner, B. A. (2011). *Garner's dictionary of legal usage* (3rd ed.). Oxford: Oxford University Press.

Gastil, J. (1990). Generic pronouns and sexist language: The oxymoronic character of masculine generics. *Sex roles, 23*(11–2), 629–643.

Gastil, R. D. (1992). Cultural regions of America. In L. S. Luedtke (Ed.), *Making America: The society and culture of the United States* (pp. 129–143). Chapel Hill, NC: University of North Carolina Press.

Gerbner, G. (1985). Mass media discourse: Message system analysis as a component of cultural indicators. In T.A. van Dijk (Ed.), *Discourse and communication: New approaches to the analyses of mass media discourse and communication* (pp. 13–25). Berlin: Walter de Gruyter.

Gibbons, J. (2003). *Forensic linguistics: An introduction to language in the legal system.* Oxford: Blackwell Publishing.

Givón, T. (1987). Beyond foreground and background. In R. S. Tomlin (Ed.), *Coherence and grounding in discourse* (pp. 175–88). Amsterdam: John Benjamins.

Goffman, E. (1967). *Interaction ritual.* New York: Pantheon.

Goffman, E. (1974). *Frame analysis.* New York: Harper and Row.

Goffman, E. (1981). *Forms of talk.* Philadelphia: University of Pennsylvania Press.

Cuyahoga Cty. Bar Assn. v. Gonzalez, 89 Ohio St.3d 470, 2000-Ohio–221.

Goodwin, C. (1994). Professional vision. *American Anthropologist*, *96*(3), 606–633.

Graddol, D., and Swann, J. (1989). *Gender voices.* Oxford: Basil Blackwell.

Green, M. C., and Brock, T. C. (2000). The role of transportation in the persuasiveness of public narratives. *Journal of Personality and Social Psychology*, *79*(5), 701–721.

Green, M. C., and Brock, T. C. (2002). In the mind's eye: Imagery and transportation into narrative worlds. In M. C. Green, J. J. Strange, and T. C. Brock (Eds.) *Narrative impact: Social and cognitive foundations* (pp. 315–341). Mahwah, NJ: Lawrence Erlbaum Associates.

Grice, H. P. (1975). Logic and conversation. In P. Cole and J. L. Morgan (eds.),*Speech acts* (pp. 41–58). New York: Academic Press.

Grimes, J. E. (1975). *The thread of discourse.* The Hague: Mouton.

Grosz, B., and Hirschberg, J. (1992). Some intonational characteristics of discourse structure. In J. J. Ohala, T. M. Nearey, B. L. Derwing, M. M. Hodge, and G. E. Wiebe (Eds.), *Proceedings of the International Conference on Spoken Language Processing* (Vol. 1, pp. 429–432). Banff, Canada: ICSLP.

Guerini, M., and Castelfranchi, C. (2007). Promises and threats in persuasion. *Pragmatics and Cognition*, *15*(2), 277–311.

Hahn, P. W., and Clayton, S. D. (1996). The effects of attorney presentation style, attorney gender, and juror gender on juror decisions. *Law and Human Behavior*, *20*, 533–554.

Hall, S. (1985). Signification, representation, ideology: Althusser and the post-structuralist debates. *Critical Studies in Mass Communication*, *2*, 91–114.

Halliday, M. A. K. (1973). *Explorations in the functions of language.* London: Arnold Publishers.

Halliday, M. A. K. (1978). *Language as social semiotic: The social interpretation of language and meaning.* London: Arnold Publishers.

Halliday, M. A. K. (1994). *An introduction to functional grammar.* Baltimore, MD: Edward Arnold.

Halliday, M. A. K. (2002). Linguistic function and literary style: An inquiry into the language of William Golding's *The Inheritors* (1971). In *Linguistic studies of text and discourse* (pp. 88–125). London: Continuum.

Halliday, M. A. K., and Hassan, R. (1985). *Language, context, and text: Aspects of language in a social-semiotic perspective.* Oxford: Oxford University Press.

Halliday, M. A. K., and Matthiessen, C. (1999). *Construing experience through meaning: A language-based approach to cognition.* London: Cassell.

Hamilton, M. C. (1988). Using masculine generics: Does generic *he* increase male bias in the user's imagery? *Sex Roles*, *19*(11–2), 785–799.

Hansen, A., and Machin, D. (2008). Visually branding the environment: Climate change as a marketing opportunity. *Discourse Studies, 10*, 777–794.

Heffer, C. (2005). *The language of jury trial.* Houndmills, UK: Palgrave.

Henley, N. M., Miller, M. D., and Beazley, J. (1995). Syntax, semantics, and sexual violence: Agency and the passive voice. *Journal of Language and Social Psychology, 14*, 60–84.

Hill, J. (1995). The voices of Don Gabriel: Responsibility and self in a modern Mexicano narrative. In D. Tedlock and B. Mannheim (Eds.), *The dialogic emergence of culture* (pp. 97–147). Chicago: University of Illinois Press.

Hobbs, P. (2003). "Is that what we're here about?" A lawyer's use of impression management in a closing argument at trial. *Discourse & Society, 14*(3), 273–290.

Hobbs, P. (2005). Unreasonable doubt: Manipulating jurors' perceptions in a closing argument at trial. In A. Sarat (Ed.), *Studies in law, politics, and society* (pp. 109–144). Oxford: JAI Press/Elsevier.

Hobbs, P. (2008). It's not what you say but how you say it: The role of personality and identity in trial success. *Critical Discourse Studies, 5*(3), 231–248.

Hodge, B., and Kress, G. (1993). *Language as ideology* (Rev. ed.). London: Routledge.

Hoey, M. (2001). *Textual interaction: An introduction to written discourse analysis.* London: Routledge.

Holmes, J. (1984). Women's language: A functional approach. *General Linguistics 24*(3), 149–178.

Holt, E. (1996). Reporting on talk: The use of direct reported speech in conversation. *Research on Language and Social Interaction, 29*(3), 219–245.

Hopper, P. J. 1979. Aspect and Foregrounding in Discourse. In T. Givón (Ed.) *Syntax and Semantics, Volume 12: Discourse and Syntax* (pp. 213–241). New York: Academic Press.

Hopper, P. J., and Thompson, S. A. (1980). Transitivity in grammar and discourse. *Language, 56*(2), 251–299.

Huckin, T. (2002). Textual silence and the discourse of homelessness. *Discourse & Society, 13*, 347–372.

Huckin, T. (2010). On textual silences, large and small. In C. Bazerman R. Krut, K. Lunsford, S. McLeod, S. Null, P. Rogers, A. Stansell (Eds.), *Traditions of writing research* (pp. 419–443). London: Routledge.

Hurwitz, S. D., Miron, M. S., and Johnson B. T. (1992). Source credibility and the language of expert testimony. *Journal of Applied Social Psychology, 22*, 1909–1939.

Hyland, K. (2002). Genre: Language, context, and literacy. *Annual Review of Applied Linguistics, 22*, 113–135.

Hymes, D. (1962). The ethnography of communication. In T. Gladwin and W. Sturtevant (Eds.), *Anthropology and human behavior* (pp. 13–53). Washington, DC: Anthropological Society of Washington.

Hymes, D. (1973). Toward linguistic competence. *Sociolinguistic Working Papers #16.* Austin, TX: Southwest Educational Development Laboratory.

Hymes, D. (1974). *Foundations in sociolinguistics: An ethnographic approach.* Philadelphia: University of Pennsylvania Press.

Irvine, J. T. (1979). Formality and informality in communicative events. *American Anthropologist, 81*, 773–790.

Irvine, J. T. and Gal, S. (2000). Language ideology and linguistic differentiation. In P. Kroskrity (Ed.), *Regimes of language: Ideologies, polities, and identities* (pp. 35–84). Santa Fe, NM: School of American Research Press.

Jackson, B. (1988). *Law, fact, and narrative coherence.* Merseyside, UK: Deborah Charles Publications.

Jackson v. State, 600 A.2d 21 (Del. 1991).

Jacoby, J., Nelson, M. C., and Hoyer, W. D. (1982). Corrective advertising and affirmative disclosure statements: Their potential for confusing and misleading the consumer. *The Journal of Marketing*, *46*(1), 61–72.

Jakobson, R. (1957). *Shifters, verbal categories, and the Russian verb.* Cambridge, MA: Department of Slavic Languages and Literatures, Harvard University.

Jakobson, R. (1960). *Closing statements: Linguistics and poetics.* In T. A. Sebeok (Ed.), *Style in language* (pp. 350–377). New York: Wiley.

Jalbert, P. L. (1994). Structures of the unsaid. *Theory, Culture and Society*, *11*, 127–160.

Janney, R. W. (2002). Context as context: Vague answers in court. *Language and Communication*, *22*, 457–475.

Jenkins, J. (1993). The Americans inns of court: Preparing our students for ethical practice. *Akron Law Review*, *27*, 175–196.

Jessop, B. (2002). *The future of the capitalist state.* Cambridge: Polity.

Johnson-Laird, P. N. (1968). The choice of the passive voice in a communicative task. *British Journal of Psychology*, *59*(1), 7–15.

Johnstone, B. (1996). *The linguistic individual: Self-expression in language and linguistics.* Oxford: Oxford University Press.

Johnstone, B. (2002). *Discourse analysis.* London: Blackwell.

Jones, L. B., and Jones, L. K. (1979). Multiple levels of information in discourse. In L. K. Jones (Ed.), *Discourse studies in mesoamerican languages*, Vol. 1. Dallas: Summer Institute of Linguistics and the University of Texas at Arlington.

Karttunen, L., and Peters, S. (1975). Conventional implicature in Montague grammar. In C. Cogen, H. Thompson, G. Turgood, K. Whistler, and J. Wright (Eds.), *Proceedings of the first annual meeting of the Berkeley Linguistics Society* (pp. 266–278). Berkeley: University of California.

Khalil, E. M. (2000). *Grounding in English and Arabic news discourse.* Philadelphia: John Benjamins.

Khalil, E. N. 2005. Grounding: Between figure-ground and foregrounding-backgrounding. *Annual Review of Cognitive Linguistics*, *3*, 1–21.

King, J. H. (1980). Prosecutorial misconduct: The limitations upon the prosecutor's role as an advocate. *Suffolk University Law Review*, *14*, 1095–1135.

Koslow, S., Shamdasani, P. N., and Touchstone, E. E. (1994). Exploring language effects in ethnic advertising: A sociolinguistic perspective. *Journal of Consumer Research*, *20*, 575–585.

Koven, M. (2002). An analysis of speaker role inhabitance in narratives of personal experience. *Journal of Pragmatics*, *34*, 167–217.

Koven, M. (2007). *Selves in two languages: Bilinguals' verbal enactments of identity in French and Portuguese.* Philadelphia: John Benjamins.

Kozin, A. (2008). Unsettled facts: On the transformational dynamism of evidence in legal discourse. *Text and Talk*, *28*(2), 219–238.

Kress, G. (1989). *Linguistic processes in sociocultural practice*. Oxford: Oxford University Press.

Kress, G., and Van Leeuwen, T. (1996). *Reading images: The grammar of visual design*. London: Routledge.

Kuo, S. (2001). Reported speech in Chinese political discourses. *Discourse Studies*, *3*(2), 181–202.

Kurzon, D. (2007). Towards a typology of silence. *Journal of Pragmatics*, *39*, 1673–1688.

Labov, W. (1972). The transformation of experience in narrative syntax. In W. Labov (Ed.), *Language in the inner city* (pp. 354–396). Philadelphia: University of Pennsylvania Press.

Labov, W. (1984). Intensity. In D. Schiffrin (Ed.), *Meaning, form, and use in context: Linguistic applications* (Georgetown University Roundtable on Languages and Linguistics) (pp. 43–70). Washington, DC: Georgetown University Press.

Labov, W., and Waletzky, J. (1967). Narrative analysis: Oral versions of personal experience. In J. Helm (Ed.), *Essays on the verbal and visual arts* (pp. 12–44). Seattle: University of Washington Press.

Lakoff, G. (1991). Metaphor and war: The metaphor system used to justify the war in the gulf. *Journal of Urban and Cultural Studies*, *2*(1), 59–72.

Lakoff, G., and Johnson, M. (1980). *Metaphors we live by*. Chicago: University of Chicago Press.

Lamb, S., and Keon, S. (1995), Blaming the perpetrator: Language that distorts reality in newspaper articles on men battering women. *Psychology of Women Quarterly*, *19*, 209–220.

Leech, G. (1999). The distribution and function of vocatives in American and British English conversation. In H. Hasselgård and S. Oksefjell (Eds.), *Out of corpora: Studies in humour of Stig Johansson* (pp. 107–118). Amsterdam: Rodopi.

LeVan, E. A. (1984). Nonverbal communication in the courtroom: Attorney beware. *Law and Psychology Review*, *8*, 83–104.

Levinson, S. (1983). *Pragmatics*. Cambridge: Cambridge University Press.

Levinson, S. (2000). *Presumptive meanings: The theory of generalized conversational implicature*. Cambridge, MA: MIT Press.

Levitt, D. P. (1991). Rhetoric in closing argument. *Litigation*, *17*, 17–21.

Li, C. N. (1986). Direct and indirect speech: A functional study. In F. Coulmas (Ed.), *Direct and indirect speech* (pp. 29–45). Berlin: Mouton de Gruyter.

Lief, M., Bycel, B., and Caldwell, H. M. (1998). *Ladies and gentlemen of the jury: Greatest closing arguments in modern law*. New York: Scribner.

Locke, T. (2004). *Critical discourse analysis*. London: Continuum International.

Longacre, R. E. (1989). Two hypotheses regarding text generation and analysis. *Discourse Processes*, *12*(4), 413–460.

Longacre, R. E. (1996). *The grammar of discourse*. Berlin: Springer.

Luchjenbroers, J., and Aldridge, M. (2007). Conceptual manipulation with metaphors and frames: Dealing with rape victims in legal discourse. *Text and Talk*, *27*(3), 339–359.

MacKay, D. G. (1980). Psychology, prescriptive grammar, and the pronoun problem. *American Psychologist*, *35*(5), 444–449.

MacMartin, C. (2002). (Un)reasonable doubt? The invocation of children's consent in sexual abuse trial judgments. *Discourse & Society*, *13*(1), 9–40.

Maher, M. (1996). Developing a winning case strategy. *Trial*, *32*(4), 42–46.

Martin, J. (2000). Close reading: Functional linguistics as a tool for critical analysis. In L. Unsworth (Ed.), *Researching language in schools and communities: Functional linguistics approaches* (pp. 275–303). London: Cassell.

Martínez Lirola, M., and Chovanec, J. (2012). The dream of a perfect body come true: Multimodality in cosmetic surgery advertising. *Discourse & Society*, *23*, 487–507.

Massaro, T. M. (1989). Empathy, legal storytelling, and the rule of law: New words, old wounds. *Michigan Law Review*, *87*(8), 2099–2127.

Matoesian, G. (1993). *Reproducing rape domination through talk in the courtroom*. Chicago: University of Chicago Press.

Matoesian, G. (2001). *Law and the language of identity: Discourse in the William Kennedy Smith rape trial*. Oxford: Oxford University Press.

Matoesian, G. (2005). Nailing down an answer: Participations of power in trial talk. *Discourse Studies*, *7*(6), 733–759.

Matthiessen, C. (1995). THEME as an enabling resource in ideational "knowledge" construction. In M. Ghadessy (Ed.), *Thematic development in English texts* (pp. 20–54). London: Pinter Publishers.

Matthiessen, C., Teruya, K., and Lam, M. (2010). *Key terms in systemic functional linguistics*. London: Continuum International.

Mauet, T. (1998). *Mauet's trial notebook* (2nd ed.). New York: Aspen Publishers.

Mauet, T. (2000). *Trial techniques* (5th ed.). New York: Aspen Publishers.

Mauet, T. (2009). *Trials: Strategy, skills, and the new powers of persuasion* (2nd ed.). New York: Aspen Publishers.

Mayes, P. (1990). Quotation in spoken English. *Studies in Language*, *14*(2), 325–363.

State v. McCarroll, 336 N.C. 559, 445 S.E.2d 18 (1994).

McDonald, S. A. (2005). When a victim's a victim: Making reference to victims and sex-crime prosecution. *Nevada Law Journal*, *6*, 248–271.

McElhaney, J. W. (2005). *McElhaney's trial notebook* (4th ed.). Chicago: ABA Publishing.

Meyer, P. N. (1994). Desperate for love: Cinematic influences upon a defendant's closing argument to a jury. *Vermont Law Review*, *18*(3), 721–749.

Meyer, P. N. (1996). "Desperate for love II": Further reflections on the interpenetration of legal and popular storytelling in closing arguments to a jury in a complex criminal case. *University of San Francisco Law Review*, *30*, 931–962.

Millar, M. G., and Millar, K. U. (1990). Attitude change as a function of attitude type and argument type. *Journal of Personality and Social Psychology*, *59*(2), 217–228.

Milroy, L., and Llamas, C. (2013). Social networks. In K. Chambers and N. Schilling (Eds.), *The handbook of language variation and change* (2nd ed., pp. 409–427). Oxford: John Wiley and Sons.

Morford, J. (1997). Social indexicality in French pronominal address. *Journal of Linguistic Anthropology*, *7*(1), 3–37.

Motes, W. H., Hilton, C. B., and Fielden, J. S. (1992). Language, sentence, and structural variations in print advertising. *Journal of Advertising Research*, *32*(5), 63–77.

Moulton, J., Robinson, G. M., and Elias, C. (1978). Sex bias in language use: Neutral pronouns that aren't. *American Psychologist*, *33*(11), 1032–1036.

Mukařovský, J. (1964 [1932]). Standard language and poetic language. In P. L. Garvin (Ed.), *A Prague school reader on esthetics, literary structure, and style* (pp. 17–30). Washington, DC: Georgetown University Press.

Myers-Scotton, C. (1993). *Social motivations for code-switching: Evidence from Africa*. Oxford: Oxford University Press.

Notestine, K. (1999). Closing arguments. *Brief*, *29*(1), 72–77.

O'Barr, W. (1982). *Linguistic evidence: Language, power and strategy in the courtroom*. New York: Academic Press.

Ochs, E., and Capps, L. (1996). Narrating the self. *Annual Review of Anthropology*, *25*, 19–43.

O'Connell, D. C., and Kowal, S. (1994). The transcriber as language user. In B. Guillermo (Ed.), *The dynamics of language processes: Essays in honor of Hans W. Dechret* (pp. 119–142). Tübingen: Gunter Narr.

O'Halloran, K. A. (2011). Limitations of the logico-rhetorical module: Inconsistency in argument, online discussion forums and electronic deconstruction. *Discourse Studies*, *13*(6), 797–806.

Pascual, E. (2006). Questions in legal monologues: Fictive interaction as argumentative strategy in a murder trial. *Text and Talk*, *26*(3), 383–402.

Payan, J. M., and McFarland, R. G. (2005). Decomposing influence strategies: Argument structure and dependence as determinants of the effectiveness of influence strategies in gaining channel member compliance. *Journal of Marketing*, *69*(3), 66–79.

Peled-Elhanan, N. (2010). Legitimation of massacres in Israeli school history books. *Discourse & Society*, *21*(4), 377–404.

Perrin, L. T., Caldwell, H. M., and Chase, C. A. (2011). *The art and science of trial advocacy* (2nd ed.). Newark, NJ: LexisNexis.

Petty, R. E., Cacioppo, J. T., and Goldman, R. (1981). Personal involvement as a determinant of argument-based persuasion. *Journal of Personality and Social Psychology*, *41*, 847–855.

Petty, R. E., Cacioppo, J. T., and Kasmer, J. (1988). The role of affect in the Elaboration Likelihood Model of persuasion. In L. Donohew, H. Sypher, and E. T. Higgins (Eds.), *Communication, social cognition, and affect* (pp. 117–146). Hillsdale, NJ: Erlbaum.

Phillips, N., and Hardy, C. (2002). *Understanding discourse analysis: Investigating processes of social construction*. Thousand Oaks, CA: Sage.

Polanyi, L. (1982). Linguistic and social constraints on storytelling. *Journal of Pragmatics*, *6*(5), 509–524.

Potter, J. (1996). *Representing reality: Discourse, rhetoric and social construction*. London: Sage.

Potts, C. (2005). *The logic of conventional implicatures*. Oxford: Oxford University Press.

Rathus, S. A. (2012). *Psychology: Concepts and connections*. Belmont, CA: Wadsworth.

Refo, P. L. (2007). Closing argument: A string of pearls. In P. A. Schwab (Ed.), *The litigation manual* (1st supplement, pp. 706–722). Chicago: ABA Publishing.

Richards, J. C., and Schmidt, R. (2010). *Longman dictionary of language teaching and applied linguistics* (4th ed.). London: Longman.

Roberts, J. H. (1999). The SEC of closing arguments. *American Journal of Trial Advocacy*, *23*, 203–214.

Roberts, F., and Robinson, J. (2004). Interobserver agreement on first-state analytic transcription. *Human Communication Research*, *30*(3), 376–410.

Rogers, M. G. (2006). *Litigation technology: Becoming a high-tech trial lawyer*. New York: Aspen Publishers.

Romaine, S. (1999). *Communicating gender*. Mahwah, NJ: Lawrence Erlbaum Associates.
Rosen, H. (1988). The autobiographical impulse. In D. Tannen (Ed.), *Linguistics in context: Connecting observation and understanding* (pp. 69–88). Norwood, NJ: Ablex.
Schiffrin, D. (1996). Narrative as self-portrait: Sociolinguistic constructions of identity. *Language in Society*, *25*, 167–203.
Schrager, S. (1999). *The trial lawyer's art*. Philadelphia: Temple University Press.
Searle, J. (1969). *Speech acts: An essay in the philosophy of language*. Cambridge: Cambridge University Press.
Shore, B. (1996). *Culture in mind: Cognition, culture, and the problems of meaning*. Oxford: Oxford University Press.
Sidnell, J. (2010). *Conversation analysis: An introduction*. Chichester, UK: Wiley-Blackwell.
Sigal, J., Braden-Maguire, J., Hayden, M., and Mosley. N. (1985). The effect of presentation style and sex of lawyer on jury decision-making behavior. *Psychology: A Quarterly Journal of Human Behavior*, *22*(3–4), 13–19.
Silverstein, M (1981). The limits of awareness. *Working Papers in Sociolinguistics*, *84*, 1–30.
Silverstein, M. (1995 [1976]). Shifters, linguistic categories, and cultural description. In B. G. Blount (Ed.), *Language, culture, and society: A book of readings* (pp. 187–221). Prospect Heights, IL: Waveland Press.
Simons, H. W. (1976). *Persuasion: Understanding, practice, and analysis*. Reading, MA: Addison-Wesley.
Sinclair, J. M., and Coulthard, M. (1992). Towards an analysis of discourse. In M. Coulthard (Ed.), *Advances in spoken discourse analysis* (pp. 50–78). London and New York: Routledge.
Smith, P. (2004). Rape and equal protection. *Hypatia*, *19*(2), 152–157.
Snow, D. A., Rochford, E. B., Worden, S. K., and Benford, R. D. (1986). Frame alignment processes, micromobilization and movement participation. *American Sociological Review*, *51*(4), 464–481.
Spiecker, S. C., and Worthington, D. L. (2003). The influence of opening statement/closing argument organizational strategy on juror verdict and damage awards. *Law and Human Behavior*, *27*(4), 437–456.
Spiro, M. (2003). *Culture and human nature*. New Brunswick, NJ: Transaction Publishers.
Stalnaker, R. (1978). Assertion. *Syntax and Semantics*, *9*, 315–332.
Stalnaker, R. (2002). Common ground. *Linguistics and Philosophy*, *25*, 701–721.
Starr, C., and McMillan, B. (2012). *Human biology* (9th ed.). Belmont, CA: Brooks/Cole Cengage Learning.
Stubbs, M. (1983).*Discourse analysis: The sociolinguistic analysis of natural language*. Oxford: Basil Blackwell.
Stygall, G. (1994). *Trial language: Differential discourse processing and discursive formation*. Philadelphia: John Benjamins.
Swales, J. (2004). *Research genres: Explorations and applications*. Cambridge: Cambridge University Press.
Sycara, K. P. (1990). Persuasive argumentation in negotiation. *Theory and Decision*, *28*(3), 203–242.
Talkington v. State, 682 S.W.2d 674 (Tex. Ct. App. 11 Dist. 1984).
Tannen, D. (2007 [1989]). *Talking voices: Repetition, dialogue and imagery in conversational discourse* (2nd ed.). Cambridge: Cambridge University Press.

Thiesmeyer, L. (2003). Introduction: Silencing in discourse. In L. Thiesmeyer (ed.), *Discourse and silencing* (pp. 1–33). Amsterdam: John Benjamins.

Thompson, G., and Hunston, S. (2000). Evaluation: An introduction. In S. Hunston and G. Thompson (Eds.), *Evaluation in text: Authorial stance and the construction of discourse* (pp. 1–27). Oxford: Oxford University Press.

Thompson, M. M., and Scheid, F. M. (1996). Neither polemical nor visionary: Language professionalization and the representation of women in the journal of adult education, 1929–60. *Adult Education Quarterly*, *46*(3), 123–141.

Thompson, G., and Zhou, J. (2000). Evaluation and organization in text: The structuring role of evaluative disjuncts. In S. Hunston and G. Thompson (Eds.), *Evaluation in text: Authorial stance and the construction of discourse* (pp. 121–141). Oxford: Oxford University Press.

Tiersma, P. (1999). *Legal language*. Chicago: University of Chicago Press.

Tomlin, R. S. (1985). Foreground-background information and the syntax of subordination. *Text*, *5*, 85–122.

Tomlin, R. S., Forrest, L., and Pu, M. M. (1997). Discourse semantics. In T. A. van Dijk (Ed.), *Discourse as structure and process* (pp. 63–111). London: Sage.

Trenholm, S. (1989). *Persuasion and social influence*. Englewood Cliffs, NJ: Prentice-Hall.

Trew, T. (1979a). Theory and ideology at work. In R. Fowler, B. Hodge, G. Kress, and T. Trew (Eds.), *Language and control* (pp. 94–116). London: Routledge and Kegan Paul.

Trew, T. (1979b). What the papers say: Linguistic variation and ideological difference. In R. Fowler, B. Hodge, G. Kress, and T. Trew (Eds.), *Language and control* (pp. 117–156). London: Routledge and Kegan Paul.

United States Code, Title 28, Part 3, Chapter 49, Section 753[b].

van Dijk, T. A. (1977). *Text and context: Explorations in the semantics and pragmatics of discourse*. London: Longman.

van Dijk, T. A. (1983). Discourse analysis: Its development and application to the structure of the news. *Journal of Communication*, *33*(2), 20–43.

van Dijk, T. A. (1986). News schemata. In C. R. Cooper and S. Greenbaum (Eds.), *Studying writing: Linguistic Approaches* (pp. 155–186). Beverly Hills, CA: Sage.

van Dijk, T. A. (1993). Principles of critical discourse analysis. *Discourse & Society*, *4*(2), 249 283.

van Dijk, T. A. (1995). Discourse analysis as ideology analysis. In C. Schäffner and A. Wenden (Eds.), *Language and peace* (pp. 17–33). Aldershot, UK: Dartmouth Publishing.

van Dijk, T. A. (1997). Cognitive context models and discourse. In M. Stamenow (Ed.), *Language structure, discourse and the access to consciousness* (pp. 189–226). Amsterdam: John Benjamins.

van Dijk, T. A. (2000). On the analysis of parliamentary debates on immigration. In M. Reisigl and R. Wodak (Eds.), *The semiotics of racism: Approaches to critical discourse analysis* (pp. 85–104). Vienna: Passagen Verlag.

van Dijk, T. A. (2005). Contextual knowledge management in discourse production: A CDA perspective. In R. Wodak and P. Chilton (Eds.), *A new agenda in (critical) discourse analysis: Theory, methodology and interdisciplinarity* (pp. 71–100). Amsterdam: John Benjamins.

van Dijk, T. A. (2008). *Discourse, knowledge, power and politics: Towards critical epistemic discourse analysis.* Lecture CADAAD, Hertfordshire, July 10–12, 2008. Unpublished manuscript.

van Dijk, T. A. (2009). Critical discourse studies; A sociocognitive approach. In Ruth Wodak and Michael Meyer (Eds.), *Methods of critical discourse analysis* (pp. 62–85). London: Sage.

van Eemeren, F. H., and Grootendorst, R. (2004). *A systematic theory of argumentation: The pragma-dialectical approach.* Cambridge: Cambridge University Press.

van Kuppevelt, J (1995). Discourse structure, topicality and questioning. *Journal of Linguistics, 31*, 109–147.

van Leeuwen, T. (1995). Representing social action. *Discourse & Society, 6*(1), 81–106.

van Leeuwen, T. (2002). The representation of social actors. In M. Toolan (Ed.), *Discourse analysis* (pp. 302–339). London: Routledge.

van Leeuwen, T. (2005). *Introducing social semiotics.* London: Routledge.

van Leeuwen, T. (2007). Legitimation in discourse and communication. *Discourse & Communication, 1*(1), 91–112.

van Leeuwen, T. (2008). *Discourse and practice: New tools for critical discourse analysis.* Oxford: Oxford University Press.

Virtanen, V., and H. Halmari (2005). Persuasion across genres: Emerging perspectives. In H. Halmari and V. Virtanen (Eds.), *Persuasion across genres* (pp. 3–24). Philadelphia: John Benjamins.

Voss, J. F., and Van Dyke, J. A. (2001). Narrative structure, information certainty, emotional content, and gender as factors in a pseudo jury decision making task. *Discourse Processes, 32*(2–3), 215–243.

Waicukauski, R., Sandler, P. M., and Epps, J. (2009). *The twelve secrets of persuasive argument.* Chicago: American Bar Association.

Wallis, S. (2013). *z*-squared: The origin and application of χ^2. *Journal of Quantitative Linguistic, 20*(4), 350–378.

Walter, B. (1988). *The jury summation as speech genre.* Philadelphia: John Benjamins.

Walter, J., and Helmig, J. (2008). Discursive metaphor analysis: (De)construction(s) of Europe. In T. Carver and J. Pikalo (Eds.), *Political language and metaphor: Interpreting and changing the world* (pp. 119–131). New York: Routledge.

Wårvik, B. (2004). What is foregrounded in narratives? Hypotheses for the cognitive basis of foregrounding. In T. Virtanen (Ed.), *Approaches to cognition through text and discourse* (pp. 99–122). Berlin: Mouton de Gruyter.

Weber, M. (1978). *Economy and society: An outline of interpretive sociology.* In G. Roth and C. Wittich (Eds.). Berkeley: University of California Press.

Wennerstrom, A. (2001). *The music of everyday speech: Prosody and discourse analysis.* Oxford: Oxford University Press.

White, P. R. R. (2006). Evaluative semantics and ideological positioning in journalistic discourse: A new framework for analysis. In I. Lassen (Ed.), *Mediating ideology in text and image: Ten critical studies* (pp. 37–69). Amsterdam: John Benjamins.

Wodak, R., and Busch, B. (2004). Approaches to media texts. In J. Downing, D. McQuail, P. Schlesinger, and E. Wartella (Eds.), *Handbook of media studies* (pp. 105–123). London: Sage.

Wodak, R., and Meyer, M (2009). Critical discourse analysis: History, agenda, theory, and methodology. In R. Wodak and M. Meyer (Eds.), *Methods for critical discourse analysis* (2nd rev. ed., pp. 1–33). London: Sage.

Wortham, S. (1996). Mapping participant deictics: A technique for discovering speakers' footing. *Journal of Pragmatics*, *25*(3), 331–348.

Wortham, S. (1999). The heterogeneously distributed self. *Journal of Constructivist Psychology*, *12*(2), 153–172.

Wortham, S. (2001). *Narratives in action*. New York: Teachers' College Press.

Wortham, S., and Locher, M. (1996). Voicing on the news: An analytical technique for studying media bias. *Text*, *16*, 557–585.

Young, L. (1990). *Language as behaviour, Language as code: A study of academic English*. Amsterdam: John Benjamins.

Young, L., and Harrison, C. (Eds.) (2004).*Systemic functional linguistics and critical discourse analysis: Studies in social change*. London: Continuum International.

Yule, G. (1996). *Pragmatics*. Oxford: Oxford University Press.

INDEX

Note: Locators followed by the letter 'n' refer to notes.